Calamities of Exile

Lawrence Weschler

Three Nonfiction Novellas

CALAMITIES OF EXILE

The University of Chicago Press

With a new Postscript

The University of Chicago Press, Chicago 60637
The University of Chicago Press, Ltd., London

Paperback edition 1999
Printed in the United States of America
07 06 05 04 03 02 01 00 99   2 3 4 5
ISBN 0-226-89393-6 (cloth)
ISBN 0-226-89392-8 (paperback)

Portions of this book originally appeared, in somewhat different form, in *The New Yorker*.

The works by Breyten Breytenbach that appear on the title page and on pages 136, 138, and 185 are reproduced with the artist's permission.

Library of Congress Cataloging-in-Publication Data

Weschler, Lawrence.
Calamities of exile : three nonfiction novellas / Lawrence Weschler. — Pbk. ed.
p. cm.
Originally published: Chicago : University of Chicago Press, 1998
Includes index.
Contents: Oedipus in Samara — The trials of Jan K. — A horrible face, but one's own.
ISBN 0-226-89392-8 (pbk. : alk. paper)
1. Makiya, Kanan. 2. Kavan, Jan, 1946– . 3. Breytenbach, Breyten. 4. Political activists—Biography. I. Title.
D849.W456 1999
303.48'4'0922—dc21   98-52316
CIP

♾ The paper used in this publication meets the minimum requirements of the American National Standard for Information Sciences—Permanence of Paper for Printed Library Materials, ANSI Z39.48-1992

For my Viennese grandparents

Ernst Toch (1887–1964)
Alice Zwack Toch (1892–1972)
Henri Weschler (1893–1963)
Angela Engel Weschler (1894–1961)

All forced into complicated exile
at about the same age
I am now

Contents

Preface

The three narratives joined together in this volume were conceived, almost from the start, as a sort of triptych: three tales, that is, about basically decent expatriates (the first an Iraqi, the second a Czech, the third an Afrikaner), each of whom tries to do the right thing with regard to the totalitarian regime holding sway over his homeland, to varyingly calamitous effect. They do that thing—the thing you or I too might have done if only we were far more courageous than we are—only to end up thoroughly bollixed.

As such, these narratives afford a sort of double cat scan into the natures both of totalitarianism and of exile. Or maybe, to shift the metaphor slightly, the decent impulses animating each of these tales can be likened to individual atoms projected into a cloud chamber, their uncanny vapor trails helping to elucidate the character both of themselves and of the supersaturated medium across which they travel.

It is not within the compass of this preface to posit some vast unified (totalizing) field theory of totalitarianism; in fact, it is the essence of my approach to insist, rather, on the revelatory aspect of the specific, the particular, the quirkily individual. One might note, however, how in all three of the totalitarian situations surveyed in this text—Iraq's, Czechoslovakia's, and South Africa's—the regime's dominance depended, paradoxically, on both the atomization and the homogenization of the subjugated population. Dictators want their subjects both to surrender all sense of themselves into the national (or class) mass and, simultaneously, to experience themselves, qua individuals, as utterly alone, cut off, both endlessly suspect and unendingly suspicious of everyone else. Pithed, in short, of even the fantasy, let alone the possibility, of any sort of independent agency. In a sense, the regime intends that its subjects experience themselves as exiles in their own homes—isolate, ineffectual, and utterly contingent. For the condition of actual exile ordinarily dictates a similar sort of double movement in its victims, toward simultaneous atomization and homogenization and this wearing down of the potential for agency. Edges get shaved away and subjectivity is continuously shorn until individuals experience themselves as little more than abject objects, tossed by a cruel and senseless fate.

The three protagonists of the tales that make up this volume, however, are very edgy guys—even their edges have edges!—and, for whatever reason, they would not allow themselves to be worn down. They are difficult men, given over, it sometimes seems, to endless complication—though perhaps such complication was essential to the very vigor of their defiance: easy men, after all, generally fell away and did nothing.

The edginess is but one of the motifs that seems to pulse uncannily from one of these stories to the next. The reader will infer countless others, from the general (the guilt-drenched nostalgia of exile, for example, or the queasy dance of interrogators and their charges, wherein it's not always clear just who is playing whom for the fool), to the peculiarly specific (English girls keep marrying exotic foreigners, for some reason, across these pages; the narratives, perhaps not so surprisingly, keep wending toward climactic scenes at airports; two of the stories involve episodes where the protagonist tries to sneak past customs in disguise, the disguise in both cases consisting in its entirety of the absence of a usual beard).

All three tales, likewise, are rooted in family dramas—two are stories of fathers and sons, the third perhaps more so that of a jagged band of brothers. If at their wider political level these are stories of tyranny and rebellion, of torment and grace, of galling, almost incapacitating failure and the transcendence of that failure—of exile, in short, and return—it's invariably also true that these wider political themes first get broached and rehearsed around the intimacy of the family dinner table, the place, after all, where we all receive our first gashed edges and in flight from which we all experience our first intimations of exile. "There was rebellion, father"—the lines from Robert Lowell's early personal/political poem kept thrumming through my head as I reported these stories and then composed these tales.

Those lines, and lines from Seamus Heaney:

History says, *Don't hope*
On this side of the grave.

But then once in a lifetime
The longed for tidal wave
Of justice can rise up
And hope and history rhyme.

The latter derive from Heaney's Sophoclean rhapsody, *The Cure at Troy,* composed in 1990, around the same time these pieces, too, were gestating, in the aftermath of that annum mirabilis, 1989, when everything seemed so much simpler and dictatorships everywhere seemed to be melting away. But then the floodtide passed over and things fell decidedly out of rhyme once again. Totalitarianism, though manifestly evil, turned out to be evil in a confoundingly complicated way, one that seemed to contaminate everything it touched—not least, all opposition to it. That, too, ends up being one of the themes of this book: how vexed and botched this business of trying to do the right thing can get to be, and then, on the far side, how simple and serene.

* * *

Speaking of confounded and complicated, the reader will perhaps imagine the mixed feelings with which the subjects of these profiles—Kanan Makiya, Jan Kavan, and Breyten Breytenbach—allowed me into their lives during the reporting of these pieces, but it would be hard to convey the sheer graciousness and imperturbable forbearance with which they did so. The same, as well, with their families (notably including Mohamed and Margaret Makiya, and Yolande, Jan, Cloete, and Rachel Breytenbach) and with their friends. I hereby extend my heartfelt thanks to all.

These pieces came into being, in the first instance, under the sheltering patronage of the late William Shawn at *The New Yorker,* though they were actually composed during the tenure of his successor, Bob Gottlieb, who kept the faith, and then published (in the last two instances) in the pages of Tina Brown's revitalized magazine. Editorial continuity was provided throughout by my unflappable master, Pat Crow, who himself has a singular talent for making the complicated (sometimes the almost impossible) appear effortlessly simple. The pieces were immeasurably improved, for that matter, by the entire editorial apparatus at *The New Yorker,* especially the magazine's legendary fact-checking department, notably including David Kirkpatrick, Alexandra Horowitz, and Liesl Schillinger.

This trilogy was virtually complete five years ago, but most publishers (spooked perhaps in part by the notorious fate of nonfiction collections) couldn't even see their way clear to considering it. My steadfast agent Deborah Karl stuck with the prospect throughout, however, and our only mistake, in retrospect, may be that we didn't approach Alan Thomas, at the University of Chicago Press, from the very start. His enthusiasm for the project was immediate, and his sage advice throughout the process of its completion has been a constant support.

I speak of family life, all twisted and fraught, and frankly, I don't have a clue what I'm talking about. My own wife Joanna and our daughter Sara continue to shower me with undiluted grace, day after day after day. I don't deserve it.

Oedipus in Samara

Kanan Makiya in and out of Iraq

1992

I

Initially not much was known about Samir al-Khalil. To be fair, initially not many people were all that interested in knowing the slightest thing about him. On the jacket of his 1989 book *Republic of Fear: The Politics of Modern Iraq,* his publishers at the University of California Press had identified him simply as "an Iraqi expatriate, . . . a scholar of history and politics," who had been working on the book "for the past decade." They also acknowledged that Samir al-Khalil was not his real name. The horrifying text, a relentlessly probing revelation of the rule of violence and state terror inside Saddam Hussein's Baathist Iraq, made it obvious why such a writer might prefer to remain pseudonymous. "I owe a handful of very dear friends a great deal in the writing of this book," al-Khalil noted tersely in the book's acknowledgments. "But things being what they are under the Baath, I can no more mention their names than I can write under my own."

Al-Khalil had had the greatest difficulty getting his book published at all—dozens of publishers passed on it between 1986 and 1988 when he was showing it around, as he subsequently told me. And when the book finally was published in the spring of 1989, it went largely ignored. The author's depiction of the dire state of public, and even private, life in Iraq and his forebodings regarding Saddam Hussein's long-term regional ambitions, for instance, seemed to sail right past the American foreign-policy establishment, which at that time was intent on a realpolitik rapprochement with

Iraq, as the region's seemingly natural counterweight to Iran, the power that was still being seen as the main enemy. During its first year, al-Khalil's book sold barely a thousand copies.

On August 2, 1990, when Saddam invaded Kuwait, the book was one of the few authoritative texts available on the subject of the Iraqi tyrant. Suddenly, *Republic of Fear* was being reviewed everywhere, and usually with high praise. The *New York Times Book Review*'s critic declared it "required reading for anyone with a serious interest in Iraq or in the political dynamics of dictatorship." Peter Sluglett, writing in the London *Times Literary Supplement,* found it "a sophisticated and brilliantly savage denunciation of Arab populist politics." Hardcover sales took off overnight, and within two months Pantheon had brought out a paperback edition, of which it eventually sold 65,000 copies. The book became a best-seller in Britain and was translated into French, German, and Arabic as well. Al-Khalil was being cited everywhere. As the crisis mounted, he contributed frequent op-ed pieces, and even allowed himself to be interviewed on both radio and TV: he wore a wig and kept his back to the camera, and his voice was passed through a series of disguising filters. Many people wondered just who this Samir al-Khalil might be.

Nobody knew; nobody was even close. One afternoon, Samir al-Khalil agreed to participate in a three-way satellite hookup over National Public Radio, with Adeed Dawisha, an Iraqi-expatriate political scientist working in Cairo, who was one of the people whose candidacy for the role of al-Khalil had been put forth. Before the taping began, Dawisha complimented al-Khalil on his book. "But, Mr. Khalil," he said, "I wish I knew who the hell you are."

Al-Khalil wasn't yet ready to reveal his identity—certainly not over a transatlantic satellite connection—so speculation continued. In January, just before the start of the allied counter-offensive, the University of California Press began circulating galley proofs of a second book by al-Khalil, entitled *The Monument: Art, Vulgarity and Responsibility in Iraq.* Some perceptive readers began to suspect that al-Khalil might be an architect, for while *Republic of Fear* had established that Saddam's entire system repelled al-Khalil, *The Monument* showed that one of the things that most repelled him about that system was the dictator's penchant for grandiose neo-Fascist architecture, and more specifically the collusion of the Iraqi intelligentsia and the Iraqi artistic establishment in the realization of Saddam's megalomaniacal, multibillion-dollar schemes. For example, in various passages al-Khalil highlighted the work of Mohamed Makiya, the founding head of Baghdad University's School of Architecture and one of the foremost architects in the Middle East, who had started out in the fifties by creating exquisite, understated modern structures appropriate to the ancient archaeological sites they surrounded, but by the mid-eighties was submitting proposals, at Saddam's behest, for projects like a huge, lavish new Baghdad State Mosque.

The immediate occasion for the book seemed to be a particular monument Al-Khalil had begun hearing about a few years earlier, a spectacularly vulgar victory arch Saddam had ordered constructed in the heart of Baghdad, the centerpiece of which consisted of two gargantuan, scimitar-wielding arms erupting from the ground.

Al-Khalil started out from that monument, endeavoring almost perversely to take it seriously as "a work of art"; he wanted to interrogate it, to see what truths it could be made to divulge about its wider context and the aspirations of its creator. But he didn't stop there. His text roiled out, broaching ever vaster considerations—the nature of art, of kitsch, of tradition and innovation, of responsibility and complicity, of irony and ideology. The book churned in anguish: Plato and Aristotle and Rousseau and Arendt and Benjamin and Auden were all brought to bear across an exposition that became increasingly subtle and tormented. At times, reading *The Monument* could get to be like lifting the lid off a wicker basket only to spy the seething cobra deep inside, coiling and tumbling upon itself, a continuous turmoil—and yet, every few moments, the two piercing black eyes peering up and out at you, you'd feel a shiver of recognition. So much seemed to be going on inside the text—and so much more just beyond—that readers now *really* came to wonder: Who the hell *was* this Samir al-Khalil?

The mystery didn't last long. As the Gulf War came hurtling to a climax, the man who went by that name, increasingly tormented by the grim turn the war and, even more so, its denouement were taking, felt he could no longer sustain his pseudonymous subterfuge. He was increasingly desperate to be able to speak out openly and clearly and under his own name. So in March 1990 he finally did come out (to use that curious locution otherwise favored by gays and debutantes), and it turned out that he indeed was an architect; his real name was Kanan Makiya, and he was in fact the son of Iraq's foremost architect, Mohamed Makiya.

And the really tough nut in all of this was that he loved his father. He admired him enormously and even cherished some of the designs the man came to concoct—his most mature work—for Saddam Hussein during the eighties. When Kanan and I first began conducting the series of conversations that would lead up to this profile, he was nowhere near as concerned about the security implications involved in shattering his own prior anonymity as he was by the possibility that a full disclosure might hurt his father or, more specifically, his father's feelings. He was still very close to him. He used to work for him and even ran his father's London-based office, Makiya Associates, through much of the seventies and into the eighties, when the then-exiled master received his first summons back to Baghdad and thereupon started working for Hussein. The son presently broke with his father, largely because of that work, and began writing *Republic of Fear*. Howling. Loving his father all the while.

It's a long story.

KANAN MAKIYA was born in Baghdad in 1949. His father was born there thirty-odd years earlier—the actual year is uncertain. "When the British entered Baghdad" is how the elder Makiya's mother used to put it, but Kanan's father says that he thinks he was born in 1916, the year before the British entered Baghdad.

"I come from medieval Baghdad," Mohamed Makiya told me one day last spring, in London. The father has been based there since 1974, and the son, who has spent the last few decades traveling between England and America, currently keeps apartments in both the London and the Boston areas. I was sitting with the father in the office of his firm, Makiya Associates, which was not the bustling place it had been in earlier years. At one point, the staff had included more than fifty people, but the firm began winding down its operations during the latter half of the 1980s, in part because Saddam Hussein, engaged in his long war with Iran, had begun running out of money to finance his gargantuan schemes; in part because Mohamed Makiya had begun to have increasingly serious reservations about working for Saddam; and in part because Kanan, who for many years managed the office for his father, had left the firm over their seemingly irreconcilable differences.

Mohamed Makiya retained the firm's office space, however, and he still visits it regularly, often just to pore over an astonishing library of antique portfolios that fill the shelves along its walls: rich leather-bound volumes, some of them with spines longer than a person's leg, including eleven folio volumes from the official record of Napoleon's expedition to Egypt (1825), volumes of David Roberts's *Sketches in the Holy Land and Syria* (1849), Prisse D'Avennes's sumptuous album *L'Art Arabe* (1877), and an enormous Russian illustrated survey of mosque architecture in Samarkand (1905). Throughout his career, Makiya has used this library as a sort of image bank, its myriad etchings and plans a trove of detail waiting for reclamation and transmutation. "Tradition isn't something nostalgic," Kanan has quoted Mohamed as saying. The quotation appears in Kanan's third book, *Post-Islamic Classicism: A Visual Essay on the Architecture of Mohamed Makiya,* a coffee-table volume that he recently published in celebration of his father's work. (Kanan is clearly ambivalent about his father's achievements.) "In Islamic architecture there is a vocabulary which I find stimulating," the quotation continues. "It uplifts me because of its intrinsic abstract quality. You can never be a good 'modern' without having gone through the long path of tradition."

The morning of my visit, several volumes lay strewn across the floors and tables of Mohamed Makiya's conference room and private office, opened to ancient maps and vistas of Iraq's cities, and especially the Shia centers in the south—Karbala, Najaf, Kufa, Nasiriya. The Shiite rebellion that flared up at the end of the war had only recently been put down, and detailed accounts of the carnage and the physical mayhem involved were just beginning to filter back through the Iraqi-émigré grapevine; Mohamed was squaring those accounts with the images spread all about him. "That block there—I hear it's completely destroyed," he said. "The dome of that mosque there . . . " His eyes were glistening. A few minutes later, we were looking through a portfolio of etchings of ancient Baghdad—the Baghdad he had grown up in—and it was then that he made his remark about coming from medieval Baghdad. "I can tell you, this life"—he pointed to a dusty street scene—"I lived it. I didn't read it. I've lived seven centuries in my life, not seven decades."

Mohamed Makiya told me that he was born on the tenth of Muharram, which is the holiest day in the Shiite calendar—the anniversary of the defeat, in A.D. 680, of Husayn, the son of Ali, whom Shiites consider the true heir of the Prophet, and whose massacre outside Karbala brought about the schism between Shia and Sunni Islam. Mohamed was steeped in his family's Shiism from birth, he said—not in its strict religiosity but in its festive spirit. "For me, religion isn't so much a question of faith as it is one of culture—a tying back to one's ancestors—and I find it an absolute necessity," he said. While he isn't particularly observant religiously, he identifies with what he sees as "the Shiite spirit."

I realized that Mohamed was telling me all this in part as a criticism of his son, who considers himself a fervent secularist—if anything, an atheist, and certainly not a Shiite. It was one of their many disagreements. But in time I came to see that Mohamed Makiya was given to such pronouncements, moving quickly from some specific subject (that of his birth and upbringing, say) to the loftiest of speculations. In *Post-Islamic Classicism,* Kanan notes, "Makiya venerates the past, and the far-away in general. At present he is working on a book he calls *Images of Baghdad: Past and Future*. The present is always significant by its absence. This is reason enough not to see eye to eye with him on many things. Nonetheless, the consistency of his disregard for the world as it is is also somehow bound up in the specificity of his achievement in architecture."

Although Mohamed Makiya sometimes seems rooted in the Shiite south of Iraq, he was in fact born in the Sabbabigh al-Aal neighborhood of Old Baghdad, a Shia enclave then dominated by the magnificent, if crumbling, minaret of Al-Ghazl—a superb example of Abbasid-dynasty brick architecture, and all that remained of a thirteenth-century mosque that had once served as the caliph's own. Mohamed never knew his father, who was a textile merchant; he died of old age when Mohamed was only a year old. Mohamed and his mother and her one other son ended up living with her brother, who ran a modest grocery store. Mohamed described this uncle to me as a big man with a knife in his belt, who expected his nephew to quit school at the age of eleven and help out in the family business. One of the ur-tales of Makiya family lore involves the way the young headmaster of Mohamed's school came barreling into the market square one morning, a short skinny man and incidentally a Jew (this at a time when fully a third of Baghdad's population was Jewish!); how he cornered the burly uncle and berated him for pulling such a gifted young boy out of school, humiliating him in front of all his customers; and how he then grabbed young Makiya by the arm and dragged him back to class. The uncle relented and never interfered in the boy's education again.

Once the British had finally secured Baghdad, during the First World War, they decided to stay for a while. They yoked three of the defeated Ottoman Empire's more far-flung and underdeveloped provinces—Basra, Baghdad, and Mosul—into a single entity, gave it the name Iraq, and installed Faisal, a Sunni emir from the Arabian Peninsula, as its king. The British retained control over Iraq under a League of Nations mandate until the end of 1932, when the country achieved nominal independence. During their fifteen years in power, the British had tended to concentrate governmental authority in the same Sunni-minority classes that the Ottomans, who were also Sunnis, had favored —much to the annoyance of the majority Shiites. Faisal, for his part, tried to temper the country's fierce ethnic resentments and ended up being resented by almost everyone; he died, in despair, at the age of forty-eight, only a year after independence. His son Ghazi ruled over an increasingly restive country for the next six years, before dying in an accident, at which point *his* son, only four years old, was crowned Faisal II, with a pro-British regent, Abd al-Ilah, ruling in his stead.

Meanwhile, Mohamed was flourishing in school. He excelled in mathematics, and his scores on his graduating year's baccalaureate exams were among the highest in the country. This was particularly fortunate, because that year a liberal and modernizing education minister launched a program to take fifty of the country's brightest young students, regardless of sect, and send them abroad on full government scholarships. It was thus that Mohamed arrived in London in 1935. He spent his entire first year there learning English, preparing for the necessary matriculation exams, and, having gone almost overnight from a world of oil lamps and open sewers to one of electric lights and indoor plumbing, trying to recover from culture shock. After that, he was sent to the University of Liverpool to begin his serious training. With no particular conviction—at first, anyway—he chose to major in architecture. Some of his teachers doubted whether a boy from Baghdad would be able to master the subtleties of Christopher Wren and Inigo Jones, but by the end of his second year in Liverpool he was one of the top students in his design class. During holidays, he would go on bicycle tours and draw elevations of churches and city streets. Slowly, the discipline was exerting a fascination over him.

"HE WAS ALREADY a fully formed architect by the time I met him," Mohamed's wife, Margaret, told me later that day. "Fully formed and very serious." Margaret had joined us for tea in an Indian café near Covent Garden, not far from the apartment where she and Mohamed now live. Walking in, she looked like a stout, no-nonsense British matron. In the course of our conversation, she remarked that Kanan was such a romantic, just like his father, and I asked if she hadn't been a bit of a romantic herself—an English girl who fell in love, gave up everything, turned her back on her family, and went off to live in Baghdad for what she thought would be the rest of her days.

"What's romantic about that?" she replied gruffly. "What could be more prosaic?"

They met in 1941, while Mohamed was doing a last year of postgraduate work in city planning at the University of Liverpool and Margaret was a second-year history student there. Her father was a strict headmaster in New Mills, Derbyshire, and her relationship with Mohamed encountered strong opposition at home. Forced to make a choice, she simply broke with her past. In 1942, Mohamed was accepted in the doctoral program at Kings College, Cambridge, and she joined him there the following year. Despite the war, this was an idyllic period: Mohamed continued to learn about modern architectural trends while plowing through his dissertation, whose title was "The Influence of Climate on Architectural Development in the Mediterranean Region," but he also spent time attending lectures by Bernard Lewis and Bertrand Russell and Harold Laski. He and Margaret didn't have much money to spare, but what little they had they spent on books.

In 1946, Mohamed received his doctorate and returned to Baghdad. A year and a half later, Margaret joined him there, and they were wed. A year after that, Kanan was born; a second child, a daughter named Hind, born in 1952, completed the family. Margaret was welcomed wholeheartedly by Mohamed's family—his mother adored her—but even so their first several years in Baghdad were difficult. "The thing you have to realize is that in 1946 there was no such vocation in Iraq as that of architect," Margaret told me. "The word didn't really exist in Arabic. There were words for contractor and builder—which was to say a sort of craftsman—but nobody had ever heard of somebody doing what architects do here in the West."

Initially, Mohamed got a job with the municipal authorities that amounted to a kind of city planning, but it paid barely enough to cover the rent on minimal lodging. Margaret also got a job. She taught English and history at the University of Baghdad. That job lasted for twenty-seven years, and in the early days she was earning more than twice as much as her husband. He opened an office on the side, but it wasn't as though he could just go out looking for clients. "That's not how things are done in the Middle East," Margaret said. "Everything's much more indirect and roundabout—a friend-of-a-friend, tentative approach, that sort of thing." When Mohamed did get work, there were no contracts, and often no detailed plans. He would have to improvise on the spot. A client frequently paid in goods, not money. Discussing the subject in advance was considered crass. Sometimes Mohamed was compensated with carpets; once, a sheik in southern Iraq gave him a cow as payment. "And a rather nasty cow at that," Margaret recalled. "Used to kick like hell."

Most of the work Mohamed did in those early years was contracting rather than designing. In the spring of 1953, while he was supervising the erection of a low-cost housing project, the Tigris overflowed its banks, as it often did then, before dams were finally built to regulate its flow. The flood was the worst in many years, and the project's entire brickmaking operation was washed away. Though work crews were up all night trying to salvage what they could, tons of other material was ruined by morning. Mohamed was personally liable for the loss, and it took him and Margaret years to recover.

The children, however, were sheltered from the precariousness of life, and Kanan remembers his first ten years with particular fondness. The family was living in a bungalow in an area of Baghdad where British officers had lived during the war. The house itself was modest, just four rooms, but a yard that it shared with neighboring bungalows had huge eucalyptus trees and wildly overgrown gardens, which made it a child's paradise. Many of the immediate neighbors were other members of the country's gradually emerging technical intelligentsia, but just beyond the bungalows was a neighborhood of *sarifah* dwellings—the mud huts of impoverished migrants pouring in from the south. (During Mohamed Makiya's lifetime, Baghdad's population has risen from less than two hundred thousand to more than four million.) Kanan spent much of his early childhood playing with children from that neighborhood. His nanny was an Assyrian, and she took him to her home so often that he became, in effect, a member of her extended family.

His father's right-hand man in the contracting business was a towering, one-eyed Kurd. Once, returning from the north, this man brought little Kanan a present, a brown bear cub. Of course, as the months passed it grew apace, and eventually it had to be chained outside in the yard. The Kurd relished coming over to wrestle with the bear—the bigger it got, the better, as far as he was concerned. At one point it ripped an arm off Kanan's beloved teddy; evenings it howled, or rather roared, at the moon. "Frightful racket," Margaret recalls. Eventually they ended up taking the bear and presenting it to the young king, who had a menagerie of his own. "Solved the bear problem," Margaret says simply. The Kurd, for his part, presently returned to the north to take part in his people's resistance; he'd return occasionally with harrowing stories. Years later, in *Republic of Fear,* Kanan would render unusually sympathetic accounts of Iraq's various national minorities and the successive persecutions they faced. If part of that sympathy arose from political conviction, Kanan is certain a large measure came from the rich exposures of his early youth (as, no doubt, did some of the political convictions themselves).

The family's lives began to stabilize, although, as Margaret says, "life never stabilizes in the Middle East. It never becomes standardized unless you're fabulously wealthy, and even then you can lose everything overnight. For all the rest of us in Iraq, certainly during those years, life was always difficult." Still, as oil revenues started trickling into Iraq in the mid-fifties, there were increasing numbers of offices to be constructed and houses to be designed, and Mohamed Makiya began to get increasing numbers of commissions. By 1959, he was even able to build a house of his own—a striking blend of International Style and purely local and traditional motifs, and featuring an ingenious round library. "That house had a wonderful intimacy," Kanan recalls. "It had no overall structure. It just grew and grew as our circumstances permitted, its morphology utterly organic—wall, brick, sheet glass—and at any moment you could hardly tell if you were inside or outside."

WHEN IT CAME to Iraq's suddenly burgeoning modern cultural activities, the Makiyas were very much on the inside. Mohamed and Margaret, back at their apartment, showed me a photograph, from 1957, of Mohamed escorting the young King Faisal II through the first modern-art exhibition of the country's Artists' Society, which Mohamed himself had helped organize. Off to one side, in the photograph, stand Abd al-Ilah, the regent; Jewad Salim, Iraq's foremost modernist sculptor and artist; and Khalid al-Rahal, another major sculptor. Uniformed men lurk in the shadows. Less than a year after that picture was taken, the king and the regent were both murdered during a brutal military coup. Salim created a large and striking bas-relief, the last masterwork of his career, as a public monument in celebration of that revolution; al-Rahal, for his part, stayed on in Baghdad, became ever more renowned, and eventually designed some of the key monuments to Baathism and Saddam Hussein.

The 1958 revolution was a watershed in modern Iraqi history. The monarchy was abolished and a "republic" declared. Ironically, it was under the monarchy that Iraq had enjoyed a parliament—one of two principal legacies of its years under British mandate, the other being the army. But in 1958 the army overthrew the parliament, and "Republican Iraq" hasn't had a parliament since. The parliament had been a vaguely effective body during its first years, in the thirties, but as the decades passed it had become increasingly corrupt and had lost touch with the Iraqi people. So had the monarchy itself; it was generally regarded as far too pro-Western. Initially, at least, the revolution enjoyed enormous popular support.

But there were two factions contending for control of the revolution, and their often bloody intrigues formed the backdrop for much of Iraqi politics in the next decade. One faction was the pan-Arabists, who wanted Iraq to merge as quickly as possible with the newly formed United Arab Republic, made up of Egypt and Syria. (The Suez crisis had occurred two years earlier, and the charismatic Gamal Abdel Nasser's populist pan-Arabism was at its peak.) This faction consisted of some of the officers who had taken part in the coup and of various other political groups, including the Baath Party, a small, fanatical organization that saw itself as the true vanguard of any eventual pan-Arabist triumph. The opposing faction comprised most of the other Iraqi officers who had been involved in the coup, including its leader, Abdul Karim Kassem, and he now emerged as both prime minister and commander-in-chief. Their line was more specifically Iraqi nationalist—or "Iraqicist," as they put it—and was supported by a mass-based Communist movement, which claimed the allegiance of much of the Iraqi intelligentsia as well.

The following year, 1959, a Baathist hit squad, including Saddam Hussein, who was then twenty-two, botched an assassination attempt on Kassem, and Saddam fled to Egypt. Kassem managed to hold on (though in the meantime he turned on his Communist allies) until February of 1963. Then a bloody combined military and Baathist coup dislodged him. There followed an unstable succession of military regimes, one displacing the next right through the Six-Day War, in 1967—a calamitous event that undercut the prestige of military regimes throughout the Arab world. Capitalizing on that defeat, the radical wing of the Baath Party reasserted itself, decrying the incompetent leadership of the military and hinting darkly at Fifth Column conspiracies. During the summer of 1968, the radical Baathists struck once again, and the regime they succeeded in installing then has survived to this day. At the age of thirty-two, Saddam Hussein, who had returned from Egypt, became the deputy chairman of the Revolutionary Command Council, in charge of internal security.

That was Iraqi political life at the top—a chaotic welter, mortally dangerous for anyone who dared step in. But the point about Iraq in the sixties is that ordinary people, by and large, didn't need to get directly involved. Governments came and went, but there was a fairly vital civil society, one of the most vital anywhere in the Middle East. Baghdad's robust cultural and intellectual life drew from the heterogeneousness of its population, which included Jews, Kurds, Shiites, Sunnis, Armenians, and Christians. There was a rich context of political discussion (including one of the largest and most effectively organized Communist movements anywhere in the Third World); writers and journalists and artists and teachers and architects were able to sustain more or less normal practices, certainly within the Third World connotations of the term. Later, things changed dramatically, and Kanan feels that failures of nerve and imagination by those same cultural figures played a considerable role in the change; but while he was growing up civil life was still possible.

The years from the late fifties through the early seventies were generally good ones for Mohamed Makiya. Many of the Makiyas' friends were far to the left, if not outright Communists, but Mohamed himself was nearly oblivious of politics; he was too busy pursuing his own projects. In 1959, he founded the University of Baghdad's School of Architecture, and throughout the next decade he served as its head, making it into one of the most highly respected such faculties in the Third World and, in the process, molding an entire generation of Iraqi architects. He recruited teachers from Britain, the United States, Czechoslovakia, and Poland, among other places, but he also required the school's students to know their Iraqi architectural heritage, sending them out to draw elevations of Baghdad and of cities and villages and archeological sites throughout the country. Frank Lloyd Wright, Walter Gropius, and Buckminster Fuller were guests in his home.

In the early sixties, important commissions began coming Mohamed's way. One of the most important of these was from the Ministry of Religious Affairs to design a mosque around Al-Ghazl, the ruined minaret in whose shadow he had grown up. He jumped at the chance, but then held out for months in an attempt to wrest from the ministry a commitment for a larger site, in keeping with the importance of the minaret. He didn't get it. "I had to build a cathedral in an area suitable for a chapel," he complains, but he nevertheless succeeded. Kanan, who vividly remembers visiting his father at the site and watching him supervise the smithies forging grillwork and the stone-carvers etching calligraphic motifs into the bricks, has described the resultant structure, the Khulafa Mosque, as "a chapel that wanted so much to be a cathedral that it ended up looking like one." The mosque seemed to be at once completely contemporary and entirely integrated into its historical setting—an early instance of the quintessential Makiya style.

Mohamed went on to design bank buildings, libraries, private residences, and government ministries for Iraq. Perhaps his most ambitious project during the mid-sixties—certainly the most important to him—was the master plan for a modern university in the ancient Shia city of Kufa. "He spent a lot of time in those days hobnobbing with the turban types, trying to accommodate their requirements in a contemporary setting," Kanan recalls. Within Iraq, his only serious rival was another modernist architect, Rifat Chadirji, but now Mohamed's work began taking him outside Iraq as well: in 1968, he won an international competition for the Chamber of Commerce and Industry Building in Manama, Bahrain—the first of a number of commissions in the small Persian Gulf states, whose coffers were beginning to swell with oil revenues. He was becoming one of the most sought-after architects in the Middle East.

KANAN IDOLIZED his father, and during those years he took every opportunity to visit him at the sites of his various projects. He was struck by the difference between the extraordinarily gentle face Mohamed turned toward his family and the fierce and often angry one with which he pursued his professional aims. Meanwhile, Kanan himself was doing exceptionally well at school, especially in math. He attended the best high school in Baghdad, which was run by American Jesuits and offered instruction in both English and Arabic.

Like his father, Kanan was largely oblivious of politics, but he does recall two incidents from those years that helped to shape his later attitudes. The first was the 1963 coup, which occurred when he was fourteen. From the roof of his house, he was able to see jet fighters attacking the Defense Ministry. Even more disconcerting was what he saw on television in the days that followed. When many of Kassem's partisans continued fighting, refusing to believe the reports that their prime minister had been killed, the Baathists responded by repeatedly televising a lengthy film clip displaying his bullet-riddled corpse. As Kanan recorded in *Republic of Fear:*

Night after night, they made their gruesome point. The body was propped up on a chair in the studio. A soldier sauntered around, handling its parts. The camera would cut to scenes of the devastation at the Ministry of Defense where Kassem had made his last stand. . . . Back to the studio, and close-ups now of the entry and exit points of each bullet hole. The whole macabre sequence closes with a scene that must forever remain etched on the memory of all those who saw it: the soldier grabbed the lolling head by the hair, came right up close, and spat full face into it.

The fear that the Baath were trying to instill in this and other instances was brutally direct. The centuries-old message was simple: he is dead, you had better believe it, we can do the same to you.

To an extent, the message had its effect on the young Kanan: it fostered in him a deep suspicion of the Baathists, and he never had any illusions about them after those 1963 scenes.

The second incident occurred in the midst of the Six-Day War, in June of 1967, when Kanan (by this time almost eighteen) was being subjected to incessant news reports of spectacular Arab successes on the battlefield, with hundreds of Israeli fighter planes already shot down. "I don't know why," Kanan said to me, "but I just remember immediately thinking, This is such bullshit, these are all such lies, we *deserve* to lose."

At the time, Kanan was finishing high school, and he very much wanted to study abroad. One of the Jesuits at his school encouraged him to apply to the Massachusetts Institute of Technology, where he was accepted, and he began classes in September of 1967. The Jesuits were expelled from Iraq the following year, after the Baath returned to power. The school was taken over by the Baath and now is attended primarily by the children of leading Party officials.

At M.I.T., Kanan continued to excel at math, but his passion shifted to the arts. He became obsessed with abstract metal sculpture, and the following summer, back in Baghdad, he embarked on a tutorial in wood carving with Mohammed Ghani, a major Iraqi modernist, who, as it happened, had had his first show in the Makiya home. At M.I.T., however, Kanan was soon gripped by another, and even more overpowering, passion—for political engagement. From fairly standard anti–Vietnam War activities he drifted into an increasingly serious involvement with the problems of his home region. He read voraciously and sought out mentors, and he soon found one in an Israeli mathematician named Emmanuel Farjoun, who was working on his doctoral dissertation in algebraic topology. Farjoun was an anti-Zionist socialist. As he told Kanan the first day they met—and subsequently told me, in London—he had been a misfit in the Israeli Army, which ended up assigning him to agricultural duties, "for everybody's sake."

While serving out his stint of alternative service as a shepherd in the hills along Israel's eastern border during the summer of 1967, he was up with the sheep the night that Israel launched its lightning preemptive strike initiating the Six-Day War. "God damn it," he cursed, watching the Israeli jets streaking toward their targets in Jordan and Syria, "this is such bullshit—we *deserve* to lose."

The only Israeli who'd wished that Israel would lose the Six-Day War meets the only Arab who'd wished the Arabs would: it was love at first sight. And, indeed, Kanan and Emmanuel have remained best friends to this day, forming and informing each other's politics, which back in the late 1960s were Trotskyist and pro-Palestinian (if not particularly anti-Israeli) in a tandem of mutually high regard. Their hope was for a revolutionary socialist transformation of the entire region, with Israeli workers and Palestinian workers and Lebanese workers and Iraqi workers all rising up together, united in their common destiny.

In the spring of 1969, Kanan met Afsaneh Najmabadi, an Iranian physicist, who was a graduate student at Harvard. She had been born in Teheran in 1946, into a famous family of Shiite clerics and scholars going back several generations (her mother, a schoolteacher, had been among the first in her family to dispense with the veil), but Afsaneh was an atheist—or, to put it another way, physics had become her religion. She was a prodigious student, and when she graduated from high school, in 1964, she scored first in the entire country on the national math exams. She enrolled in the University of Teheran to study physics, but by the middle of her second year she realized—as she told me when I visited her in Cambridge, Massachusetts—that she wasn't going to earn any Nobel Prizes staying there. She applied to several American universities and was awarded a full scholarship to Radcliffe.

There Afsaneh continued her studies, advancing to graduate work in particle physics at Harvard in 1968, but she, too, was soon being drawn to politics—in particular, toward the incipient feminist movement, the anti-Shah campaign, and the Palestinian cause. One day in the early spring of 1969, she attended a teach-in on Palestine cosponsored by Harvard and M.I.T., and there she came upon a young man deeply embroiled in a political argument. "He didn't look like an Arab," she recalled. "He had incredibly bushy brown hair in those days, like a halo, and I thought he must be an American Jew, and I was struck by the progressive stands he was advancing. I went up to him afterward and introduced myself, and told him where I was from. He gave his name—Kanan Makiya—and said he was an Iraqi. 'But Shia,' he immediately added, to put me, an Iranian, at ease."

They began going out together. A few weeks later, they climbed into her beat-up VW Beetle and headed for a ride out onto Cape Cod, with Afsaneh driving. Halfway along, something happened, the car spun out, tumbling over and over. Kanan was safe, but Afsaneh was seriously injured. On the ambulance ride to the hospital, Kanan leaned over her crumpled body and for the first time declared his love to her. She recovered, they moved in together, and soon they were wed. Afsaneh, too, joined the Trotskyist movement.

Kanan began to bend his academic studies in the direction of architecture—in part, perhaps, because of his father but also in part because politically he was having a hard time justifying his purely formalist aesthetic interests. Architecture offered a way of blending those interests with some kind of social utility. In 1971, he took a year off and spent it in Bahrain, as an apprentice in his father's growing operation there. Afterward, he returned to M.I.T. and completed his thesis for an architecture degree—"something," he recalls, "about how anything really worth doing architecturally can't possibly be done because of the conditions of late capitalism."

IT WASN'T "late capitalism," however, that was threatening the possibilities of architecture in Iraq around this time. After the Baathists stormed back into power, in 1968, no sphere of Iraqi life was any longer allowed to exist outside politics. Everything, including architecture, became intensely political —and only one type of politics was allowed. Within months of the Baathist resurgence, Mohamed's beloved Kufa university project was shut down: the Baathists saw no reason to be encouraging Shia particularism, or, for that matter, any cultural expression outside their control. No sooner had they canceled that project, however, than they tried to commission Mohamed to rebuild Babylon right on top of its archeological ruins. He immediately confronted the minister in charge. "I told him, 'This is crazy. You are asking me to turn Babylon into a tourist trap with a Ziggurat Hotel—this is a crime against history!'" he recalls. "The man was my worst enemy at the time—he was the one who had ordered Kufa shut down—but he listened, and I managed to convince him. Later, they killed him."

Other possibilities had begun opening up for Makiya—in Bahrain and Oman and Qatar. His Gulf practice was thriving, and he began spending increasing amounts of time in his Bahrain field office, supervising all those new projects. Luckily, he happened to be in Bahrain in the spring of 1972, when, back in Baghdad, his name showed up on one of the Baathists' lists of suspected Fifth Columnists. The Baath had been conducting periodic sweeps for some time, terrorizing the populace through successive discoveries of ever-wider conspiracies: Jewish traitors, Jesuit subversives, British agents, Iranian spies. People would be swallowed up, disappear for months or years, and often die in prison or, even worse as it sometimes seemed, finally get themselves released. Margaret recalled for me the case of a family friend, the former ambassador to the United Nations: "They got him and held him for years. When they finally let him out, he had the mind of a five-year-old."

So one day, while Mohamed was off working in Bahrain, Margaret received word that his name had shown up on a list of those who were going to be dragged in as part of the next round of arrests. The Baath had unearthed yet another dastardly conspiracy, this time one of *Freemasons!* (Mohamed was no Freemason, but their next-door neighbor apparently was, and he'd been arrested some months earlier, tortured . . .) Margaret managed to get word to Mohamed not to return. He didn't.

For her, a truly dreadful year followed. "I was like Isabel Burton," she recalls. "'Pay, pack, and follow'—that was her motto, and it became mine." As unobtrusively as possible, she worked to pack her family's belongings and ship them, one by one, out of the country. Every object, every book, had to be inventoried; every form required a separate protocol of signatures. "I was lucky," she says. "I'd been teaching twenty-seven years by that point—twenty-seven times, say, a hundred students a year. That made for a lot of contacts in the various ministries, and I had to draw on every single one of them."

A few years earlier they'd moved out of the house Makiya had built (it had been taken over by a top Baath official who proceeded to destroy the place). Now she was having to sell their new home, on a lovely site along the river, under obviously distressed conditions. Kanan never even saw the place. It was commandeered by the Baathist defense minister. Later they killed him, too. But finally Margaret managed to make it out, joining Mohamed first in Bahrain and then in Muscat, Oman, where he'd taken a job redesigning the town's entire city plan.

Meanwhile, Kanan was completing his thesis for a master's in architecture at M.I.T., and Afsaneh had begun work on her doctoral dissertation at Harvard. At this point, however, she abandoned her scientific studies: she had done extremely well on her orals, but she had lost interest in physics and decided not to complete the dissertation, instead throwing herself wholeheartedly into politics. By that time, she and Kanan were tiring of the United States. Both Trotskyist and Middle Eastern–expatriate politics seemed far more vital and more sharply focused in Europe, so in the fall of 1974 Kanan entered a yearlong postgraduate program in urban and regional planning at the London School of Economics, and Afsaneh joined an active group of Iranian expatriates in London who were beginning to coordinate protests against the increasingly wobbly regime of the Shah in Teheran. Kanan, for his part, spent much of that year working on behalf of the Kurds in Iraq, who during this period had mounted an anti-Baathist insurrection—an uprising that was championed, if only momentarily, by secretary of state Henry Kissinger and his main regional ally, the Shah.

That same year, Mohamed Makiya decided to establish an office in London, and Margaret decided to establish the family's new home base there. (Mohamed was traveling continually in those years, from one Gulf project to another.) Kanan, who was far more practical than his father, shepherded the London office through its various registration procedures, helped find office space, and even began hiring a staff. After completing his year at the London School of Economics, he started working for his father full time, running the entire office, though not without some trepidation. "At a certain level, this was a ridiculous situation," Kanan told me during one of our talks. "There came a point—our work load was steadily increasing all through here—where I was in charge of coordinating the efforts of forty or fifty people, most of them far more experienced than I was. Actually, this situation was not an uncommon one in the Middle East during those years, as the oil money poured into all these essentially family businesses. But it was awkward." Still, by all accounts, Kanan was an unusually competent administrator.

And, by all accounts, Mohamed was an unusually difficult man to administer *for*. To him, his project was everything, and he could be curt and dismissive with both underling and client; Kanan's job was to pick up the pieces, to try to finesse the damage. His job was also to coordinate the office's work on upward of a dozen projects simultaneously—a library in Abu Dhabi, a mosque in Rome, a market in Qatar, various private residences in Bahrain, a housing complex in Oman. Almost from the start, Kanan abandoned any thought of making a creative contribution. "Can two artists hold the same pen and write?" is how Emmanuel Farjoun framed the problem for me. "Both Kanan and his father are artists at heart." So Kanan ceded the field to his father, but at times he chafed under that self-imposed restriction. And at times he chafed at doing this sort of work at all. On the side, he went on with his political work, writing long, sophisticated analytical articles on various Middle Eastern themes. "My friends were all trying to deal with the concrete problems of the world," he commented to me. "More often than not, I was stuck dealing with the worldly problems of concrete."

But not all the time. In 1978, with a group of Lebanese friends—onetime Trotskyist colleagues who had returned from the Lebanese civil war shell-shocked and drained of illusion—he founded Al Saqi, an Arabic-language bookstore and cultural center in Westbourne Grove, in West London. (*Al saqi* means "the water bearer," and the store's insignia is a drawing of a water seller offering drinks to two children.) Al Saqi was intent on being as inclusive and nonsectarian as possible, and since the only other such outlets in England at the time were aligned with various warring political factions, Kanan and his friends found themselves under attack from all sides. But they persevered, and eventually they launched a publishing program as well, which they conceived of in part as a bridge between East and West, offering important Arabic titles in English, and vice versa. At one point, for instance, they decided to publish an English version of Tawfiq al-Hakim's great modern Egyptian novel *Maze of Justice*. It turned out that a fine out-of-print translation already existed—by the former Israeli foreign minister Abba Eban. The directors met to try to decide what to do. Should they publish it and simply leave the translator's name off? Kanan insisted that they publish it and emphasize the translator's name, which is what they did.

Later, during the Salman Rushdie affair, Al Saqi made a point of continuing to sell *The Satanic Verses* right through the entire controversy, the only such Arabic outlet to do so. Meanwhile, Kanan's father opened an exhibition space in the back of the store that would specialize in Middle Eastern themes, and called it the Kufa Gallery. Mohamed and Kanan designed the bookstore and the gallery together, and Mohamed moved his own operation into the building as well.

Kanan spent a lot of his spare time on that enterprise, and a good deal of what was left on Iran. In 1978, Afsaneh began making extended stays in Teheran, and became increasingly involved in the political ferment there. The Trotskyists supported Ayatollah Khomeini as a way station on the path toward a more authentic revolution; after all, the masses couldn't be wrong. But Kanan and Afsaneh became less and less sure of the wisdom of that position. As Khomeini returned and the mullahs' ire was directed at women in particular, forcing them back into roles of virtually medieval servitude, Afsaneh grew restive. Kanan tried to alert their friends in London, but, by and large, he was ignored. Afsaneh, meanwhile, would return to Iran, rejoining her embattled colleagues, helping to edit their paper and organize their rallies, trying to salvage what she could.

The offices of Makiya Associates, however, were claiming more and more of Kanan's time; and he began to devote himself to a single huge project. "In 1976, we submitted an entry in an international competition for Kuwait," Kanan told me. "It was for—and this, I swear, was the client's name for it, prominently displayed on all the announcements and stationery and later on all the plans and blueprints—the Kuwait State Mosque and Multi-Storey Car Park. And, actually, that is perfect: it absolutely sums up Kuwait, that country of extravagant public piety and air-conditioned automobiles. Anyway, our entry won, and the further plans and the actual construction of the thing took up the better part of the next several years."

This was the biggest project Makiya Associates had yet realized. The firm had to work within certain client-specified parameters: the emir, for example, wanted his own private entrance. And then Mohamed had certain requirements of *his* own. The parking lot was supposed to be underground, but he couldn't accept the idea that Muslims, prostrate in prayer and hugging the earth, as the Koran commands, would in truth be hugging a vault filled with six hundred automobiles. So he had to find a way to sequester the cars over to one side. Enormous complications arose as the project went along: foul-ups regarding the color of the setting concrete, impediments occasioned by the colossal air-conditioning ducts, cost overruns of all sorts, the interference of countless layers of bureaucrats (all of them Palestinian, incidentally: the Kuwaitis never sullied themselves with anything as mundane as actually administering how their millions were being spent).

Finally, after six years, the building was completed. The emir arrived to survey his structure for the first time, took one look at the sleek swaths of barely adorned concrete—a key element of Mohamed's conception—and ordered a small army of mosaicists brought in from Morocco to make it look the way the king's palace looks there. Today, Kanan washes his hands of the whole affair, saying, "After the emir's mosaicists had got through with the place, they'd given it all the patina of a cheap Tangier hotel."

THE KUWAIT STATE MOSQUE, with its myriad complications, was causing a considerable drain on the finances of Makiya Associates, and the firm was actively soliciting projects elsewhere. At the end of 1979, Kanan was approached by a Lebanese firm to consult on the design aspects of a competitive bid for three thousand units of low-cost housing, including schools and other facilities, for construction in Baghdad. Kanan threw the office into this new project with enthusiasm. At the time, he had no moral compunctions about participating (the Lebanese firm's proposal eventually lost out), and even today he defends the decision, on the ground that this was in any case a valuable contribution to the lives of common people in Iraq. "Somebody had to do it, and it might as well have been done well," he told me. "I see no problem with that." Still, the project gnaws at him, because it might have been one of the factors that brought Mohamed Makiya's name back to the attention of Iraq's Baathist officials.

For 1979 was also the year in which Saddam Hussein consolidated his hold on power in Iraq, through a purge of his onetime senior colleagues in the Baath Party. Hundreds of them were killed, including fully a third of the Revolutionary Command Council. (In a move of typically ruthless cunning, Saddam arranged to have some of the surviving ministers and Party leaders execute their former colleagues, thereby assuring their complicity in the new order.) His authority thus in place, Saddam looked toward the future, where two imperatives focused his attention. One was the sudden ascendancy of his archrival, Ayatollah Khomeini, earlier that year in neighboring Iran. Both men were aspiring to hegemony over Middle Eastern politics: Saddam as the head of a pan-Arab (though not particularly Islamic) coalition, one that would by definition exclude non-Arab Iran; Khomeini as the head of a fundamentalist Islamic revival, but one of a distinctly Shiite complexion (and hence one that would undercut Saddam in both his Sunni and his secularist aspects).

At any rate, Saddam found it increasingly necessary to start covering his Islamic flank, as it were. To his rapidly proliferating and ubiquitous images —one day he would appear in dashing military garb, the next in the sleekest of European-cut trappings—he added the simple white robes of the humble Muslim penitent. He began frequenting mosques, including the superb little mosque that Mohamed Makiya had created early in his career around the thirteenth-century Abbasid minaret. In passing, Saddam asked his aides, "Who did this?"

Second, Saddam was looking toward 1982, the year when Baghdad would serve as the site of the triennial Conference of Nonaligned Nations and he himself would assume the mantle of that movement's leader for the next three years—in effect, as he saw it, becoming the leader of the entire Third World. The 1979 nonaligned meeting had taken place in Havana, and Fidel Castro would be visiting Baghdad to acknowledge the transfer of leadership. With this conference in mind, Saddam surveyed his capital city and found it wanting. He and his Baathist colleagues had two years in which to transform it into a gleaming modern metropolis worthy of the coming convocation. No expense would be spared: oil revenues were booming, and whatever sums were necessary would be diverted to the task. As Mohamed subsequently heard the story, Saddam summoned his aides and asked them which Iraqi architects could be called upon to spearhead such a program. "There are two," he was told. "One is in"—in prison, that is. This was Mohamed's old friend and rival Rifat Chadirji, who was serving a sentence on trumped-up charges of economic sabotage. "And one," Saddam's aides continued, "is out."

AND SO IT WAS that on a morning late in the spring of 1980 an envelope postmarked Baghdad arrived in the London offices of Makiya Associates. It contained a letter from Samir Mohammed Abd al-Wahhab, the mayor of Baghdad, to Mohamed Makiya, informing him that the Iraqi government had decided to rebuild Baghdad and was inviting him to come home and participate in the planning, and perhaps even the running, of the entire operation.

"With that earlier housing project, I'd always felt that it seemed safe, interesting, nothing directly to do with the regime, nobody would have to physically be there, and, anyway, what could be wrong with a simple housing project?" Kanan told me one afternoon. "But this one—it was obvious from the start what it was. A letter coming from the highest levels of the Baath Party, from the mayor of Baghdad, a famously crude and thuggish man, one of Saddam's most loyal operatives. I was against it from the start. My father's feelings were mixed. On the one hand, he, of all people, was aware of the sheer risks in terms of security—he hadn't forgotten what it was like having his own name appear on that list. He was aware, as we all were, that this was a tough regime. And yet, for my father, this was also a dream offer—the reconstruction of Baghdad! It embodied everything he'd fantasized about and worked toward since he founded the School of Architecture at the university. It drew on both his architectural and his city-planning sides. It was perfect.

"But, as I say, it was scary, too. We went round and round. We hesitated. We argued. We procrastinated. Finally—it was getting into the summer now—we decided to decline the offer, but even that was scary, because how did you do so without offending them, and what would they do if you did offend them? We ended up sending a polite note begging off, on the ground of my father's health. We said he was unfortunately too ill to take on such a challenge at this time."

Almost immediately, Makiya Associates received a second dispatch, this time by telex and not from the mayor's office but from the Revolutionary Command Council itself, repeating the offer and adding several explicit guarantees: The past was to be put away. He would be met at the airport and housed in the finest hotel. "We assure you of your safe return," the telex read, and it was signed by one of Saddam Hussein's top aides, Tariq Hamad Abdullah, who included his personal phone number.

"'We assure you of your safe return,'" Margaret Makiya commented in recalling the telex. "That was the most chilling part."

"Now we were really thrown into consternation," Kanan told me. "I was still against it, but my father felt that he had to go. Others were telling him it would be more dangerous for him to refuse than to accept—he still had family and friends in Iraq. That business with the phone number was particularly unnerving—and very Middle Eastern—because we all knew, and we knew that they knew, that for him to call would in effect be for him to agree to go. And he couldn't very well not call—because, I mean, how sick could you be that you couldn't even call? They bulldozed right past all our excuses."

A few weeks later, in August of 1980, Mohamed Makiya took a first-class seat on an Iraqi Airways jet bound for Baghdad. Father and son agreed from the outset that, no matter what, Kanan would not join him on this trip to Baghdad or any other. Not only was Kanan against the whole undertaking to begin with, but it was likely that his various opposition activities in exile were known to Baathist security agents, and, besides, he could face immediate conscription if he returned.

"I arrived at dawn," Mohamed told me. "What can I say? In Baghdad again for the first time in almost ten years, the sun coming up—it was all very moving. There was a man there from the Office of the Presidency to meet me, which was a bit frightening. He whisked me through customs, he had a car waiting outside. He kept my passport neatly tucked in his shirt pocket, which was scary, and laid a revolver on the seat between us, which was even scarier. He quickly drove me to the city's best hotel and installed me in an eighth-floor suite with a magnificent view of the river. And a few minutes later I was being taken to the Presidential Palace to meet with Hamad Abdullah. While I was sitting there in the waiting room, two of Saddam Hussein's bodyguards came in. 'Why would somebody like you leave here to go work in Kuwait?' one of them challenged me. 'Yeah, leave a country like ours with such a great army?' the other said. Nervously, I tried to explain that the Iraqi image outside the country was also important."

Eventually, Mohamed was taken in to meet with Hamad Abdullah; four other members of the Revolutionary Command Council joined them, and presently the mayor of Baghdad as well. Hamad Abdullah assured Mohamed that he was there as their guest, saying, "We are proud of you." ("Hamad Abdullah was very nice and kind," Mohamed recalled. "Later, they killed him.") The mayor told Mohamed that the country had built up a huge cash reserve, and was ready to devote billions of dollars to returning Baghdad to its former Abbasid glory. Could he develop a general proposal and have it ready within a week? Hamad Abdullah then informed him that in four weeks the government would convene a four-day conference on the theme of tradition and modernism in the reconstruction of Baghdad. Would he stay on for the conference? Could he recommend any other participants? They wanted to start working immediately on a waterfront-renewal project in downtown Baghdad. Did he have any ideas? And they wanted to rebuild the neighborhood around the Khulafa Mosque.

Mohamed was drawn in. Working by telex with his London office—Kanan recalls the entire office churning away, TV monitors tuned to the royal wedding (of Charles and Diana) in the background—he did manage to throw together a general plan in a week. Mohamed took time off to revisit key historical sites, like Samarra and Basra, in an act of spiritual and creative replenishment. He visited with old friends: in one case he was shocked to find a close friend distinctly anxious, talking only in a whisper for fear of being overheard by a four-year-old grandchild playing off in the corner. He continued meeting with city officials and planners, many of them former students of his. He informed the mayor that he wanted to maintain his base in London, and wanted not to be chief architect for the entire scheme but only to design specific projects for it. Meanwhile, Saddam Hussein ordered Rifat Chadirji released from prison, and Chadirji agreed to serve as the mayor's counselor in charge of the reconstruction of Baghdad, on the condition that he be allowed to leave the country after the meeting of the nonaligned nations in 1982.

Mohamed remained in Baghdad for the four-day conference, which opened on September 19 and took place in the Presidential Palace, with scores of top Party and state planning officials participating. Every few hours, Saddam Hussein dropped in briefly, and then left again. "At one point, I was in the middle of giving a talk, and suddenly I noticed one of the ministers gesticulating frantically," Mohamed recalled. "Saddam had just walked in, and the protocol apparently was that I should stop, and start all over again from scratch. I stopped and waited until he had sat down, like a professor waiting out a tardy student, but then I just went on from where I'd paused. The minister almost went mad with his frantic exertions. One of the other days, there was a big luncheon, and I was trying to hang back unobtrusively, but someone came up and told me that the president himself wanted me to join him at his table. I was taken there and told to be seated—we were the only two at the table. He was very polite, very clever, but he would never allow any cross-chatter while he was conversing—in fact, everybody was expected to simply stand around awaiting instructions. It was all very eerie, all his cabinet members standing around stiffly like that, like servants—people like Tariq Aziz. Hussein didn't even bother to introduce them." Tariq Aziz went on to become Iraq's foreign minister.

"So, anyway, he was in and out of the conference the whole time," Mohamed said. "Listening, interjecting, commenting, summarizing. In the end, only *his* comments were allowed to stand. The fourth day, however, he didn't show up, and, in fact, the whole conference was moved to a different place. Something seemed to be going on, but I couldn't figure out what. Early the next morning, however, I was awakened by a terrible whooshing noise. I rushed to my balcony, and there below me—I was *above* them—two Iranian fighter jets went zooming by on what must have been their first revenge flights. It turned out that Hussein had launched his war against Iran during the night. He must have been planning it all through the conference, and yet he'd had the time and the confidence to attend almost all our deliberations, and he never gave any indication."

II

Mohamed had been intending to fly back to London a few days hence, exactly the way he'd arrived, by Iraqi Airlines, first class. One look at those two Iranian fighters streaking by beneath his balcony, however, and he changed his mind immediately, organizing an overland taxi caravan to Amman, Jordan, for that very afternoon. On his way out of town, he had his taxi pause at a friend's to say goodbye. No sooner had his car stopped than it was immediately surrounded by security police: "Why are you stopping here? Let us see your papers." Maybe it was the war, everybody all tense, security stepped up. Maybe it was just how it always was (and his other friend had been right after all about the grandchild). He didn't know. He thought about it a bit later on the long drive west across the desert. But mainly he was thinking about the reconstruction of Baghdad. His mind was already brimming over with projects. Surely this war wouldn't last, it would be over in a matter of days and everybody could get back to the serious work at hand.

Back home, the arguments between Kanan and his father took a serious turn. "I said we shouldn't be doing this," Kanan recalled. "We just shouldn't be doing it. As I say, I hadn't been giving that much thought to Iraq during the years immediately before that—Israel, Lebanon, and of course Iran had been much nearer the forefront of my concerns. But the year before, I'd heard a story from an Iraqi friend that had left a *deep* impression—in fact it's the one I use to open my book."

"Salim was about to sit down to dinner when the knock came," is how Samir al-Khalil launches the first chapter of *Republic of Fear* (a footnote acknowledges that names and a few details have been changed).

The two men did not come in or identify themselves. They confirmed Salim's identity and politely told him to accompany them for a few questions. His wife asked too loudly whether anything was wrong, what was the problem, they hadn't done anything, and so on. Salim reassured her as though he knew all about it; he stepped outside with the men, and gently pushed the door shut in her face. Salim remembered his hands turning clammy in the car, although it was not hot, and feeling his stomach had caved in on itself although he was no longer hungry. The car stopped at the local Amn *[secret police] headquarters.*

. . . He remembered waiting for a long time. Although still ignorant of the reasons for his being there, he was becoming more and more afraid. Eventually he was ushered into an enormous office. Screen monitors dotted the entire space, and their flashing images impressed him more than anything else about the room. Whether they were there for effect or for function made little difference.

Salim was offered tea and spoken to politely throughout. An important-looking man, whose office this was and whose name he never found out, looked at some papers before him and asked where he had been on a particular day many months ago. Salim didn't remember.

There follows a long and harrowing account of the questioning, the way license plate numbers and the like were produced, to ever more vertiginous effect, until Salim, to his great relief, realized that he'd been laid up all that week with a foot injury and had lent out his car and therefore couldn't have been driving it at all.

To his astonishment, the explanation appeared acceptable; in fact it seemed to come as no surprise. More questions followed as though to pin down the matter, and then the interrogation was over. Relief covered Salim's face until the bombshell struck.

The important-looking man wanted Salim to vacate his house within ten days—clothes, furniture, and all. Salim was to drop his keys at another office in the building and register his new address; he would be contacted when his story had been checked out. Further questions and polite remonstrations were ruled out; the man's demeanor began to show irritation. Salim was escorted to the street and returned home.

The house was vacated, and the keys delivered. Months later a telephone call from Salim's local Amn *headquarters informed him that he could collect his keys from the office where he had deposited them and return to his house.*

Not a single official piece of paper was proffered, or for that matter asked for. Salim, having recovered from the mechanics of his tribulation, shoved the matter aside as one might the weather or a natural disaster of some kind, and pressed on with his otherwise perfectly mundane life.

"So, anyway," Kanan continued, "it was against that sort of backdrop that we were having these conversations, that and the fact that this crazy war was going on, even if it was just going to be a short one, as everybody thought at the time. My father would say, 'This is for history. It's not for the people there now. It has nothing to do with them—they'll be gone. This is for Iraq—it's for the future.' And, in a way, in all this he was simply being consistent with his usual approach: he always showed total disdain for the client—because he wasn't doing this for them, it was always for the future! Architects are such megalomaniacs. Ayn Rand got it exactly right: it's in the deepest marrow of the profession."

Though a lot has happened in the decade since—a lot more tearing, a lot of mending—the argument still seemed fresh, as immediate and pertinent as ever, the day I talked with Mohamed Makiya in his office. "I wanted to work for Iraq again," he told me. "For the previous eight years, I hadn't been able to. I'd been working everywhere else in the Gulf, only not there, not in my own home. Iraq was *my* home, not theirs. They said as much themselves. The minister of public works, whom I had known when he was a student at the university, came up to me and said, 'This is *your* golden age, not ours.' I felt I owed something to my country: here my homeland was, momentarily blessed with the opportunity of all that wealth from the oil boom, and there I was, with my forty years of experience and skills, the blessing of having been sent out from the country to acquire those skills. I *owed* it to my country—it had nothing to do with the regime. What did they matter? They'd be gone. But who knew if Iraq would ever have such an opportunity again?

"And even people who opposed Saddam would come up to me and whisper that I should do it. 'If you don't do it, imagine the alternative if they get one of their sycophants to do it,' they'd say. There was all that, and then, as the years went by and several of these commissions were won by way of international juried competitions, there was simply this feeling of pride in being an Iraqi artist competing against all these international eminences and besting them, defying the conventional prejudice against Iraqi inferiority. I also had to think of my office as a whole—over forty coworkers. They didn't care if it was Saddam or Margaret Thatcher or whoever—it was work. But for me, mainly, it was that I'm an architect, this is what I do, I create—I love to create, and these were the greatest opportunities of my creative life. The authorities were giving me a completely free hand, and I was in the position to be doing all of it for my country."

Since we'd been speaking quite frankly in our conversation that day, I asked him to compare his vocation in this instance with that of Albert Speer. "The question you have to ask about Speer," Mohamed replied, not in the least offended (he'd obviously thought about it himself), "is how much was he working out of his being a Nazi rather than as a human being, a humanist, an architect working at the human scale out of love of the human past and the human future of his country." And, of course, Mohamed had a point. He was manifestly no Speer, and the buildings he came to design in the years ahead were no simple fascist excretions. They were steeped in the history of their country. But, in a way, that was precisely what made them so problematic.

For that's the kind of architect Mohamed was. Wherever he went, he tapped into the deepest historical traditions of the place he was dealing with, no matter how "modernist" the transmutations he eventually effected upon these traditions. "What I really hate," he told me one day, "is those international-style modernist architects who show up at some new Third World site and proceed to erect the same generic building wherever they are, maybe just slapping on some local allusion at the end: 'Oh, this is the Baghdad airport, so we'll put up a mural of a flying carpet.' That's not what architecture should be about. The history of the place has to shine through every aspect of the design." In the case of Iraq, he was naturally drawn to the period of what he took to be the country's greatest archeological glory—the Abbasid era. In several of his submissions he was explicit on this point. Other architects submitted charts, plans, site elevations, simulated vistas, a maquette or two. Mohamed did all that, and then submitted an entire treatise as well, including long expositions of history, complete with maps showing the vast sequential expansions of Iraqi rule, culminating with the founding of Baghdad as the seat of the Abbasid caliphate in 762. The text evoked, for example, the glory of a time when "travelers came [to Baghdad] from all over the known world in search of an education or fortune or to witness the caliph Al-Muktader and his parading force of 160,000 horsemen and footmen, 7,000 slaves, 700 chamberlains and 100 lions."

"This was my father to a T," Kanan commented to me. "He wasn't pandering, not in the least. That vision was always the authentic wellspring for his work, long before the Baath." Nevertheless, it dovetailed perfectly with the Baathist vision and, in particular, with Saddam Hussein's own vision of Baghdad as the once and future center of the world. "The glory of the Arabs stems from the glory of Iraq," Saddam had proclaimed in 1979. "Throughout history, whenever Iraq became mighty and flourished, so did the Arab nation," he went on, alluding to the Abbasid hegemony. "This is why we are striving to make Iraq mighty, formidable, able, and developed, and why we shall spare nothing to improve welfare and to brighten the glory of Iraqis." For Saddam, however, the model of the Abbasid caliphate was to be emulated in more than its physical expanse and geopolitical strength: he was also attracted by the Abbasid style of governing—all power radiating from the center, the caliph, with everyone else subservient.

WHEN MOHAMED got back to London, he and his staff set to work. Kanan's misgivings having been overridden, the Makiya Associates office began pouring its creative energies into projects for Baathist Baghdad. The first was an elaborate proposal for the downtown waterfront area; then came a detailed set of designs, undertaken in conjunction with a prominent German architectural firm, for Al-Rashid, a modern university that the Baathists were preparing to start from scratch. No problems here, for the work was completely apolitical, with the exception of a few odd requirements, such as the fact that no building in one area of the Al-Rashid campus could exceed a certain height lest its top-floor occupants be able to look down upon a neighboring nuclear-research facility.

The same could not be said for Mohamed's major triumph during this period: victory in an architectural competition to design the Baath Party headquarters. As far as Mohamed was concerned, of course, this was simply going to be a particularly important government building—albeit one with its own odd requirements, such as a bomb shelter. He had no doubt, he now says, that by the time it was built the Baathists would be long gone. And, in fact, he went out of his way to ventilate the design, providing, for example, large open courtyards and soothing fountains. This was the Party's administrative headquarters, not its police headquarters. The interior was to be filled with conference halls, not torture chambers. Still, it was *the Baath Party headquarters*—and Kanan was dead set against the firm's having anything to do with the project.

From the start of his father's new involvement in Iraq, Kanan moved to establish firebreaks of various sorts, both between the office and the Baath and between himself and the office's work. In the former instance, he set up ever more elaborate arrangements for delegating work to other firms and to subcontractors, so that Makiya Associates itself would have minimal exposure inside Iraq. As for the latter, he brought new people into the firm, so that he could arrange to have nothing to do with any design aspects of the work. "I didn't draw a single line," he assured me, before adding dolefully, "I just organized the whole thing."

Kanan had considered leaving outright. "He knew that he was central to the administration of the whole office," Afsaneh recalls. "He knew that if he had just quit he could have brought the whole thing to a halt." At the same time, he was devoted to his father: he couldn't do that to him.

Throughout this period, he saw his father every day at the office. In addition, they lived next door to each other in Wychcomb Studios, and their fights spilled over from office to home. "The most bitter experiences of my life were the terrible fights between Mohamed and Kanan around that time," Margaret confided to me. Emmanuel Farjoun similarly recalled that Kanan was "flipping out," and added, "The pressures were enormous. He didn't approve of the work the office was doing. In fact, he was agonizing over it. No doubt he'd have had to leave someday, in any case. The Iraqi business was just bringing matters to a head."

Afsaneh was not in much better shape. Luckily, she hadn't been in Iran the day Saddam attacked: if she had been, as the wife of an Iraqi (and a leftist activist to boot) she might well not have made it out alive. Rather, she instantly realized that as the wife of an Iraqi she could not return to Iran. (During the following months, she was able to get her parents out.) Still, even before Saddam's invasion her idealism regarding Iran and her hopes for her country's regeneration had faded substantially. She and Kanan had been among the first members of their leftist group to see that Khomeini's fundamentalism was not merely an incidental step on the path toward a more radical revolution—instead, it *was* the revolution. And that realization was devastating. On her last trip to Teheran, in July of 1980, she recalled, she had had to wear a scarf over her head; the city was rife with rumors of vigilante violence. "It was terrible," she told me. "But that wasn't the worst part: One day, three weeks into that last visit, I was walking along a city street when, for some reason—a draft or something—my scarf slipped, momentarily uncovering my head. For a moment, I panicked—I felt a tremendous surge of fear. But do you know what I really felt? I felt *ashamed.* I felt profound shame, and that feeling *really* scared me."

After September of 1980, Afsaneh went through a period of desolation in London: not only had all her political hopes been dashed, but many of her fellow activists had been lost in the maelstrom—imprisoned, executed. And now, in addition to everything else, her homeland was at war with her husband's, the two sides piling up corpses along their common border in an almost unprecedented frenzy; and, in addition to *that,* her husband was in misery about the work his firm was doing for the man who had started it all. If the urgencies of the world had once drawn her out of academe, its horrors now drove her back in: she threw herself into a second Ph.D. program, this time in sociology, at the University of Manchester, and she got her degree in less than two years. At the same time, she retreated into family life: she became pregnant, and Kanan's and her first child—a daughter, Bushra (the name means "good tidings" in Arabic)—was born in 1981; a son, Naseem, was born four years later.

In any event, it was clear to both Afsaneh and Kanan that it was past time to be cutting their ties to Makiya Associates. Kanan worked as quickly as he could, but it still took him over two years. He had to establish a board of directors to oversee the operations of the office (he retained a position on the board); he had to bring in new people; and, most important, he had to find someone who could take over his own day-to-day managing role and had to train that person in all its intricacies. Finally, in 1983, they did leave. They headed back to America and settled, for the time being, in a house in the Riverdale section of the Bronx, where Kanan began work on a book.

THE SEED for the book had actually been planted a couple of years earlier, in London, when one of Kanan's former Trotskyist colleagues, Neil Belton, who was then an editor at Verso–New Left Books, commissioned him to prepare what both of them thought was going to be "a quickie"—a straightforward report on Iraq that would "explain to people the peculiar intensity and violence of Iraqi nationalism," as Belton described it to me in London recently. Belton and Kanan had initially assumed that the manuscript would take about two years to write, and that its interpretation would be grounded in good, solid Marxist categories, such as competing class interests and the debilitating contingencies imposed on development by the capitalist world order. "It ended up taking quite a bit longer," Belton said. "And, of course, what finally emerged was something very different from what we had expected."

"So New Left Books came up with this offer," Emmanuel Farjoun recalls. "A seemingly light commission for your standard, general programmatic overview. But Kanan's a serious guy. He read and he read. The book continued and the war continued. The whole scene in the Middle East got worse and worse. He discovered things as he went along, discovered the inadequacy of his earlier way of looking at things—of *our* earlier way, because he ended up taking me with him. He was incredibly tenacious. And I think that a part of what was driving him was surely the shame he'd felt in working on those Iraqi commissions back in his father's office. He felt a deep guilt, and the book, in part, was his way of coming to terms with that."

"There's a great irony here," Afsaneh remarked to me one day. "Because the truth is that before 1980 Kanan hadn't been all that involved in Iraq. Lebanon and Palestine and, later, Iran were far more to the fore in what we were struggling over. But then it was as if the Baath came to him. If his father had not been invited back to Iraq, Kanan would probably never have written that book. It was his being involved, even tangentially, in designing the Baath Party headquarters that actually got him thinking, seriously thinking, about the Baath."

And there was a further irony. Throughout his years of running his father's office, Kanan, who was in charge of setting everyone's salaries, had behaved as any self-respecting socialist would have under the circumstances, and set his own salary ludicrously low—even below that of the office secretary. When he was establishing the board of directors to oversee things after his departure, however, he awarded himself a sizable stipend as a member of that board, in justifiable compensation, as he saw it, for all his years of undervalued service—a sort of pension. Thereafter, he would be getting a slice of the office's annual profits—enough, for example, to allow him to go off and write a book about Saddam Hussein. In effect, Saddam Hussein became not only the principal subject of Kanan's book but, unwittingly, its principal sponsor as well.

Kanan felt that, with the exception of Afsaneh, Emmanuel, and a few other close friends, he couldn't speak with anyone about what he was doing. Perhaps his fears for his own safety and his family's were exaggerated, but the deeper he got into his research the less reason he had to think so. Those were years in which Iraqi agents were regularly going around the globe killing people they thought of as enemies.

In beginning the book, Kanan was able to pore through his own files, which were substantial. On top of that, he began visiting libraries—notably, while he was still in London, the superb collection of the University of London's School of Oriental and African Studies, and also his neighborhood public library.

"It was in my neighborhood library that I stumbled upon Hannah Arendt's *Origins of Totalitarianism,* and it completely bowled me over," he recalled. "I devoured it and all her other books, and then, it seems, the books of everyone she ever referred to—Benjamin, Valéry, Auden. Arendt and Auden were completely unknown in Arabic, and I lobbied hard over at Al-Saqi"—the London bookstore and publishing house he had helped found—"to get them to bring out Arabic translations of *On Violence* and *The Poet and the City,* which they've recently done. All those people became tremendously important to me."

Later, in America, Kanan unearthed a large cache of Baath Party pamphlets and documents in the New York Public Library. ("Who knows how they got there?") Despite their bombast and rhetorical excess, these papers became a central resource for his work. In a "Note to the Reader" he offers several "general assumptions about political behavior" that have informed his labors. First among these is his contention that "what leaders, parties, and citizens think and expressly say about politics matters." He explains, "The words that people use are not a 'reflection' of some hidden reality; they are themselves part of that reality. . . . Despite the proclivity of those in public office to propaganda, rhetoric, chicanery, and lies, on the whole even they usually end up saying what they mean and meaning what they say."

Kanan also took to frequenting seminars at the New School; one was on Hannah Arendt's *The Human Condition,* and another one set him to reading Hobbes. "I realized that I didn't know any of the classics," he told me. "I had read all of Marx, Trotsky, Lukács, but none of Plato, Aristotle, Rousseau, Locke"—a situation he proceeded to rectify. Leaving Riverdale after a year, Kanan and Afsaneh returned to their old haunts, in Cambridge, Massachusetts. Afsaneh began teaching at several of the local universities and writing for academic journals, and Kanan began attending seminars at Harvard, most notably those given by the political scientists Judith Shklar and Stanley Hoffmann. "I just started sitting in on everything either of them taught, completely illegally," he said. "I'm sure they had no idea who I was or what I was doing there." He also spent long sessions in the Widener Library.

"It's strange," he recalled for me one day. "Even though the stuff I was exploring and discovering was almost unremitting in its morbidity and gore and, in fact, was getting worse and worse the further I went along, still, the work itself was greatly enjoyable. I felt like this is what life is all about, this is what everybody should be doing." Another time I heard him describe the years he was working on *Republic of Fear* in America as "an idyll."

Idyllic though they may have been, they were also terribly difficult. Guilt-ridden before over the work he had been doing for his father, he was hardly less guilt-ridden now over having abandoned him. "In the Middle East, relations with fathers are incredibly complex and *never, ever,* get questioned," Kanan told me one day. "A son is expected never to criticize his father. You can be as militant as hell in every other aspect of your life—in fact, such militancy is prized—but you never turn it inward and attack your father."

A few months after their return to America, Kanan and Afsaneh had invited his parents to visit them in Riverdale. The day before that visit ended, Mohamed came upon part of his son's manuscript, and stayed up late into the night reading it. The next morning, as they were waiting for a taxi to take them to the airport, an obviously tense Mohamed exploded in the worst rage that any of them had ever experienced. Betrayal! How could his son betray him like this? Oddly, Mohamed wasn't as much upset by the attack on Saddam Hussein or the Baath—that didn't seem to bother him at all—as he was by what he saw as a vicious slur on Shiism in the pages he had read, a gratuitous slur on religion itself. "You should never do anything to insult your father's religion, no matter what you think," Mohamed scolded Kanan. "Don't you know that in doing so you are striking at the root of everything?" Kanan didn't even know what his father was talking about: his references to Shiism had been straightforwardly secular, but then that may have been part of the basis of Mohamed's fury. (Kanan had also been critical of Khomeini's actions in Iran, and one of the stranger aspects of this whole period in their lives, according to Kanan, was that Mohamed, the Shia, continued to maintain a certain reverent regard for Khomeini the entire time he was working for Saddam.) From there the fury spilled in all directions: how such a book could compromise the office's work (Kanan assured his father that he would publish the book under a pseudonym); how Kanan had betrayed him by abandoning the office, how he had never really been devoted to the office at all; how he had probably enlisted in the first place just to obtain a work permit; and so forth. It was a horrendous scene, culminating in a complete rupture of relations: they neither spoke nor wrote to each other for the next eight months. Even today, almost a decade later, they're still trying to sort it out. They talk about it, both marveling, but the memory impinges and they wince.

"The fact that I'd broken with my father is not unrelated to how I was simultaneously breaking with my earlier politics as well," Kanan concedes, referring to Marx, Trotsky, Lukács. He and his friends were clearly undergoing a radical reevaluation of everything they had previously taken for granted: Lebanon, Palestine, Iran, Iraq. "All of us were reeling from the way the world was not conforming to our expectations," Kanan told me. "I mean, for instance, in Lebanon my friends and I—especially my very close Lebanese friends—had all started out supporting the so-called progressive forces, the coalition of the various leftist, nationalist, and Palestinian groupings in their uprising against the Christian Maronites. But things quickly degenerated—like the Spanish Civil War, only worse. By the end, all those involved were identical, each faction its own little mafia, every one of them doing equally horrible things to everyone else. Or Iran: over and over again, the left got it wrong—within our organization, Afsaneh warning and nobody wanting to believe her. Afsaneh and I finally broke with our Trotskyist allies over Iran."

In May of 1984, he wrote to his friend Emmanuel, "Could it be possible that a Marx today in a Middle Eastern political context is far less of a revolutionary than, say, a Voltaire?" He expanded on this theme for me. "We in the Middle East had taken over certain themes from the West wholesale—Germanic nationalism, Marxism, the imperative toward industrialization—but we'd never experienced the Enlightenment, in which these themes needed to be grounded if they were going to make any real sense. Liberalism is a nasty word in the Middle East, but I came to feel that liberalism in the sense of the fight for individual rights, the claims of the part as against those of the whole—that that was precisely what needed to be asserted in the face of the Baath. It wasn't so much any economic category, for example, that needed to be put at the top of the agenda as it was, say, the category of violence."

Kanan also tried to avoid those accounts of Iraq's history and current impasse that laid the preponderance of blame at the feet of Western imperialism. "I vigorously eschew all variations of the conspiratorial view of history," he wrote in his "Note to the Reader," "particularly as these are applied to relations with the West. Instead I single out for consideration the demonstrably inverted relation between the common Iraqi perception of the pervasiveness of a hateful Western influence and the factually diminishing ability of the West to influence local events in the modern period."

When I challenged him on this point recently—saying something to the effect that even paranoiacs have real enemies and that profoundly delusional systematic constructs often have their origins in truly crazy-making contexts—Kanan retorted, "But the point is that often the craziest systems develop where there's been the least occasion. I mean, look at a country that's maybe suffered the most under colonialism and imperialism—India. Four centuries of occupation. Read the last chapters of the first volume of *Kapital*—horrible stuff. By contrast, take a country that's suffered among the least—Iran: never colonized at all. Now, compare the sheer levels of delusion in the two places. Fine, so you have the United States throwing its weight around in Iran in the more recent period—1953, Mossadegh, the Shah, Kissinger, SAVAK. Still, let's have a sense of scale here—the interference was substantial and manifestly deleterious, but the resultant rhetoric is right off the charts. That total imbalance, it seems to me, has something to do with Islamic culture—going back to the Crusades in the case of the Arabs generally, to the originary wound of Shiism among the Persians. This zealously guarded sense of victimization, of having been wronged. The reality is there, but it pales in significance compared to the rhetoric that's gotten generated alongside it.

"Let's try to ground that reality," he continued, "at least with regard to the contemporary period, when what's going on through much of the Middle East, including Iraq, is the exact opposite of imperialism: untold wealth is pouring *into* the region; the sweat of workers' labors elsewhere is pouring into, not out of, the Middle East. And, as far as the Iraq case goes, oil there's been nationalized since 1960, and the whole place has been sealed off since 1967. No, we can't always be blaming the outsider; at some point we have to start taking responsibility for ourselves."

Kanan's position reminded me of some of the progressive activists I'd met in Latin America who bridled at the notion that all the region's woes were the fault of the United States—that Americans, for example, had been responsible for training their security officials in the use of torture. "What?" they'd challenge me, almost taking nationalist umbrage, "You don't think our monsters were smart enough to come up with all of that stuff by themselves? Hell, our monsters taught *your* monsters a thing or two." In both cases, that position has a certain amount of truth and, indeed, serves as a corrective to lazy habits of prior thinking. Future historians are invited to sort out the specifics. But in both cases a position that insists on asserting one's own, as opposed to everyone else's, responsibility for a given situation has heuristic value: it makes possible a future politics that otherwise might become lost in a bottomless sense of victimization and despair. Harvard historian Roy Mottahedeh, former head of the university's Middle Eastern Studies Center, has pointed out to me that the fierce intellectual battles swirling "around this question of the reconstruction of the Iraqi past"—arguments in which al-Khalil's contributions have figured prominently—"are, in fact, all arguments about Iraq's future." And, within that context, Kanan has been insisting that to the extent that Iraqis come to see themselves, at least to some degree, as responsible for their own predicaments, they can also begin to imagine themselves as the possible authors of their own eventual salvation.

THE MANUSCRIPT that would eventually become *Republic of Fear* began with a harrowing depiction of institutional violence in Baathist Iraq, surveying the state and Party structures (police, military, surveillance networks, prisons, torture chambers) devoted to maintaining "security"—or, rather, to guaranteeing that every Iraqi citizen perpetually feel insecure and isolated. The ideal of such a regime, Kanan wrote, is "the transformation of everybody into an informer."

Next, he set out to explore how his homeland could ever have come to such a pass. His approach was, in effect, one of excavation; indeed, true to his own vocational origins, he seemed to cast an architect's eye over the history of Iraq, examining its deep foundations, highlighting its far-flung symmetries, finding and testing its key stress points. He was pursuing a conceptual deconstruction of the regime for which his father was simultaneously busy elaborating visionary constructs.

In all this, Kanan's extended analysis of the development of the Baath Party ideology played an important part. He saw in the Baath the pan-Arab populist worldview taken to its logical extreme—the notion that freedom, for example, existed only within the group, since one could be truly free only in one's true Arabness, "Arabness" being defined as anything the Baathists chose to say was Arab, while anybody they chose to subjugate was by definition not Arab and hence not worthy of freedom. Kanan demonstrated how from the beginning the Baathists saw their politics as one of love—that is, the unquestioning dissolution of the individual self into the idealized mass, torture in this context becoming a form of therapy in which the lapsed one is vouchsafed an opportunity to be reclaimed and allowed back in (hence the Baath's astonishing name for their torture division: "The Instrument of Yearning").

Kanan acknowledged the remarkable extent of modernizing development that had occurred under the Baath. But if, for example, more and more people were now able to read, it was also the case, Kanan noted, that, owing to the pervasive censorship, more and more they were able to read only one thing. Similarly, while Kanan was willing to grant that Iraqi women had had their status raised almost to the equal of men's—in fact, to a degree unprecedented in the Arab world—he also noted that this had occurred within the context of a political system in which both men and women had been utterly denuded of intrinsic rights.

He went on to explore the way in which the logic of Baath governance—fear progressively feeding upon itself—dictated a relentless concentration of power into smaller and smaller circles, and finally into the person of just one man, the absolutely revered leader, Saddam Hussein: "the only genuinely free man in Iraq." That leader—and hence the entire state, whose essence he personified—Kanan portrayed as fundamentally delusional, imagining enemies everywhere and acting on those imaginings in an endless vortex of self-fulfillment. In his final chapter, on the Iran-Iraq War, Kanan analyzed the way in which the two regimes—one based on "faith" and the other on "love"—though they had entirely succeeded in enforcing their respective deranged worldviews within their own borders, had collided disastrously in trying to extend those worldviews beyond those borders.

THE WAR: it ground on and on; and back in London it was turning the work of Makiya Associates inside out. At first, there had been a tremendous hurry to complete the proposals, designs, and layouts for dozens of buildings, so that construction on all of them could begin in time for the Conference of Nonaligned Nations. But, with the war continuing, the nonaligned movement decided to shift the venue for the conference, since it couldn't very well hold its meeting in the capital of one of its principal members while that state was at war with another of its principal members. So the nonaligned nations met in 1983 in New Delhi; and meanwhile, in Baghdad, the sense of urgency that had animated many of the projects began draining away—and so, for that matter, did much of their funding. Money that was supposed to have gone into the rebuilding of Baghdad was instead being lavished upon the demolition of Iran.

But Saddam Hussein was still having his big ideas. In 1982, in part to further cover his Islamic flank in his confrontation with the Ayatollah, he had announced an international competition for a Baghdad State Mosque—one that would, naturally, have to be among the grandest mosques in the world. For example, the Islamabad Mosque, in Pakistan, could contain upward of thirty thousand faithful in simultaneous prayer, so Baghdad's mosque would have to be at least as big. That was the brief. Mohamed, for his part, felt that it lacked ambition.

Architects from all over the world—including Robert Venturi, from the United States, Ricardo Bofill, from France, and Minoru Takeyama, from Japan—converged on Baghdad. Many of them complained that the mosque's proposed site was a mistake—too far from the center of the city, in a sprawling, raggedly developed backwater to the west. But Mohamed noticed that the site happened to lie almost directly over the spot where Abu Ja'far al-Mansur, the eighth-century Abbasid caliph who founded Baghdad, had erected his great, round, walled fortress of a city, with a mosque and his own palace at its very center. This coincidence afforded Mohamed an occasion to tap directly into the entire Abbasid legacy: not only would he design a mosque unprecedented in its scale, but he would reorient the entire city of Baghdad in the process, returning it to its roots, imposing a new structure on its present slapdash expanse. In effect, he solved the problem of the mosque's off-center site by simply making it the city's new center. The treatise he submitted in conjunction with his proposal began with the passage cited earlier, that evocation of the glorious moment over a thousand years ago when Abbasid Baghdad briefly constituted the center of the world; it went on to a detailed analysis of the entire city as it currently existed, and outlined how it might be transformed, looking toward the year 2000, by the construction of this new focal point, from which residential and industrial and commercial and cultural districts would radiate in a vast new urban conception, the whole to be interlaced with a picturesque network of canals and waterworks. This was unquestionably architecture with a sense of scale.

A sense of scale, however, was something distinctly lacking in the three- day televised conference at which the competition entries were judged. According to Mohamed, each contestant was allowed to make only a twenty-minute presentation, without slides. Saddam Hussein himself drifted in and out of the proceedings, his mind seeming to be only half there. In the end, it looked as if the commission would be awarded to the Jordanian entrant, with the French submission as runner-up. (It turned out that those selections were being advanced by Saddam himself, primarily because at the moment he happened to be involved in delicate diplomatic overtures to both Jordan and France and required all the leverage he could muster.) Then this outcome was suddenly reversed, and word came down that six of the seven contestants should somehow pool their efforts into a single new plan. (The Japanese contestant was excluded, because he alone had chosen not to come to Baghdad to present his submission in person.) Mohamed Makiya and Robert Venturi both refused to participate in such a travesty. Mohamed fumed to the competition's functionaries, "This was my present to the city as a Baghdadi, and I won't participate in a bazaar of distributed spoils." Within a few years, the entire project expired of its own ludicrousness.

Mohamed, meanwhile, was offered a sort of consolation prize—the inside track on an international competition for a project that was perhaps of even greater importance to Saddam personally: the Military Parade Ground outside Tikrit, his home town. With the war still raging, Saddam had decreed that each province would have its own military parade ground where he could review his troops marching in victory, as they would no doubt be doing any day now—phalanxes a hundred thousand strong.

Of course, the question haunting this competition was why any rational person would want to come out into the middle of the desert simply to watch a hundred thousand troops marching by under a merciless sun. The preposterousness of that premise, however, proved seminal to Mohamed's solution. Drawing for his formal inspiration on an Abbasid ruin in nearby Samarra—a square-walled structure diagonally bisected by a rutted path—Mohamed proposed having the parade tarmac cut through a mammoth square pavilion at a similar angle. As he went along, the avenue itself took on less and less importance, shrinking in width from scheme to scheme, while the surrounding walls took on volume, incorporating splendid cultural venues—cinemas, theaters, art galleries, poetry-reading amphitheaters, libraries, nooks for religious meditation. The required cantilevered reviewing stand was there, but much more important in Mohamed's conception was the world of cultural possibilities he managed to fit in underneath the stand. The central military parade tarmac was relegated almost to the status of a back alley compared with the cultural concerns spread throughout the structure. "They had commissioned a military parade ground," Mohamed told me, "and I gave them a mosque."

Alone among eight international competitors, Mohamed was invited to have a personal audience with Saddam Hussein. The president had clearly been studying Mohamed's submission carefully. "I put it bluntly," Mohamed recalls. "I said it would be better for his own pride to have a social rather than a purely military ground, and he nodded. 'Come,' he said. 'Let's sit over here.' And he came out from behind his desk and we sat in two easy chairs over to the side. I asked him why children should visit the archeological wonders of antiquity. If the people of Samarra were alive today, what would *they* be designing? The point is to compete not only with one's contemporaries but with antiquity itself. Here we are speaking of the rugged north of the country, so we move from clay to stone—to the strength and nobility of stone. He kept nodding. I was there for three-quarters of an hour, selling the project, and he appeared to be buying. He asked several smart and pertinent questions—about the blankness of the walls, for example—and I explained my reasons. He struck me as a very intelligent man, very. He sees himself as the soul of Arabism, and, gazing upon the maquette of the parade ground, he saw himself as the author of the whole project. As I was leaving, he turned to one of the senior aides who had been standing stiffly over to the side the whole time, and said, 'See? Who but an Iraqi could think like that, with such a depth of understanding? In the future, we should use only Iraqis, or, if we use foreigners, have them work under Iraqis like this.' And presently it was announced that our office had won the competition."

And thus they continued, the architect and the tyrant, each convinced that he was the one who was using the other. But the war continued as well, draining lives and funds, and Mohamed's festive parade ground in Tikrit was never constructed.

BACK IN THE United States, Kanan was completing *Republic of Fear*. This was now the spring of 1986. He sent a copy of the finished manuscript to his British publisher, Belton, who didn't know what to make of it—this certainly wasn't the book he thought he'd commissioned. Belton, in turn, showed it to Fred Halliday, a renowned Middle East authority, who found it "both too thick and too thin" (too thick on the theme of violence, too thin on economic analysis and everything else). Belton finally declined the book, and Kanan undertook an ever more dispiriting search for a publisher. To begin with, hardly anybody cared about Iraq, but even among those who were open to publishing a book on such a manifestly peripheral subject (principally the university presses), this particular manuscript was just too idiosyncratic: it was more of an interpretation than an explication; it wasn't attempting to describe Iraq so much as to probe its *meaning* (and so it appeared to require specialized knowledge of the place, thereby further narrowing its potential audience). Among those who *did* care about Iraq, the book's interpretation was decidedly controversial—it seemed to step on toes everywhere. It turns out that Middle Eastern Studies is as rancorous an academic enclave as any, and many of the text's academic reviewers zeroed in on the pseudonymity of its author, speculating, variously, that he must be a Jew, a Mossad agent, a Saudi agent, a CIA agent, a Communist, or a lapsed Baath official. Some of those willing to believe that the author was in fact an Iraqi dismissed him as a self-hating one, and some of those even went so far as to attack the manuscript as a slur on the entire Iraqi nation. The text had its proponents as well, but still it languished for almost two years, netting one rejection after another, until it landed on the desk of Lynne Withey, a young editor at the University of California Press.

Withey was new on the Middle Eastern desk at that press, so her pile of manuscripts was somewhat lower than it might have been when this new one arrived uninvited. She was therefore able to spend a bit more time on it than she otherwise might have. She was particularly taken with the text's "combination of deep research and *fire*," as she subsequently told me, and she was also intrigued by the "cloak and dagger" aspects of the whole project. She sent the manuscript out for review, receiving several quite fine responses, including one from an Oxford Middle East specialist who said he'd certainly assign the book in his classes but that its author stood a good chance of getting himself killed for having written it. All interactions between Withey and the mysterious Mr. al-Khalil were routed through a post office box in Cambridge, Massachusetts. The directors at the University of California Press had never before published a pseudonymous text, and they deliberated long and hard about the precedent. Finally they required that Mr. al-Khalil furnish the names of at least two reputable third parties who could at least vouch for his existence. After he had done so, they decided to go ahead with the book's publication. It eventually came out in the spring of 1989.

KANAN HAD RETURNED to London. His marriage with Afsaneh suffered a crisis in the spring of 1986, just as he was completing the book, and they separated soon afterward, with Afsaneh staying on with the children in Massachusetts (where she was now a postdoctoral fellow at Harvard's Center for Middle Eastern Studies). They remained good friends, however, and he frequently returned to visit, lodging at her house for weeks at a time, partly so as to retain his ties with the children. Eventually, he got an apartment of his own nearby and started spending about half the year there.

While he was in England in 1986 and 1987, the next major phase of his career opened out unexpectedly. He took to visiting his father's office again, catching up on its activities and mending wounds. The office was by then beginning to wind down. With the war still dragging on, Saddam had run out of money. Mohamed, meanwhile, had become more and more distressed over the character of the regime he had been dealing with for more than five years. "Around this time, my father entered an increasingly religious phase," Kanan told me. "He returned more deeply than ever to his Shia roots. Visitors began calling him at home—Shia men so observant that they wouldn't even acknowledge my mother's presence, let alone shake hands with her." Whether Mohamed's retreat from Saddam was part of the cause or the effect of this deepening Shia involvement is not entirely clear. It is clear, however, that his final break with Saddam was precipitated by the fate of Sayyed Mahdi al-Hakim, a greatly revered Shia clergyman and fellow exile in London. In January of 1988, Baath agents lured Mahdi al-Hakim to an Islamic conference in Khartoum, Sudan, and assassinated him, in the lobby of the Hilton Hotel there. The Iraqi-expatriate community back in London exploded in anger. A protest march was organized, and Mohamed, for the first time in his life, took part in such an event. Marching past the Iraqi Embassy, he knew that in all likelihood he was being photographed and his association with the Baath was thus being irretrievably sundered. After the march, he started letting the Kufa Gallery be used for anti-Saddam meetings.

During his visits to his father's offices, Kanan had begun leafing through the plans and layouts that had been generated in his absence—he paid particular attention to those for the Baghdad State Mosque and the Military Parade Ground in Tikrit—and one afternoon he realized, to his horror, that these were the most significant works of his father's career and, indeed, summations of everything that had gone before. "A twenty-year-old dream [going all the way back to Khulafa] was realized on paper in the language of physical dimension," he subsequently wrote, recalling his sudden reaction to some of the drawings of the Mosque.

I knew then that I had not understood this dream before. I felt little and mundane beside my father's magnificent capacity to think big and live a fantastic dream. . . . He [had] ended up with the monument to beat all monuments: the mother monument of them all. This can be seen in the whole conception and how it relates to all the details. Nor is there a single Arab or Western contemporary who can compare with him. Late modernism's inability to idealize the city on a big scale is intimately bound up with its unwillingness to create public spaces and grand gestures of the order of the Baghdad State Mosque. Just for a moment I experienced something of a revelation; I stood outside my thinking self, totally immersed in the forms which now filled me with awe. A moment is all it took to comprehend visually, clearly and for the first time, how consistent he was as an architect, how good, maybe even how great.

It's not as if this discovery made things any easier for Kanan. He resolved to write a book about his father, in part to help sort out his own contradictory feelings. And it was just as he was setting out to do so that he began hearing rumors about another military parade ground, Saddam's own, in Baghdad: the Monument. Saddam had announced his intentions regarding the structure in a speech in April of 1985, which outlined the Monument's form and scale. It was to consist of a victory arch, which was to be constructed, according to his own design, to celebrate the Iraqi victory over Iran—a victory that at the time of the commission wasn't even remotely in sight. A pair of sixty-foot-high bronze arms would seem to erupt out of the earth on either side of a vast parade ground, brandishing a pair of mammoth, gleaming steel scimitars that would meet a hundred and forty feet above the tarmac. The arms themselves were not to be sculptured by any artist; rather, they would be created by engineers working from plaster casts of Saddam Hussein's own arms, precise to the hair follicles and pimples. No Iraqi factory was going to be able to handle the commission, so the arms would instead be forged at the Morris Singer Foundry, in Basingstoke, England—one of the art world's largest and most distinguished foundries. Once the arms were implanted in the ground, Saddam's conception went on, their base would be overstrewn with five thousand Iranian war helmets, fresh from the front. As Kanan would subsequently note, "To look at the helmets in the knowledge that their scratches, dents, and bullet holes were made by real bullets, that actual skulls might have exploded inside, is just as awe-inspiring as the knowledge that these are not anybody's arms but the President's own."

At first, Saddam had put Iraq's eminent sculptor Khalid al-Rahal in charge of realizing his vision. When al-Rahal died, his role was assigned to Mohammed Ghani, the man who had been Kanan's private tutor in wood carving during his first summer break from M.I.T. During this period, Ghani was making regular visits to the Basingstoke foundry, and as Kanan began hearing rumors about the project, he became more and more fascinated by it. "It was Saddam's obsession," Kanan explained, "and it became mine." At parties, he questioned Iraqi visitors about the Monument's progress. He got in touch with the foundry, claiming to be a journalist doing a piece on Iraq and incidentally asking for photographs, but he encountered "an absolute wall of secrecy," he said, "as if this were some sort of military project of the highest order." The client demanded "extreme security," he was told emphatically. Kanan also spoke with the occasional journalist who had managed to get into Baghdad. He collected bits and pieces as he could. Meanwhile, his curiosity expanded to include some of the other monuments that were being built, the trajectories of other artists, the collusions of other architects (both Iraqi and foreign), the fate of cultural life generally under the Baath Party.

He intended to link all these themes with the work of his father—his father in the wider context, his father as an instance of the wider scene. He ended up dividing the two discussions and writing two books—*The Monument,* under the name Samir al-Khalil, and *Post-Islamic Classicism,* under his own name. But he remained consumed by ambivalence, and both texts seem strangely torn between love and misgiving.

Although Mohamed Makiya rated only seven mentions in *The Monument,* some of Kanan's most trenchant critiques of his father's work occurred there, if in veiled form. Exploring "art, vulgarity, and responsibility" in contemporary Iraq, al-Khalil discusses those aspects of pre-Baathist culture in Iraq which, as bracing and even laudatory as they were in themselves (and al-Khalil is enormously sympathetic to Iraqi culture's modernist surge during the late 1940s and 1950s), nevertheless contained the germs of their own eventual co-optation by the Baath. Al-Khalil subjects the crucial notion of *turath,* the almost romantic devotion to the nation's prior tradition, to a particularly skeptical reading. In the hands of a modernist master like Jewad Salim (a sort of Iraqi Henry Moore), the *turath* proved an inextinguishable source of inspiration, but by the end of Salim's career it was degenerating into a bombastic idealization of the nation's heritage that proliferated in the work of his successors and was embraced by the Baathists. In *The Monument,* the figure of Jewad Salim often seems to stand in for that of Mohamed Makiya. The implied critique of Mohamed was not lost on his old rival, Rifat Chadirji, who, finally released from Hussein's clutches and allowed to emigrate during the late eighties, one evening attended a lecture by Kanan in London on the subject of Jewad Salim and applauded loudly and pointedly at all the appropriate moments.

Meanwhile, Mohamed still could not let Baghdad go. Even after his practice there had closed down, he continued to be flooded with visions. In notebooks, on random scraps of paper, on a napkin, a tablecloth, he jotted down his schemas and sketches, only now he was expanding from the point where his State Mosque proposal had left off. He was reconceiving the entire city, concocting new plans for entire neighborhoods, contriving new conceptions of the relation of courtyard to home and home to neighborhood and neighborhood to township, of river to city, of walkers to roadways. "A Thousand and One Images of Baghdad" he titled a manuscript into which he began pouring these visions—visions that night after night were keeping him up.

WHILE KANAN was working on *The Monument* and *Post-Islamic Classicism, Republic of Fear* was at last wending its way toward publication at the University of California Press. Looking for a British outlet, Kanan once again showed the galleys to Neil Belton (who'd in the meantime shifted publishing houses). And Belton in turn showed them once again to Fred Halliday, who was flabbergasted. "Is this the same book?" Halliday asked Belton, disbelieving. Much had changed during the intervening two years—Hussein's gathering strength in the wake of his marginal triumph in the Iran-Iraq war and, perhaps even more pertinently, the manifestly growing crisis of post-totalitarian rule in Eastern Europe and the Soviet Union. "I was wrong," Halliday told Belton, who decided to go with the book after all.

Republic of Fear was published in the spring of 1989, to no reviews whatsoever and few sales. During its first year it sold barely a thousand copies in the United States, and not even that many in Britain. Visiting Britain one gets the impression that during its first year of publication most of the copies were bought by members of the tightly knit Iraqi-expatriate community, where the book caused quite a sensation. "It was like a bombshell," one member of the community recalled for me, "a bombshell that brought life rather than death." While the few Westerners who came in contact with the book tended to be amazed by its stories, the Iraqis were most impressed by the new *analysis*.

The question of who this Samir al-Khalil might be became a staple of expatriate conversation. No one suspected Kanan Makiya, who had generally been dismissed as an incomprehensible failure ever since he'd abandoned his father's prestigious office ("And for what? *for what!?*"). After he returned to London, his marriage having evidently collapsed, he was variously construed as a dandy, a playboy, a *fils à papa,* at any rate not a serious person—a persona that Kanan didn't object to, for it made it easier for him to sustain his disguise. A colleague of Kanan's at the bookshop Al Saqi recalls one customer who happened to despise Kanan but at the same time venerated Samir al-Khalil and couldn't stop talking about him. Kanan's parents would host dinners at which conversation would invariably turn to the question of the identity of this mysterious al-Khalil fellow: his English is so good, the speculation would run, he must be a Jew, or an Assyrian, or a Kurd, or an Armenian. (Iraqis were so intrigued and, in some cases, offended by al-Khalil's evident sympathies for the victims of the various pogroms of Iraqi national minorities that they guessed he must be such a victim himself.) He was certainly not a Shia (various incontrovertible proofs would be proffered). "Yes, yes," Margaret would cluck. "My, who *could* he be?"

Kanan finished the manuscripts of *The Monument* and *Post-Islamic Classicism* almost simultaneously and sent them off to publishers, but he then grew despondent at how poorly *Republic of Fear* was being received outside Iraqi circles. In part to rouse himself from that despondency, he conceived the idea of a book on the great cities of the Middle East—Cairo, Beirut, Baghdad, Mecca, and, notably, Jerusalem. But before Kanan could begin working on that project, Saddam Hussein invaded Kuwait. Kanan happened to be in London on August 2, the day of the invasion, and suddenly he was famous—or, anyway, his pseudonym was. A few months earlier, Belton had decided to go ahead with a paperback edition of *Republic of Fear,* despite the hardcover edition's meager sales. That first paperback edition had reached the stores at the end of July, and it now sold out in a matter of days; subsequently, twenty-five thousand copies were printed and sold. In the United States, the University of California Press hardcover edition sold out almost overnight, and Pantheon rushed to issue its paperback edition in October.

Though Saddam's invasion of Kuwait horrified Kanan, it did not surprise him. If anything, the last chapter of his book, with its dissection of the political psychology of the Iran-Iraq War, had virtually predicted such a move. From the outset, Kanan felt that the invasion was an absolutely fundamental challenge, particularly to the Arab world—and he was convinced that Saddam would not be deterred by anything short of war. As an instance of one sovereign Arab state's simply swallowing up another (in complete violation of all the canons of pan-Arabist mutual regard), Saddam's actions were unprecedented—as momentous for the region, Kanan felt, as anything since the fall of the Ottoman Empire, including the Suez crisis and the Six-Day War. As far as he could see, Saddam was making a power grab of historic proportions: he was not going to be satisfied with Kuwait alone; he was taking advantage of what he saw as the moral bankruptcy of the Gulf states and the strategic exhaustion of the West to begin extending the Baathist hegemony and, in time, the Baathist yoke as well throughout the region. He was intent on becoming a major world player.

"Everyone I respected, anyone who was a friend or whom I'd ever want to have as a friend, it seemed, immediately gravitated toward the peace position," Kanan told me. "And with almost every fiber of my being I longed to be there with them. Only, in this instance I couldn't be. It was an incredibly painful time."

Kanan became increasingly anxious—and, again, publicly so—after October, as President Bush raised allied troop levels on the ground and then forced his arbitrary January 15 deadline through the United Nations Security Council. Though Kanan had foreseen the necessity for some sort of war, this was decidedly not the sort he had envisioned. (He had hoped that the sanctions would be allowed to continue in place, sapping Saddam of his strength, until such time as the Arabs themselves finally recognized their true interests and took the lead in evicting him from Kuwait.) And yet passages from his own book were increasingly being marshaled by editorialists and politicians to justify the rush to battle. At one point, Kanan received word through his publishers that some prominent members of Congress would like to meet with him, and he agreed to such a meeting. Among those present were members of the so-called bipartisan group that was moving to back President Bush's initiative, and the meeting left Kanan unnerved. Some of these people, he felt, didn't care in the least about Iraq; their bloodlust was rising; they were going to get to kill Arabs and decisively weaken Arab strategic interests. That was all it was for them. Kanan began suffering from a kind of moral whiplash. Now it was his turn to experience how one's own heartfelt labors could momentarily come to serve the requirements of people with altogether different agendas and intentions.

ON JANUARY 17, 1991, when the allies began bombing Iraq, Kanan was in Egypt, attending the twenty-second annual Cairo Book Fair. There he came upon two separate pirated editions of *Republic of Fear,* in addition to the nonpirated one he'd personally authorized. He wasn't entirely sure what to make of all the sudden interest: one of the pirated editions was said to be the work of the Saudi secret service. The book was flanked by ravings of all sorts—astrological ecstasies, fundamentalist screeds, translations of *The Protocols of the Elders of Zion,* and another title, *Oil and Blood,* which purported to trace the virulence of Baath rule in Iraq to the supposed preponderance of Jews in the party's leadership.

On hearing of the allied air campaign, Kanan greeted the news with considerable ambivalence. For the next several days, he later told me, he walked the streets of Cairo, a transistor radio wedged to his ear. On the one hand, he was experiencing a sense, verging on elation, that Saddam had finally miscalculated so disastrously that now his days must definitely be numbered. On the other hand—and as the weeks passed, this feeling became more and more pronounced—he was horrified by the scale and the intensity of the bombing program. His father, like many other Iraqi expatriates in London, was similarly distressed. For all his misgivings about Saddam, Mohamed couldn't understand why the allies had to take out all those bridges over the Tigris, for example, and most particularly one key suspension structure, which, as an architect, he had long prized. "What was the military sense in that?" he later asked his son in anguish. "All that did was hurt common people in their daily lives, all that did was deface our common heritage."

By the middle of February, Kanan had returned to the United States and, still under his pseudonym, was again regularly speaking out on radio programs, but he was beginning to feel an increasing pressure to dispense with the subterfuge, that is, to break out of his isolation, to speak in his own voice. In part, the security constraints that had formerly prevented his doing so seemed to be lifting: Saddam Hussein and his security agents surely had more important things to worry about at the moment than Samir al-Khalil's true identity, and, besides, there was a good chance that they would all soon be removed from power. His cover was beginning to unravel in any case: an Egyptian newspaper was publicly speculating that Samir al-Khalil was a prominent Iraqi architect. Sometime later, he would even hear that the Baath had concluded that the meddlesome Samir al-Khalil must in fact be his father, Mohamed.

But most pressing of all for Kanan during the latter days of February was his growing horror at the shape the war was taking and at the Bush administration's apparent indifference to its certain aftermath inside Iraq. Although President Bush had always maintained that America had no quarrel with the Iraqi people, the brunt of the war's terrible violence was being borne in the first instance by a conscript army ranged in the Kuwaiti theater's front lines, most of whose members had no desire whatsoever to be there, and in the second by the Iraqi population as a whole, whose sacrifices over generations to build up a basic technological infrastructure were being systematically laid waste in a matter of weeks. President Bush had urged the Iraqi people to rise up and overthrow "Saddam Hussein, the dictator," but his State Department was refusing any contact with the Iraqi-expatriate opposition community, members of which were desperately angling for such a meeting, so that they could present their various visions of a federated, democratic future for the country.

Kanan wanted to be able both to speak out openly against these trends, lending the weight of his now considerable prestige to the argument, and to meet openly with fellow Iraqi oppositionists, to take part in their dialogues, and to help further their programs. Just as he was preparing to emerge from clandestinity, in late February, the war was suddenly over, although fighting continued for some weeks, in the form of uprisings by the Iraqi people, both in the Shiite south and in the Kurdish north, against the regime they clearly held responsible for their country's debacle. The Iraqi people rose up, but the allied forces froze in place, trying their best to act as if they had had nothing to do with the developing chaos.

It was against this backdrop that, on March 7, at a symposium put together by Harvard's Center for Middle Eastern Studies, Samir al-Khalil made his first flesh-and-blood public appearance, along with three prominent Iraqi oppositionists who had recently flown over from England in yet another futile attempt to make contact with the State Department. The center had had time to put up only a few posters advertising the event, but Samir al-Khalil's name was a definite draw—most of those in the know realized that by appearing he would be giving up his anonymity—and, as the meeting convened, hundreds of participants showed up, most of them Middle Eastern expatriates, many of them with copies of al-Khalil's book tucked under their arms (for autographing purposes), and the entire event had to be moved outside of the meeting room to a large foyer. Kanan was extremely nervous. His life was being turned inside out: a decade of the deepest and most circumspect seclusion was being transformed overnight into the most public of exposures.

"It was a very moving event," Professor Roy Mottahedeh, of Harvard, who was one of the evening's organizers, recently recalled. "All four of the speakers were tremendously eloquent. Besides Kanan, we had a Kurdish leader and two Shiite activists, one of them a prominent mullah. Everyone in the room was mesmerized, as much as anything by the wonder of why these people hadn't been heard from all along. The speakers were clearly both thoughtfully coherent and passionately concerned. And then Kanan spoke, last and longest, and the audience was completely focused, entirely intent."

Finally, Samir al-Khalil had a face—a surprisingly young one, it turned out. He was of medium stature, mildly stooped, with a large head, going bald but with dark thick curls fringing the sides and back; he had dark-brown eyes, high and prominent cheekbones, vaguely sunken cheeks. His voice was unusually mellifluous—a British-American accent laced with Middle Eastern undercurrents. It was a quiet voice, and people leaned forward to hear.

Near the end of his talk, Kanan called on the United States to suspend its ceasefire negotiations with the Iraqi military and instead march on Baghdad immediately and flush out Saddam Hussein and his cronies once and for all. This proposal (coming from a prominent Arab intellectual) met with a wide spectrum of responses that evening—most favorable, generally, among Iraqi expatriates, least so among Palestinians.

Kanan went on to raise his challenge in a variety of forums—on "Nightline," in the *New York Review of Books,* and in the *New York Times*—during the ensuing weeks. He repeatedly invoked the specter of the utter devastation wrought by the allied campaign upon the common people of Iraq. He quoted Richard Reid, an observer of the United Nations Children's Fund who, on returning from a reconnaissance mission to Baghdad, described that city of four and a half million as "essentially unmarked, [like] a body with its skin basically intact [but] with every main bone broken and with its joints and tendons cut." After citing that characterization one evening on a local Boston television broadcast, Kanan went on to note how the mayhem had hardly been random: "The bones weren't crudely and wantonly smashed—no, they were crushed with surgical precision, the precise choosing of which nerves and which tendons to cut and where. That was the nature of this particular war. And that is what the U.S. is priding itself in with today's celebrations." Around the same time in his long piece in the *New York Review,* he raised the question of proportionality: "Did so many Iraqis who did not want to fight have to die? And did an entire country have to be left 'brain-dead' [again quoting Reid]? . . . Why was Baghdad being bombed so intensively while the Iraqi army was in full rout? Does an entire country have to be crippled to enforce a 'principle'?" From such questions he would frequently move on to descriptions of the current carnage being visited upon his countrymen as Saddam's shock troops, now unimpeded, went about their business of annihilating the various uprisings in one town after the next.

He'd repeat his contention that at its outset the crisis launched by Iraq's invasion of Kuwait had principally been an Arab concern. The United States would have been justified back in August, he suggested, had it simply washed its hands of the whole affair. Such a position would have been morally consistent, in Kanan's estimation. But in getting involved in a massive way, he insisted, the United States had incurred massive obligations to help those it had now crippled.

He pointed to the denouements of the First and Second World Wars—the First, in which a vengeful peace had been followed by isolationist revulsion and remove on the part of the victors, with staggering consequences; the Second, in which a more humane peace had been furthered by the victor's intimate involvement in the democratic reconstruction of the two principal vanquished nations. Which model was going to hold in this instance?

The Iraqis at that moment were simply incapable of saving themselves: there'd been both too much devastation generally and too little damage done to the regime's security apparatus. The Iraqi people desperately required outside assistance. "General Schwarzkopf," Samir al-Khalil proclaimed in a prominently featured op-ed piece in the *New York Times* of March 27, "has to acquire the vision of a General Douglas MacArthur and march on Baghdad."

Such positions riled Kanan's onetime allies on the Left. "Out of despair," wrote Alexander Cockburn in the *New Statesman and Society,* "comes mental pandemonium." Tariq Ali, the noted British-Indian New Leftist and another of Kanan's onetime (and similarly lapsed) Trotskyist comrades, told me how "Kanan wasn't betrayed by President Bush so much as by his own illusions. There are aspects of his work which I respect enormously" (Ali had produced a half-hour documentary version of Kanan's *Monument* essay for British television long before it had even found a publisher), "but when it comes to Great Power politics, I'm afraid he's an innocent, a complete babe. The people like him who set their store in 'enlightened imperialism' have not been proved right. The Americans were never going to support democracy in Iraq, if for no other reason than that the Saudi and Kuwaiti royal families were dead set against it, and it's impossible to imagine democracy ever coming to just one country in that region."

When I mentioned Tariq Ali's comments to Kanan, he countered that his prescription had never been as naive as it might have appeared. "The U.S. should have gone into Baghdad out of humanitarian interests and out of moral debts incurred—but also in its own self-interest," he said. "The whole point is that this war has been an unprecedented earthquake for the entire region, shaking all prior relations and presuppositions to their roots. And if now the situation is simply left to fester, if the Arab world is left to see that all this violence was simply for the purpose of destroying Iraq as a state and a nation and a culture with no other vision whatsoever, then the consequences for the entire Middle East will be catastrophic. Iraq and the rest of the Fertile Crescent will become increasingly unstable as fundamentalist and nihilistic movements proliferate, and, as always before, instability in the Fertile Crescent will inevitably spread throughout the Arabian Peninsula. And then where is the U.S. going to be? No, I think the real possibility is precisely the opposite of the one Tariq describes, for I firmly believe that a democracy installed and encouraged in Iraq—previously the most totalitarian state in the Arab world—could have a catalytic effect throughout the region, and in particular upon Kuwait and Saudi Arabia."

Edward Said wasn't buying it. In a blistering interview published some months later in the *Middle East Report,* the Columbia University–based Palestinian intellectual recalled hearing similar comments of Samir al-Khalil's during a recent panel discussion: "What struck me as extraordinarily sad, not to say desolate, was his appeal to the United States, which had just devastated his country militarily, to enter further into Iraq and unseat Saddam Hussein. . . . He is intelligent, fluent, but unable to attach himself to anything but an issue of the moment, with no realism in perspective. He's suddenly discovered he's got to do something, and what does he do? He appeals to the United States . . . to come and rescue him! It's astonishing."

Much later, when I mentioned Said's interview to Kanan—by then, most of the American troops had returned home—he said, "Let's even impute the worst motives to the Americans—let's assume their march into Baghdad would have occurred with full imperialist and colonialist banners flying. Still, it would have been better than what we have now, if for no other reason than that tens of thousands of lives would have been saved. Saddam's security forces would have been broken up and their reign of terror terminated, the sanctions could have been lifted and food allowed to flow in, the Army Corps of Engineers would have been in there repairing irrigation canals and reviving the country's agricultural sector, the medics would have been in there vaccinating children and regenerating the dialysis machines. Said and his friends were all eager to denounce me and to claim I'd gone mad. But how was what I was proposing so very different from what they themselves were demanding around the same time—that the United States Army ought to intervene to protect the Palestinians in Kuwait from the terrible reprisals being visited upon them by the returning Kuwaitis? If such human intervention was appropriate on behalf of the Palestinians in Kuwait City, why wasn't it just as appropriate for the Shia citizens of Basra, just sixty miles away?"

KANAN RETURNED to England in April, and it was soon thereafter that I first visited him and his father in London. It was a remarkable time to be doing so, for if Samir al-Khalil was a controversial figure in the Arab world generally, he was enormously valued by his confederates in the Iraqi-expatriate community. (One young woman told me how seeing him on TV the first time, so eloquently arguing her people's cause, she had gotten "goose prickles and pin-pricks" all up and down her spine.) Some people began treating him almost like a confessor; victims of the Baath who had somehow escaped the country, with dismal tales of violation and repression, and had found a sheltering validation in the pages of *Republic of Fear,* wanted to meet its author and unburden themselves of their own tales. Kanan became a sort of one-man clearinghouse of desperate narratives.

I went with him one afternoon, for example, to meet with two expatriate businessmen. One of them had happened to be abroad in 1969, tending to their firm's business, when the other, his colleague, had been arrested in Baghdad as part of one of the early "Fifth Column" sweeps. This second fellow had thereafter been horribly abused, subjected to a farcical show trial, remanded to over a decade in prison under conditions of unspeakable wretchedness, finally released but not allowed to leave the country for another fifteen years. Now an old man, but hardly broken, he seemed uncannily centered, maintaining his powerful self-assurance the entire time he was relating his appalling story; his friend looked on in awe. He told us, for example, about how, at his show trial, the prosecution's key piece of evidence had been a letter seized from their office files in which a British exporting firm had designated him as their Iraqi "agent." "This single word 'agent,' you see," he explained. "Five letters. They said, 'Aha! That proves you were a British spy~!' I tried to explain the business meaning of the term, but they'd have none of it. Because of their ignorance regarding common English usage, I ended up having to spend the next decade of my life rotting away at the bottom of some dark hole."

He'd been repeatedly tortured, he told us, but he'd never broken, never groveled, never signed any of the fabricated confessions repeatedly shoved in his face. Why? we asked him. How did he account for the success of his resistance? "Because I am *a man,*" he replied, with fierce self-evidence, "and a man doesn't break." Describing several other prisoners who had broken, he seemed to despise them even more than the tormentors they'd all shared. His face curled with contempt: "They broke because they *weren't* men. They were disgusting, all of them. If I ever saw one of them again, I would spit in his face, or worse." (I shuddered momentarily for Iraq's future. For all his nobility, this man briefly seemed to me the mirror obverse of Hussein himself, whose uncanny poise and self-assurance on the various video clips leaked out of Iraq during and since the crisis have been one of the eeriest, most disconcerting features of the entire affair. Oh, that blighted country with all its manly men. Kanan, with his tormenting self-doubts and wide-open vulnerabilities, seemed to come from a different universe.)

The man went on to describe his release and his years after prison, the mistrust of everyone on the outside, the continual intrusions of the security forces into people's daily lives. One man, a friend he'd acquired in prison who'd also been released around the same time as he was, had subsequently had his case mentioned in passing over Iranian radio during the Iran-Iraq War. "A few days later the police picked him up and dragged him back in for questioning. Luckily—or so we thought at the time—he was released again just a few days later. Only now his health went into a sudden and terrible decline. He became bedridden. He went blind. The skin about his face and genitals fell off. He went deaf. When he died, six months later, he was incoherent, a virtual skeleton with intestines, nothing more. I'm sure they poisoned him. They have entire labs experimenting with exotic biological mixtures. They poisoned him to get back at him for having had his case featured over Iranian radio, even though he'd had nothing to do with that, and also, mainly, as a way of letting all the rest of us know that we mustn't talk, that they had their people everywhere." He fell silent. (I have, of course, disguised some of the particulars of this account.)

The ex-prisoner's friend looked on through all of this, teary-eyed. He had believed he'd never see this old friend again, and yet here he was. Except for the fluke of his having been abroad at the time, all of this could have happened to him, too. (I thought of Kanan's father in Bahrain in 1972.) As we were preparing to leave, the friend came up to Kanan and whispered, "He's been here for over half a year now. We've been together the whole time; we're almost inseparable. Never until today, with you here, did he so much as mention any of this. Thank you for your book."

Out on the street, Kanan commented that he'd been having countless experiences like this. "It's strange," he said. "You know the Iraqi press is not hesitant to report on violations of human rights; in fact, it's saturated with accounts of such violations, not there in Iraq, of course, but everywhere else around the globe—the more gruesome the account the more extensive the coverage. Day after day. It's all part of the mix, intended to demoralize the population, as if to say, 'This is how it is *everywhere,* this is man's fate, don't even fantasize about any alternative.'"

We talked to another recent émigré, who described the atomization of daily life inside Iraq, with everyone distrusting everyone else. It must be terribly difficult, I commented, having to live with such double-mindedness. "Double-mindedness?" he shot back. "I *wish* it were only double-mindedness. I myself lived at least five lives, each securely walled off from all the others. There was the me-at-work" —he began counting them out on his fingers—"the me-with-my-friends, the me-with-my-children, the me-with-my-wife, and then," he tapped his closed fist against his sternum, "there was *me*."

It wasn't only the Iraqis who sought Kanan out: Kuwaitis too seemed eager to find him. One of them, who'd just emerged after having spent the entire occupation inside Kuwait City, told him about the deadening transformation of Kuwaiti television, how it quickly became a nonstop paean to the glories of the revered leader Saddam Hussein. "Only once a week," he related, "did the propaganda let up for a few hours, and instead they'd broadcast a regular movie. The streets would empty and everybody would rush home to enjoy that little respite. One time—this must have been in December or so, the crisis was already well along, the allied armies were all dug in along the southern border—they showed us *The Good, the Bad and the Ugly,* you know, the Clint Eastwood western. The whole movie went along, quite engrossing and enjoyable, and then, in the last scene, Eastwood walks into this ambush in a seemingly deserted town, his poncho slung over his shoulders. Suddenly he's being fired on from all sides, dozens of people shooting at him, only *they're* the ones who start collapsing dead all around. He just stands there, untouched. Finally everything falls silent and he lifts off his poncho to reveal a cast-iron bullet-protector wrapped around his chest: the bullets had all just ricocheted off him and instead killed the ones who'd been doing the shooting. Eastwood then took off this metal shield, set it aside, and the camera zoomed in on it. The End. Only—and I swear this happened, even though I can still hardly believe it myself—as the camera zoomed in on the shield, the image of Saddam Hussein's smiling face materialized right in the middle. His technicians had even figured out a way to sabotage that little bit of our respite!"

Kanan subsequently told me of another Kuwaiti encounter he'd recently had, this one back in Cambridge, Massachusetts, with the son of the senior iman of the Kuwaiti State Mosque, of all people. This young man had been studying in the United States when the invasion occurred and had immediately volunteered to take part in the liberation of his homeland. He'd undergone intensive military training and then been dispatched to Saudi Arabia to serve as an interpreter. As such he was attached to one of the forward units that spearheaded General Schwarzkopf's flanking maneuver from the outset of the hundred-hour campaign. His job had been to monitor and translate the Iraqi army's radio traffic—but throughout the hundred hours there hadn't been any. The Iraqis were observing blanket radio silence. Eventually his unit came to a halt, as victory was unilaterally proclaimed and the war declared over. Almost instantaneously the Iraqi radio waves came alive, crackling with urgent orders, the various Republican Guard elements communicating frantically with each other regarding the uprisings that were breaking out all over, directing tank columns from one to the other. "The Americans subsequently said they'd had no idea what the Iraqis were up to behind their lines those first few days," Kanan elaborated, "and claimed that's why they were so easily hoodwinked in their various cease-fire concessions. But it's not true. This guy told me how he and his interpreter colleagues in other units were keeping Schwarzkopf's people completely apprised every step of the way."

IT WAS REPORTS of the uprisings themselves—the Iraqi Intifada, as it came to be known—that Kanan seemed most eager for. He opened a file on the subject and in no time it was bulging. At first the atrocities all seemed to be the work of Hussein's own forces as they put down the revolts in one town after the next, often flattening entire neighborhoods, demolishing mosques and libraries and other previously sacrosanct sites, progressively cutting off the lifelines to the tens of thousands of refugees hiding out in the southern marshlands, or provoking the now famous exodus of Kurdish throngs into those freezing mountain passes in the north. As the weeks passed, reliable reports of earlier carnages inflicted by the rebels themselves during their brief ascendancies began filtering through: thousands of Baath party operatives captured and tortured, their bodies mutilated, their carcasses strung up from chandeliers inside those same mosques, which had already become slaughterhouses even before being attacked by the resurgent Republican Guard. "The level of hate twenty-two years of Baath party rule has left in its wake, the anger, the recrimination," Kanan commented to me one afternoon as we leafed through these files, "it's incredible. And of course it has terrible implications for the future."

Kanan was keeping another set of files as well, one documenting the response to the Iraqi Intifada among the Arab intelligentsia throughout the Middle East and abroad, though those files were disconcertingly thin. "You know what that response has been, for the most part?" he challenged me at one point. "A massive, unprecedented, spontaneous uprising by the population of one of the Arab world's most important states against a deeply entrenched, if utterly discredited, dictator and his regime, and what is the reaction from the majority of the Arab intelligentsia? The same as it was to the Iran-Iraq War, or the poison-gassing of Kurdish villages which occurred in that war's wake. Which is to say, nothing. No expression of solidarity or even concern. *Silence*. They wrap themselves as usual in 'the beautifying lie,' as Kundera calls it somewhere—you know that passage: 'Gazing into the mirror of the beautifying lie and being moved to tears of gratification at one's own reflection.' Endlessly they intone their odes to the Nation, the Unity of the Nation, refusing even to acknowledge the evidence right there before their eyes—the stench, the rot. It's all gone so rotten."

Kanan commented that he'd decided to launch out on a book about the Intifada and the world's reaction. *Cruelty and Silence,* he was going to call it. "And it's not only the Arabs," he went on. "All these instant books are now beginning to come out in the West as well. I just got this new *Gulf War Reader,* for example. And they all stop cold with the end of the hundred-hour campaign, as if that end had resolved anything, as if anything had ended on February 28. Everyone seems all too willing to bury the shame of the Intifada and the world's paralysis."

A few days later, Kanan gave a passionate lecture along these lines at Oxford University, focusing on the bankruptcy, as he saw it, of the Arab intellectual response to the Intifada and the crushing bankruptcy of the pan-Arabist ideal. "Arabs today need to discover that which they have in common with the rest of the world," he insisted, "not that which sets them apart." During the question period following his talk, a young Arab woman student got up and listed the ailments currently afflicting the Arab world, all the impediments blocking the way toward any authentic democratization in one country after another. "It's all so hopeless," she concluded. "How can you not be hopeless?"

"I don't *want* to be hopeless," Kanan replied simply.

And it struck me that a crucial element alongside Kanan's vision of an alternative Arab future is his sheer willfulness, a refusal to give in to the despair sucking darkly at his feet. Not that he constantly succeeds: there were several moments during the various encounters I had with him during that terrible spring and summer when he appeared almost defeated: disoriented, listless, indeed hopeless. But he usually struggled back within a few hours, and the key to his politics seemed to be a kind of philosophy of as-if: the resolve to go on acting, no matter what, *as if* one's actions still held some promise of affecting the scene. It was a mindset that I'd encountered before: in Eastern Europe during the darkest days of the Brezhnevite miasma.

Uncannily, Kanan himself seemed to be thinking along similar lines. As it became increasingly obvious that no one was coming in to rescue Iraq and that the country, savaged as it had already been, was going to be left to its own devices, Kanan called a series of meetings of the London expatriate opposition. (His father attended every one, sitting in the back, puffing thoughtfully on a pipe.) Kanan told his confederates that the time had come for some kind of decisive gesture, some sort of acknowledgment of what "1991" had come to mean in the history of Iraq and some codification of a vision of the future. Not a constitution exactly, but a kind of charter—a statement, open to signing by as many as felt they could do so, a movement pointing *toward* an eventual constitution. He proposed to dub both the document and the campaign "Charter 91" in self-conscious homage to its Czech antecedent—Vaclav Havel's Charter 77 campaign, which, against all odds, had eventually triumphed in 1989's Velvet Revolution. His fellow oppositionists seemed enthusiastic, if a bit wary. They asked him to work up a draft in consultation with as many interested parties as he could find, and it was to this project that he devoted much of the late spring and early summer. In August, he emerged with two single-spaced typed pages, which read as a sort of countertext to *Republic of Fear*—Paradiso to that book's Inferno: a new foundation, as it were, laid out across the ruins. Boldly asserting at the outset that "people have rights for no other reason than that they exist as individual human beings," it spelled out Iraq's need for a system of democratic government based on an acknowledgment of those rights and on a radical toleration for difference—a toleration extending even to minorities of one. The document called for the establishment of a parliamentary democracy and an independent judiciary, the banning of torture, a moratorium on capital punishment, and a drastic diminution in the role of the army and the security forces. It concluded with a coda, inviting signatures: "By its existence this Charter is proof that the barrier of fear has been broken: Never again will we Iraqis hang our heads in shame and let violence rule in our name." The first signature on the document was that of Mohamed Makiya.

The charter is an impressive, humane document, but, in the light of the bloodthirsty vengeance and vicious counterreprisals that have characterized Iraq since the war, it runs the risk of seeming otherworldly. At one point I asked Kanan whether his vision of a Republic of Tolerance wasn't wildly unrealistic in the current Iraqi context.

"It's precisely the Intifada that gives me hope," he replied. "I mean, of course the uprising opened up the prospect of awful sectarian violence farther down the line, as the Baath regime eventually crumbles. Iraq may well yet make Lebanon look like a Sunday picnic. Hell, we could yet have another Cambodia on our hands."

He was silent for a few moments. "On the other hand," he continued, "it was the very violence of the Intifada that gives me hope—because Iraqis were offered a chance to see the horrors they are capable of, the horrors to which the Baath has reduced them. They're never going to embrace the ideal of toleration because of some sudden revelation concerning the 'better' way offered by the West. Rather, if they ever do so it will be in the same way the West chose it during the Enlightenment: because the alternative—in the West, the wars of religion—had simply become too horrible to bear, to conceive. That's the hope I still have for Iraq—that, faced with such an alternative, it can rediscover its destiny as a richly various and pluralistic society, a meeting ground of all sorts of creeds and groupings. That's the hope that sustains me."

ON MY LAST DAY in London, I was again talking with Mohamed Makiya in his office. He had been walking me through the designs for the Baghdad State Mosque and the Tikrit Parade Ground, and the plans lay strewn about the desk between us. I asked him whether he was now glad that they had never actually been built.

He sighed. "Yes, of course, yes, no, yes," he said. "Try as I might have to avoid it, to have them be for all Iraq, they would probably have been seen as glorifying him—that *war criminal*. I mean, if he's not a war criminal, who is?

And had they been built . . . " He was silent for a few moments. "And, anyway, the plans exist. Perhaps someday people will be able to return to them, to draw on them. It's not important." His voice trailed off.

"I was so embarrassed when Kanan left the firm, so hurt," he said. "I thought that his leaving was for other reasons. I thought, What is he doing over there, just taking care of the children while his wife goes off to work? He's wasting his life. But I was wrong. Because anything that can help bring democracy to Iraq, that's worth a thousand of these." His gesture took in all the plans on his desk. "That's what will make thousands of others possible." Then, jabbing a finger in the direction of a copy of *Republic of Fear* lying on a side table, he said, "*That*. That was the important thing. That's the most important thing our family ever did for Iraq."

The Trials of Jan K

Jan Kavan in and out of Czechoslovakia

1992

I

It was the most velvet of occasions: champagne all around. March 16, 1991, at Expo, the posh restaurant pavilion in the hills overlooking Prague from the far side of the gently meandering Moldau River. The weather was marvelous, one of the first sunny days of the coming spring; and the city was gleaming—a Kokoschkian expanse. Wedding guests had converged from all over Europe—from London and Rome and Hamburg and Paris—a grand reunion of veterans from the student movement that preceded and in many ways provoked the Prague Spring of 1968. Most of the guests were now in their forties, and many were veterans of over twenty years of often perilous clandestine struggle against the normalizing regime clamped over Czechoslovakia after August 1968, when the uprising had been brutally suppressed by the Warsaw Pact forces. As, indeed, was the guest of honor, or one of them anyway—the bridegroom, Jan Kavan.

Kavan had spent those twenty years abroad, in London mostly—his life, as it were, on perpetual hold as he scrambled to invent and then to maintain one of the indigenous Czech movement's most effective lifelines. To begin with, he'd managed, with no apparent prior experience, to jerry-rig a quite sophisticated smuggling operation—for many years the biggest and most reliable of its kind—secretly ferrying tons of books and records and journals and medicines and cameras and duplicating machines and printing supplies into the country and then tons of manuscripts and manifestos and videotapes back out. He'd established the Palach Press Agency—named after Jan Palach, the student who in January 1969 set himself alight in downtown Prague's Wenceslaus Square in protest over the apathy engulfing his once vibrant homeland. By way of his Palach operation, Kavan worked relentlessly to spread awareness of the plight of his friends and allies back home. Without let-up he nudged editors and journalists and human rights activists and diplomats. He made a continuous pain of himself, and of his homeland's situation. He personally copyrighted and distributed many of the key documents of Charter 77 and the rest of the opposition, including Vaclav Havel's seminal "Power of the Powerless." He cofounded the *Eastern European Reporter,* a journal designed to chronicle the distinct evolutions of each of the Soviet bloc's constituent regimes, and of their oppositions. He was instrumental in forging links between many of those oppositions. He was a one-man clearinghouse of desperations and dreams.

Kavan's own house, meanwhile—the modest council flat from which he masterminded these various operations—was a perpetual shambles, as those at the party who'd ever witnessed the spectacle now recounted for the others. "Bloody hell," they recalled affectionately. "Getting a cup of tea was a nightmare." The walls seemed to bow under the weight of tottering piles of documents and files and videos; a mattress (Kavan's unmade bed) lay scrunched between copying machines and computers. Kavan's finances were as precarious as was his health, and his personal life was more chaotic yet. He'd apparently had dozens of girlfriends in ever more bollixed configurations, and it was rumored that he had several illegitimate children as well—no one was quite sure how many, people took bets. But all this chaos bespoke a fundamental rootlessness: twenty years into his exile and he still couldn't resign himself to it. He was perpetually on edge, with everything on hold, hopelessly waiting to go home.

And then suddenly, the miracle of November 1989 simply blossomed. Kavan was the first of the Czech exiles to make his way back into the country, arriving by jet at the Prague airport on the afternoon of November 25. Startled customs officials summoned interior police, who detained him for over twelve hours before eventually allowing him into the city, and the first thing the next morning he made his way to the Magic Lantern Theater. In no time he was helping to run the Civic Forum's press relations operation. ("He was so happy," recalls an American human rights monitor who came upon him early on in those days, "that I didn't even recognize him at first. It was such a total change. There was such a—what's the word?—a *lightness* to his demeanor.") In the months thereafter he was honored with a slot on Civic Forum's parliamentary slate, he won his Prague district seat, he reported for duty in the country's new federal parliament, and he quickly became a key member of the parliament's foreign affairs committee.

And he fell in love. He'd actually met his bride, Lenka Mazlova, a university student twenty years his junior (he was taking up *exactly* where he left off, some of his wedding guests joked), a few weeks before the Velvet Revolution, at the end of October 1989 in Wroclaw, in southeastern Poland, at a Czech-Polish solidarity festival he'd helped to organize. Three thousand Czechs had managed to get through (another two thousand were turned back on the still resolutely normalized Czech side of the border). For several days they gathered to listen to banned music, swap long-banished ideas, marvel at Poland's already cascading openness, and wonder how long it would take before even a hint of such openness would ever penetrate Czechoslovakia. Kavan mentioned some books to the young woman and promised to smuggle copies to her by way of one of his courier operations before the end of the year. Instead, within a month, he was able to deliver them in person.

He called her up from his churning Prague office, she came up from Brno to help out, and they fell in love. And this time, his friends surmised and he concurred, it was different. He was clearly ready to make a home, to have a family (Lenka was already quite evidently pregnant at the time of the wedding, and a daughter would arrive by the middle of the summer). Of course he was still in the thick of things—most of the conversation at the wedding was intensely and vividly political—but he also seemed ready, for the first time in his life, to try to lead a normal life. He was home, and clearly at peace.

And then, six days later, on March 22, 1991, he was being denounced in parliament, over a live nationwide television feed, as a longtime and knowing collaborator of the international division of the Statni tajna Bezpecnost (the StB), the Czech Communist regime's secret police.

JAN KAVAN SAYS—and how could it have been otherwise?—that when he was confronted by fellow deputies (many of them his former allies) with the claim that he'd been an StB informer and that Interior Ministry files in their possession proved the charge beyond the slightest doubt, the first thing that occurred to him was the memory of his father's ordeal almost forty years earlier. Both those who insist that Kavan is innocent and those just as certain he's guilty agree that his father's arrest, when Jan was only five years old, had to be the defining moment in the young boy's life.

Jan and his parents and brother had been sleeping in their spacious new quarters on the ground floor of an elegant villa in the Smichov district of Prague when the knock came early one morning in July 1951. Until a few months before, Kavan's father, Pavel, had been serving as press attaché in the Czech Communist government's London embassy. Jan himself had been born there in October 1946; his brother, Zdenek, had followed a few years later. Jan's earliest sense of his father was one of hushed awe—this important man who left early and came home late carrying a briefcase bulging with documents the children were forbidden even to touch. By the summer of 1951, however, Pavel and his wife were already living in terror of an ever-expanding witch-hunt that was swallowing up one close friend or colleague after another, as yet without any apparent pattern except that nearly all the victims had seemed to be dedicated Communists, many had worked in the Foreign Ministry, many of those in the London embassy, and a disconcertingly high proportion of the victims were, like Pavel himself, of Jewish descent.

"The house was unusually quiet that morning," Jan Kavan recalls. "The two men who came to take my father away talked briefly with my mother, and then others came barging in, doing precisely what we had been strictly forbidden ever to do, rifling through the papers on my father's desk and in his briefcase in the most disrespectful way. My mother looked on anxiously, and wasn't giving us any satisfactory answers."

For a year, virtually nothing was heard of his father or any of the others who had disappeared. The endless entreaties of wives were met with blank bureaucratic demurrals: the investigation was proceeding on course, their husbands were being detained for questioning. And then suddenly, on November 20, 1952, the authorities launched their great trial of the "Anti-State Conspiratorial Center." Fourteen top Communists, including the former Party general secretary himself, Rudolf Slansky, were revealed to have been operating a plot to undermine Czechoslovakia and its Communist future. Scores of witnesses were paraded forth—their painstakingly choreographed and harrowing testimony broadcast over the radio and plastered across the newspapers. One of the witnesses was Pavel Kavan, who, after being characterized by the prosecutor as "a Zionist bourgeois nationalist and Titoist," proceeded to admit, in an unnerving monotone, to having indeed acted as a key intermediary in the plot while serving as press attaché in London. (Like many of the witnesses, he employed awkward, wooden Czech locutions of the sort normally deployed in newspaper propaganda.) Others implicated Pavel Kavan himself in various schemes to use his London posting as a base for smuggling in and out of the country various goods and documents detrimental to the well-being of the nation. Of the fourteen core defendants, eleven, including Slansky, were sentenced to death. In the follow-up trials, most of the witnesses received stiff penalties themselves. Kavan was sentenced to twenty years' hard labor.

Pavel's wife, Rosemary, and the children were evicted from their home and assigned lodging in a cold, dilapidated, two-room tenement, a five-story walk-up without private toilet, in the middle of town. Smoke from passing trains aggravated young Jan's pronounced allergy to dust. Rosemary was fired from a succession of jobs and only secured enough money, from week to week, to provide her small sons with the barest necessities. Heda Margolius, Rosemary's closest friend at the time and another victim of the trials (her husband, Rudolf, had been executed as part of the core group, and she too had been left with a small son), recently told me how anguished she herself would feel watching Rosemary divide a single boiled egg into three equal segments, one for each of their three boys. She also recalled how the various widows and jail-widows had a single hundred-crown note which they seemed to pass among one another at times of greatest emergency.

Rosemary of course knew the toll the ordeal was taking on her family. In her posthumously published memoir, *Love at a Price,* she would recall, "My heart bled to see the boys paying with their health for the injustice perpetrated on their father. . . . They had been bright and beautiful youngsters when we left England. Now they were pale and listless." She'd describe going to the daycare center attached to their school and asking the woman there to administer the drops prescribed for an eye infection afflicting one of her boys. The woman

refused point blank to lift a finger "for the son of a traitor."

"But children should not suffer for the sins of their father," I protested.

"Mine did," she burst out unexpectedly. Her children had been denied secondary education and her husband had lost his job in 1948 because he was a member of a rightwing party. "My family suffered at the hands of the Communists, people like your husband," she cried.

For his part Jan recalled those school years for me in fairly stark terms. "The atmosphere was always tense," he told me. "The teachers treated me differently. Every time anything went wrong—if one of the other kids broke something and I wasn't even there, if something disappeared from the teacher's table—I was the one who got blamed. The teachers despised me for being the son of a traitor. My classmates, on the other hand, hated me for being the son of a Communist. Once during a break, one of the boys began beating me up and several of the others took to shouting 'Bolshevik Jew! Bolshevik Jew!'"

THE JEWISH BUSINESS, ironically, is central to an understanding of Jan's father's own Communism. I say "ironically" because Pavel hardly considered himself a Jew at all, at least while he was growing up. He came from a thoroughly assimilated Czech-Jewish family (his own father having changed names from Kohn to Kavan some years earlier). Nor, for that matter, did Pavel consider himself a Communist in his early days as a student activist during the darkening late 1930s. I had occasion to speak with one of Pavel's fellow victims from the days of the Slansky trials, Eduard Goldstücker, a noted academic and veteran diplomat. (He'd been a colleague of Pavel's in the London embassy, where he served as counselor, before being dispatched as Czechoslovakia's first ambassador to Israel and subsequently being called back just in time to play his own painful role in the trials.) Goldstücker had been a devoted Communist from as early as 1933, but he recalled how his fellow student union activist, Pavel Kavan, was in those days still a social democrat, a partisan of Edvard Beneš's Czech Socialist Party. Kavan emigrated to England almost immediately following Hitler's invasion of Bohemia and Moravia in March 1939 (less than six months after the Munich Agreements of the previous September). Goldstücker for his part held back, finally fleeing to Poland in July. Kavan then began to work frantically to get Goldstücker a visa of his own to England, arguing that, given Goldstücker's position as the highest Czech Student Union official abroad at the time, his participation in an upcoming international students' conference was going to be essential. He succeeded, and Goldstücker was let in just weeks before Hitler's invasion of Poland—a fact that allows Goldstücker to credit Kavan with possibly having saved his life. Both young men threw themselves into Czech émigré student politics in England, but following the German invasion of Poland, Kavan volunteered to serve in the Czech government-in-exile's armored battalion in France. (Goldstücker as a Communist felt constrained from doing so owing to the Nazi-Soviet Nonaggression Pact.) Following Hitler's invasion of France, the remnants of the Czech battalion straggled back to England by way of Bordeaux.

"And on his first day off from the unit's reconstituted encampment," Goldstücker recalls, "Kavan came up to see me in Oxford. He was—how to describe it?—a profoundly disturbed, deeply troubled man. We conversed all through the night. He told me of his experiences with the Czech armored battalion and how horrified he'd been—he was physically shaking, in tears as he told me—by the virulent anti-Semitism he'd encountered among both the soldiers and the officer corps there. His loyalty to Benes had counted for nothing—the corps positively reeked of anti-Jewish prejudice. And it was from that moment forward that he began to move toward the Communist Party, because the Communists, with their resolutely internationalist outlook, were the only party untainted by anti-Semitism."*

At any rate, Kavan and Goldstücker, after 1939, worked together more and more closely in Czech émigré student politics, especially following the Nazi invasion of the Soviet Union. Kavan edited a journal entitled *Student at War,* and the two of them tirelessly publicized the plight of their fellow countrymen left behind the lines. They noticed, for example, that the anniversary of November 17 was fast approaching. On that date in 1939, the Nazis had raided Charles University in Prague, killing a student named Jan Opeltal in the process. In the turmoil that followed, the Germans executed the top eight student union leaders still in the country and deported over two thousand others to concentration camps. Kavan and Goldstücker, by way of their own national student union, of which Kavan was vice-president, lobbied the various other national student unions to have November 17 declared International Students Day, which it was, as of 1942. (Following the war, or rather with the onset of the cold war, the day got commandeered by Moscow, and by the mid-fifties it was being celebrated on a regular basis only within the Communist bloc.)

*There is a tendency among historians today—especially in Czechoslovakia—to start the clock, as it were, in 1948, and to be amazed at the naïveté with which so many intellectuals, particularly Jews, embraced Stalinist ideology and practice. What could these people have had in their captive minds? But it's important to understand those deformations of misplaced idealism in the context of the Holocaust, which preceded and, indeed, formed them. The only place many Eastern European Jews could flee to, late in the game, was the Soviet Union—the American borders had long been closed. In many cases, Stalin saved these people's lives: no wonder they were loyal. The conveniently foreshortened view of history manifests itself as well in some of the restitution programs currently under way in Eastern Europe—again, especially the one in Czechoslovakia, which sets its clock running in 1948, decreeing that anyone whose property was confiscated by the Communist government after that is entitled to get it back. Such a policy ignores the fact that in more than a few cases the villas or factories or storefronts in question had, eight years earlier, belonged to Jews, and that many of 1948's so-called "owners" had been only too happy to gorge themselves on such questionable windfalls. It's a complicated story.

It was during this period that Pavel met a twenty-year-old Englishwoman, a schoolteacher and the daughter of middle-class Labourites, at an August 1943 conference on postwar European futures. It may have been her relative innocence that captivated him; his worldliness, his air of tragic heroism, that captivated her. Pavel and Rosemary fell in love; he went off to war once again with the Czech battalion soon after D-Day; but in April 1945, upon his return to England, the two were married, and he easily convinced her to join him on his return to Prague.

Two years later they were back in England once again, with Pavel serving as press attaché at the embassy and Rosemary raising their newborn son, Jan. Nowadays when Jan is asked to gauge the extent of his father's complicity in Czechoslovakia's descent into the Stalinist mire (and Czechoslovakia arguably descended deeper into that mire than any other Eastern European country during that period, perhaps because the Czechoslovakian Communists had the greatest claim to legitimate governance, having won a clear plurality of votes in the crucial 1946 elections), he becomes circumspect. Some people say that if Pavel Kavan hadn't been dragged under by the Slansky proceedings himself, he might have been one of those managing them. Such was probably the case with Slansky himself, who in fact did manage the ruthless early stages of the very witch-hunt that eventually destroyed him. But for Jan the charge seems untenable in his father's case; after all, Pavel was a relatively small-fry official at the London embassy while much of the machinery was being hauled into place. He didn't direct its erection; he did continue, Jan notes, to serve as the regime's apologist while that erection and many other horrible things proceeded. Pavel didn't live into the mid-1960s but Jan would like to think that, as with many of his contemporaries, his father would have evolved into a so-called Reform Communist. Among reasons for Pavel's moral obtuseness at the time, in addition to the Jewish theme, Jan lists lingering anger over Munich and Czechoslovakia's abandonment by the West, gratitude toward the Soviet Union, utopian hopes for the future. "But these are explanations," Jan admits, "not excuses. And the point is that during the sixties, as I was growing up, I condemned the whole of my father's generation for its silence during those Slansky trials; and, I suppose, being consistent, I would have to be equally critical of my father's silence in the years before."

Questions of his political culpability aside, Pavel was a very difficult man in personal terms. The stirring romance of their early courtship quickly gave way, in Rosemary's account, to something considerably more dispiriting. Pavel was prickly, peremptory, oblivious, driven. Of course, there *were* ghosts driving him: he'd lost virtually his entire family to the Holocaust, and in many ways Rosemary's portrayal of him in her autobiography is reminiscent of Art Spiegelman's portrait of his own survivor-father in *Maus*. Pavel not only was a workaholic but was secretive and given over to intrigues and infinite complication. He could be an ungrateful and ungenerous prig, and he was a male chauvinist. It was one of the tragedies of Rosemary's situation, following his arrest, that she was forced to expend the full force of her vitality on behalf of a man for whom she'd developed, at best, conflicted feelings.

By late 1955 (Stalin having been dead for more than two years), the Czech regime was under increasing diplomatic pressure, from within the Communist world itself, to empty its prisons of the remaining Slansky-era prisoners. It did so, but with as little fanfare as possible. A few days before Christmas, Pavel Kavan was handed a flimsy sheet of paper containing a terse declaration by the Czech Supreme Court abrogating the original verdict in his case and clearing him of all charges; and without so much as an apology he was thrust out into the cold night air. He showed up at his family's door "tired, pale, and haggard," as Jan recalls, "but a big, grown-up man!" The family's life was once again turned upside-down.

In many ways, both Kavan's health and his spirit had been broken by his prison ordeal, the full dimensions of which only now became evident to his family. (A key chapter of Rosemary's book, in which she recalls Pavel's own account of the inexorable process by which he was brought to his abject confession, reads like a concentrated version of Koestler's *Darkness at Noon*.) Over the next several years he attempted to fashion a new life for himself, foraging odd jobs—writing, editing, and translating. But there were blockages everywhere. He had already suffered one coronary in prison, and now he suffered a succession of others. By 1960 he was officially deemed "unfit to work" and relegated to an invalid's pension—another crushing blow to his pride. The more his worldly stature diminished, the more brusque and tyrannical he seemed to become at home. His relationship with Jan—the two had idealized each other out of all proportion during the years of their separation—was particularly troubled. Jan's own health had been devastated during the years of his father's incarceration—he suffered repeated bouts of pneumonia, bronchitis, and migraines—and consequently he'd fallen somewhat behind in school. Pavel showed no sympathy: he was dismayed by Jan's mediocre intellectual performance, which he deemed well beneath the standards he expected of his firstborn, and he had no hesitancy in telling the boy so. The two quarreled constantly.

As Rosemary later realized, Pavel, cheated of his life, needed a target for his bitterness. He couldn't bring himself to deny the very sense of that life by turning on the Party, so instead he lashed out at his family, at Jan, and, increasingly, at her. By 1960 they were considering divorce, though Pavel vacillated from thunderous rages to abject dependency. Finally Rosemary suffered a complete nervous collapse, and by the time she came out of it a few days later, Pavel had died of a final heart attack. He was forty-five years old. Jan was fourteen.

IN THE YEARS following Pavel's death, Jan threw himself into his studies, determined to prove his father wrong; and indeed, despite continuing illnesses, he succeeded in rising to the top of his class. Meanwhile, curiously, he seemed intent on following in his father's footsteps, finding himself increasingly drawn to matters political. On completing high school, in 1963, he enrolled in the journalism and social science faculty of Charles University in Prague and, like his father before him, soon became active in student union politics.

Given his life up to this point, one could easily have understood Kavan's becoming a rabid anti-Communist and rightwing reactionary (as many of his contemporaries soon did). He credits his mother's influence for the alternative evolution of his politics. Throughout their worst struggles, Rosemary, drawing on her own family's British Labour Party roots, clung to an ideal of democratically achieved social justice. "She used to explain to us," Jan recalls, "that we shouldn't equate what the Communist Party said and did with the ideals of socialism, and that in our situation, fighting for those ideals would mean opposing the practical policies of the Communist Party if we could only find the way."

For Jan Kavan, paradoxically, that way initially involved joining the Communist Party itself. He did so, he says, in part because he wanted to try to reform the party from within, but mainly because he wanted to pursue what was becoming the passion of his life, the vindication of his father and his father's fellow victims by way of an open ventilation of the facts surrounding their trials. He saw the two ambitions as not unrelated. Long after the Soviet Union and most other Eastern European countries had experienced at least some measure of de-Stalinizing thaw, Czechoslovakia still remained icebound in neo-Stalinist orthodoxy. (The gargantuan statue of Stalin that used to dominate the Prague skyline from the far side of the Moldau was erected two years *after* Stalin's death!) Many of the architects of the purges, including Party general secretary Antonin Novotny, remained firmly in power. In many cases these people had ascended into their current positions only by arranging for the executions of their predecessors. Grudgingly, they had released most of the surviving purge victims from prison, but they had no intention of rehabilitating the victims' reputations or truly compensating them for their past suffering. Before his death, Pavel Kavan, after considerable struggle, had wrested half of his back wages from the government, but only on condition that he then turn around and repay the regime thirteen crowns' room-and-board for every day he'd spent in prison.

By the mid-1960s, Novotny's strictly centralized and dogmatically regimented economic program was beginning to unravel; the Party itself was starting to fragment; and, perhaps most disconcertingly of all, the cream of the new generation, as represented by the students at Charles University, was becoming increasingly restive. Jan befriended many of the early leaders of that student movement—slightly older activists like Jiri Müller and Lubos Holocek—and Rosemary's apartment became an informal meeting place for the whole gang, the "Kavan Commune," as it came to be known. (By this time Rosemary had secured slightly better living quarters, along with a job as the English-language editor of *Czechoslovak Life*.) Thus Jan became a key figure in the student rebellion that would soon play a crucial role in bringing down the regime he held responsible for having destroyed his father's life.

As late as mid-1967, however, Novotny's regime was still fighting back tenaciously. During the summer, both Müller and Holocek were expelled from the university and drafted into the army. A sympathetic dean called Kavan in, warned him that his own expulsion was likely, and suggested that now might be an opportune time for him to take the year's leave he'd been planning so as to pursue research in England on his master's thesis. Somewhat reluctantly, Kavan accepted the advice. Arriving in London in early October, he secured employment as an orderly in a hospital and burrowed into the archives of the British Museum during his off hours. His thesis topic was the political history of the Czech émigré student movement in London during the war.

On October 31, back in Prague, the Party's Central Committee was locked in a second day of heated internal debates. On that same day, for the umpteenth time, the city's inadequate electrical grid shorted out, plunging the entire university district into darkness. In spontaneous and almost lighthearted fury, the students—unaware of the goings-on in the Central Committee—poured out of their dorms and marched toward the Presidential Castle, chanting, "We want light! We want light!" The police might have been forgiven for misinterpreting this demand as blatantly political; at any rate, they violently overreacted, charging into the crowd with truncheons raised, and the ensuing melee continued into the early morning hours. The reformists in the Central Committee immediately latched onto this incident, demanding a full investigation of the police riot, and in the ensuing weeks succeeded for the first time in forcing Novotny to back down.

Kavan, sensing the significance of the mounting crisis, rushed home to Prague, only to have his passport summarily confiscated at the airport. (During interrogation, the police let on that they suspected he'd been recruited by British Intelligence and that they were going to be keeping a close eye on him.) He reported back to the university and was soon elected to the student-faculty committee charged with coordinating the protest activities of the school's various departments, and it was in this capacity that he first met such young faculty activists as the sociologist Jirina Siklowa and the law professor Petr Pithart.

On January 5, 1968, Novotny was replaced as Party secretary by Alexander Dubcek (by March he'd be forced to resign the presidency as well). Novotny's fall opened the way for initiatives to oust Stalinists at all levels of governance and mass organization—Kavan and his confederates, for example, gained control of the Czech Student Association (SVS). Meanwhile, among the Dubcek regime's first initiatives was a full-scale investigation into the circumstances surrounding the purge trials of the early fifties.

Kavan's passport was returned to him, but he stayed on in Prague for several months, increasingly active in SVS affairs. His father's old friend Eduard Goldstücker had in the meantime assumed the leadership of Kavan's own faculty of philosophy and journalism. "Whenever Jan ran into troubles," Goldstücker subsequently recalled for me, "he'd come to me for advice. 'You know,' he'd say, 'I consider you my father's representative, so I come to you for fatherly advice.' So we'd sit down and analyze his situation down to the last detail, we'd conclude that he should proceed in such-and-such a manner. And it never failed: No matter what we came up with, he'd immediately go out and proceed in exactly the opposite direction. It was as if he *needed* to court complications and difficulty."

By April 1968, it was becoming clear that what Jan needed to do was get back to England to complete work on his thesis. He did so—continuing to organize Czech students there as well. During May he visited Paris and befriended the likes of Regis Debray and Daniel Cohn-Bendit in the midst of their great passion. Returning to London, he soon realized that, what with all these world-historical distractions, he was never going to finish his thesis by the academic year's end. So he negotiated a further year's tenure at Saint Anthony's College, Oxford, to start in the fall, and dutifully reported this fait accompli to the education officer at the Czech embassy in London. This man, named Frantisek Zajicek, presented himself as an enthusiastic Dubcekite and may even have been one, but he was also, under the code name "Zachystal," an undercover operative for the First (foreign) Directorate of the Czech StB, the secret police.

Kavan remained in London during the fateful summer of 1968 as events back home were moving toward their climax. Students and intellectuals were pushing Dubcek to liberalize the regime at an ever faster clip ("Our group was arguing," as Kavan has noted, "that democratization—the slogan of the Reform Communists—wasn't enough, that what was required was *democracy,* by which we meant workers' councils and enterprise councils and so forth, democracy closest to its grassroots"). Soviet leader Leonid Brezhnev and several of his principal vassals (including East Germany's Walter Ulbricht and Poland's Wladyslaw Gomulka) were becoming increasingly nervous. A crunch negotiation of Warsaw Pact leaders took place in Bratislava in the first week in August, after which the sense of impending doom seemed momentarily to subside.

The SVS in the meantime received an invitation to send a representative to the upcoming Kansas City convocation of the American National Students Association. The SVS executive board decided that since Kavan in London "was already virtually halfway there," and since he had fluent command of English, he would be the delegate. His presentation was scheduled for August 21. The Warsaw Pact invasion of Czechoslovakia began the night of August 20.

Robert Scheer, at that time an editor of *Ramparts,* the vanguard New Left monthly, was so impressed with Kavan's passionate denunciation of developments in Czechoslovakia that he invited him back to San Francisco to work up a version for the magazine. While there, Kavan made contact with various members of Students for a Democratic Society and other student activists at Berkeley. On his way back to Prague, later that week, he stopped off in Chicago. It is not true, he insists, as all the stories have it (stories tend to foliate all about Kavan), that he was beaten up by Chicago cops outside the Democratic National Convention hall on this visit. He did, however, address a rally of demonstrators in Lincoln Park, and he did make further valuable contacts with various activists.

By early September he was back in Prague. Nothing was as clear at the time as we now tend to remember it. Although Brezhnev may have intended to decapitate the Dubcekite movement, he was shocked by the near-universal resistance (passive though it may have been) that Warsaw Pact forces encountered among Czechs from the outset, and he hesitated. Dubcek, for example, who had been kidnapped to Moscow, was now returned, still nominally in charge as Party general secretary, though at the cost of what concessions was not immediately evident. The SVS was not instantaneously disbanded; its executive committee continued to meet and to strategize over what might still be salvaged, and Kavan, as a member of the committee, took an active role in those deliberations. (Once harsh critics of the timidity of Dubcek's Action Program, the SVS now rallied behind it as a minimal demand.)

In October, Kavan reported back to Oxford for the start of the year's first term—encountering no problems as he left—but by the end of November he was back again in Prague, and in early January 1969 he was dispatched to Budapest as the SVS's representative to a conference of international student unions on the subject of European security. In the midst of a speech denouncing imperialism—"You know, Portugal, Greece, and all that," as he reassured his anxious mother—Kavan also got in several jabs at the Warsaw Pact invasion of his own country. Rosemary cringed when she heard this (while he'd been in England, normalization had been proceeding apace, and it was now illegal to use the word "invasion" in any public speech). Sure enough, the police increasingly focused attention on his activities thereafter.

It was a few days after Kavan's return from Budapest, with full normalization taking hold and the Czech population lapsing into a sort of stunned apathy, that Jan Palach set himself ablaze in downtown Prague's main square. He didn't die immediately. He survived long enough to request an audience with Lubos Holocek, one of the SVS's top leaders and one of Kavan's closest personal friends. Kavan accompanied Holocek to the hospital and waited outside the door of Palach's room. Inside, in physical agony, Palach urged Holocek to publicly convey his plea that no other protesters attempt to follow him on this path, his dying message being, "Tell them to join you in a living fight." Palach's mammoth funeral was organized entirely by the students, including Kavan (who delayed his scheduled return for Oxford's second term); and the SVS negotiated with the government over the wording of a public appeal to Palach's potential followers, which Kavan himself was then asked to read over the radio. (Kavan still gets choked up describing this incident more than twenty years later. "The fact that out of the whole society he picked the students, and the radical students in our group in particular, gave me a feeling of great responsibility," he recalls, one which, he contends, was to animate his work for years to come.)

When a representative from Bertrand Russell's Stockholm Tribunal on the Invasion of Czechoslovakia (a sort of follow-on to the Russell-Sartre Vietnam tribunals) arrived in Prague, looking for speakers, the SVS board nominated Kavan, who quickly rerouted his return to England by way of Stockholm. Rosemary, for her part, grew increasingly anxious. "Stockholm on top of Budapest would really be pushing his luck," she subsequently recalled thinking. "The Kavans never know when to draw the line."

Kavan left for the airport the morning of January 31, 1969. He slunk back into the Commune later that same afternoon. "Don't you at least want to hear what happened?" he pleaded with his furious mother. ("Pavel's voice and Pavel's question" was the gloss she subsequently placed on that moment in her autobiography. "Genetics had done a good job.") Customs officials, rifling through his luggage, had discovered a cache of hard currency (his Oxford stipend and payment for the *Ramparts* piece) that he'd forgotten to leave in England before returning to Prague two months earlier. The penalty for the currency violation was simple: immediate confiscation. But the officials had also discovered copies of his *Ramparts* article, along with over three hundred documents he was intending to disseminate in Stockholm. So once again he was placed under investigation, and his passport once again was confiscated. The immediate penalty here was the forfeiture of his Oxford term—with a horizon, perhaps, of much worse.

Up to this point, Jan Kavan's story is fairly straightforward—most people agree on its basic contours. From here on, however, interpretations bifurcate. Some of those in Prague and elsewhere who believe that Jan is guilty contend that this is where the StB got its tentacles into him. According to the StB file, an undercover agent named Stanislav Patejdl (code name "Pavlasek"), who'd first introduced himself as a sympathetic Dubcekite foreign ministry employee, expressed concern over his case and offered to try to intervene behind the scenes. It's not clear whether he did (there are some indications in the file that matters were sorting themselves out of their own accord—there were, after all, hundreds of similar cases around this time), or whether Kavan inferred that he had done so; it's not clear that any quid pro quo was involved; it's definitely not clear that Kavan realized Patejdl was an StB agent or that Patejdl allowed him to realize as much. The fact is, however, that Kavan's passport was returned to him in late March, that he was allowed to report back to Oxford in time for the start of the spring term, and that soon thereafter he began a regular series of meetings with Zajicek at the Czech embassy, the coverage and analysis of which ran to more than five hundred pages in the StB's Kavan file. (It turns out, as well, that the StB superior to whom Zajicek was reporting in Prague was Patejdl.) Kavan insists there's a reasonable explanation for these meetings, that as the SVS's only executive officer in Britain he'd specifically been delegated to establish a British branch of the organization, and that as part of his responsibilities he'd been ordered to establish liaison with the embassy's education officer, Frantisek Zajicek (in connection with such matters as extensions of permission for out-of-country residency on behalf of a population of students who were understandably in considerable anguish at that moment). Zajicek, for his part, according to Kavan, continued to present himself as an anguished Dubcekite—he may even have been one. He was recalled in late 1970 at a time when other Dubcekites were being purged out of embassies throughout the world and even, for that matter, out of the StB. Yes, Kavan confirms, their interactions were relatively cordial and wide ranging. He doesn't remember talking with Zajicek about various British contacts, though he doesn't deny that it could have happened. He insists that he revealed nothing that wasn't fully public knowledge, that he had no idea Zajicek was an StB agent recording every nuance of his conversation (to the tune of five hundred pages!), and that he certainly wasn't serving as a conscious informer. The trouble is, a lot of people don't believe him.

ON AUGUST 21, 1969, Kavan, representing the SVS (which had had its charter revoked as of June 1969, a revocation that was still being appealed and wouldn't be finalized until September), approached the podium of an international student conference in Dubrovnik. "Today it is exactly a year since Prague students defended freedom and their blood was spilled in their struggle against foreign occupation," he began. He continued in that vein for another ten minutes—members of the various Warsaw Pact delegations storming out of the hall in protest all the while—until he revealed that he'd been reading a long extract from a declaration issued by Czech students in London on November 17, 1940.

The StB cable traffic back and forth between London and Prague, trying to figure out what the hell to make of Kavan's Dubrovnik speech—whether it was a good or a bad thing that he didn't specifically mention the Warsaw Pact invasion while instead clearly alluding to it by way of a comparison to, of all things, the Nazi occupation—would presently fill several densely packed pages of disputation in his file.

In Czechoslovakia, normalization was proceeding apace. In April 1969, Dubcek was finally eased out as Party general secretary. His replacement, Gustav Husak, initially seemed not the worst of the alternatives, for he too had been one of the victims of the Slansky era (indeed, at one point he'd shared a prison cell with Pavel Kavan). People could still hope, at least for a little while, that a full-scale Stalinist retrenchment might yet be avoided. As the months passed, however, the various ministries and Party organizations were ever more thoroughly cleansed of reformists; 54 of 115 members of the Party Central Committee were sacked, and the party itself shed over a quarter of its members through rigorous loyalty checks. Theaters were shut down, newspapers purged, and student activists (including most of Kavan's colleagues) expelled from the university. The slanders against former oppositionists grew ever more shrill. The historical account of the Slansky era once again reversed polarities, with the victims newly vilified and the victimizers celebrated all over again.

With his year at Oxford ending, Kavan enrolled for the 1969 fall term at the London School of Economics, in part so as to secure a legitimate extension of his Czech exit permit. He continued to work on behalf of his colleagues back home, though less and less as student union representative. Following the dissolution of the SVS back in Prague, Kavan's interactions with Zajicek appear to have dwindled; the two held their last recorded conversation in July 1970 (though Zajicek tried to entice Kavan into another meeting, this one at a pub outside the embassy in the following October; Kavan failed to appear, and no further contacts are listed in the file). Meanwhile, Kavan worked to forge alliances with various British leftists—peace and student and labor activists, along with young journalists. A group of them established the Committee to Defend Czech Socialists. "Social*ists*," Edward Mortimer, a member of the Committee, recently pointed out to me. "Not socialism. Defending social*ism* was *their* job, we figured. It was our job to try to defend them." Mortimer had first met Kavan in May 1968, in Paris, where they'd found themselves sharing a general sort of New Left vantage. (In the years since, Mortimer's politics have mellowed somewhat and he has become one of Britain's most respected foreign correspondents, based at the *Financial Times*.) According to Mortimer, the Committee in those days tended to divide between those who, while denouncing the Warsaw Pact invasion, wanted to avoid denunciation of the Soviets themselves (so as not to provide fodder to more conventional Cold Warriors)—and those who felt no such compunctions. "It's ironic in light of the allegations he's currently facing," Mortimer recalls, "but Kavan was always one of those in favor of taking the most radical public actions in the context of the most explicitly anti-Soviet line."

Despite the intensity of his British involvements, Kavan was wracked by guilt over the fact that he wasn't in Prague, bearing the full brunt of the regime's offensive alongside his fellow activists. Several of his friends were urging that he not return: after all, he had probably been the single SVS board member most involved in foreign contacts (what with his speeches in Budapest, Dubrovnik, Kansas City, Chicago, and London). Inasmuch as one of the principal themes of the Husak regime's developing propaganda offensive involved the supposed foreign wellsprings of the Prague Spring, Kavan could easily find himself being used, like his father before him, in a show trial designed to demonstrate precisely that thesis. Kavan acknowledged these misgivings. On the other hand, as Mortimer recalls, "He was extremely reluctant at the prospect of becoming an exile. He had a largely correct sense about the nature of political exile—the way in which exiles became prone to vicious internal disputes, all the while losing touch with the real situation back in their home countries. Again, it's all so ironic in light of the turn things have recently taken for him. But back then this was emphatically not a life he wanted to lead."

Time was running out for a decision. Kavan's oft-extended Czech exit permit would expire at the end of August 1970, and if he stayed beyond that, the decision would be made for him: he'd automatically be stripped of his Czech citizenship and ineligible ever to return. Feeling the need to consult personally with his friends back in Prague, he took advantage of the fact of his British birth and applied for a British passport—but under a different name. He had recourse to a bureaucratic procedure known as deed poll by which, through a simple one-page application and payment of a modest fee, a British citizen can change his or her last name legally. (Curiously, the first and middle names, according to British common law, are deemed to be "God-given" and hence immutable.) Kavan further benefited from the fact that the registrar of his original birth certificate had recorded his name as *Ian*—Ian Michael Kavan—so that it became a fairly easy matter for Jan Kavan to have himself recast as I. M. Frazer, and for Mr. Frazer, in turn, to procure a British passport (into which he was subsequently able to affix a Czech travel permit, obtained at the Czech consulate in Budapest).

Generally speaking, Kavan's Prague friends—those he was able to contact—seemed to think he could make his most effective contribution abroad. By 1970 they knew they were in for a long struggle—Czech society at large had been almost entirely pacified, and any opposition would have to begin small and isolated and proceed by tiny increments. Foreign awareness and support were going to be crucial. Kavan was eager to hear the opinion of his mentor, the veteran student leader Jiri Müller, but Müller, under obvious surveillance, was unable to make his way from his native Brno up to Prague and instead passed word by way of an intermediary. "The gist of Müller's message," Kavan recalls, "was that the only way I was going to be useful abroad would be to accept the discipline of meeting the needs of the opposition as the opposition itself defined them. It would be for them to define those needs, not for me. My role would be to meet their needs. This made a lot of sense to me. So I accepted and said this is what I would do."

They established a rudimentary basis for further communications. Kavan returned to England and a few weeks later received his first assignment, to purchase a duplicating machine and find some way of smuggling it back into Czechoslovakia.

Around this time Kavan wrote a letter to his old father figure Goldstücker, who'd emigrated to Britain and established himself at the University of Sussex (he's one of the world's foremost authorities on Kafka). Kavan passed along greetings from their mutual friends, mentioning that he'd just been in Prague and would soon begin smuggling back such items as duplicating machines; he concluded by soliciting a financial contribution toward the project. "And after that," as Kavan recalls, "all hell broke loose. I got back a very tough letter from Goldstücker saying that he didn't know if I was just being some kind of incredibly irresponsible adventurer, running incomprehensible risks, or else I had to be working with the StB—but until the day when the archives would be opened and he could know the truth, he was suspending all contact." Goldstücker still sputters with rage as he recalls the incident. "What on earth was he doing?" he asked me. "Was he insane? A prominent opposition activist returns to Prague under a false British passport? And yes, indeed, I did seriously entertain the thought that he might be working for the StB, or else why hadn't he been captured? I told him, from now on I forbid your using my name in any connection with what you do. And I added that I was convinced that one day that copying machine would figure against him as evidence in a court case."

Kavan obviously wasn't going to be getting any help from Goldstücker.

The Czech émigré scene was already breaking up into a welter of suspicions and cross-recriminations, so Kavan endeavored to steer an independent course. Müller, in his message, had suggested that Kavan try to smuggle the machine in by way of some British company's entry in the upcoming Brno International Trade Fair, but Kavan quickly realized the naïveté of that suggestion: no commercial enterprise was willing to run the risk. On the other hand, Kavan was just an inexperienced academic and sometime student activist—what did he know about running a smuggling operation? He began putting out feelers through some of his contacts in the British peace movement, specifically the Campaign for Nuclear Disarmament (the CND), which is how he made his way to Michael Randle.

This whole account again presupposes that Kavan wasn't in fact working for the StB all through this period and hence actually did need to find some top-secret way of smuggling his duplicating machine into Czechoslovakia. The StB Kavan file is silent on this question; or rather, the (presumably) thousands of pages of StB Kavan files that might shed light on it are conspicuously missing. As is the case with records on most of the other top oppositionists, most of Kavan's StB files were removed—destroyed? stashed away? —during the months just before or immediately after the Velvet Revolution (the surviving 1969–70 swath constitutes an exception—an inadvertent oversight? an intentional plant?). Everyone admits that such files on Kavan existed: the controversy is over whether they constituted so-called agent files or rather subject files (that is, whether he was the one informing or the one being informed on). Some of those in Prague today willing to grant that Kavan wasn't working for the StB do so only because they're convinced that in fact he was working for the KGB, and these people usually point to Randle's involvement as their best evidence.

For Michael Randle *did* happen to have recent experience in smuggling large bulky objects through the Iron Curtain. He'd been one of the masterminds behind the at-that-time still notoriously unsolved 1966 prison break of the Soviet master spy George Blake; in fact—again, still unknown to anyone at the time—he'd been the one who drove the van (with Blake stashed, nearly suffocating, inside a secret compartment) all the way to the outskirts of Berlin, where he let the spy out so that he could make his way back to Moscow.

Randle today forcefully denies ever having had any affiliation with the KGB and no one (including the jury that eventually heard his case) seriously believes he did—though such niceties carry little weight among some of

Kavan's more highstrung critics back in Prague these days. Randle was in fact something of a pacifist-anarchist, the sort of fellow who used to chain himself to missile silos, that sort of thing. For all his troubles he was condemned to serve a year, beginning in 1962, in the Wormswood Scrub Prison in Central London, which is where he first encountered the notorious Blake, who'd started serving a forty-two-year sentence of his own the year before.

Randle and a fellow pacifist prisoner, Pat Pottle, didn't in any way approve of Blake's activities—they were, as Randle recently told me, disgusted with the whole espionage racket on *both* sides—but they also disapproved of the outrageously vengeful sentence he'd been meted, which they considered a fundamental violation of human rights. During the next several years, following their own releases, as they continued to be active in various pacifist initiatives, their thoughts would occasionally return to their old prisonmate Blake and they'd toy with the idea of trying to spring him. And then, in 1966, they proceeded to do just that, in astonishingly amateurish fashion. (When Randle's wife, for example, suggested they reinforce the rope ladder they were constructing by using metal knitting needles in the rungs, she didn't mean for them to go out and buy all five hundred pairs of needles at the same store!) Once they'd sprung the spy, Randle proceeded to refit his camper van with a secret compartment behind the drawers underneath the bed, stuffing Blake inside, and along with his wife and two small children (who spent most of the journey sleeping on top of the bed) headed off for East Germany.*

By 1968, a few years after his Blake escapade, Randle belonged to that wing of the British peace movement that became as incensed over the Soviet bloc's invasion of Czechoslovakia as they'd already been over U.S. involve-

*The Blake escape proved one of the most sensational tabloid stories of the year in Britain. Police rushed into action. Amid widespread speculation that they were dealing with one of the most sophisticated KGB operations ever mounted, police nevertheless assured the public that they would be cracking the case any day now. Any week now. Any month now. Months dragged into years, and the case remained unsolved. There is some speculation today that at a certain point, when it finally began to dawn on investigators that they were dealing not with some highly sophisticated foreign intelligence operation but rather with a band of rank amateurs, they intentionally contrived not to solve the case, for everybody's sake.

And, indeed, the case remained unsolved until 1989, when Randle and Pottle published their own bestselling account of the adventure, *The Blake Escape*. At this point, the British authorities were virtually shamed into action. They brought a stiff indictment against the two culprits, and in June 1991, their case went before a jury in the Old Bailey's legendary Courtroom Number One. Randle and Pottle, who dispensed with counsel, instead choosing to defend themselves, started

ment in Vietnam. In fact he personally took part in a famous action wherein teams of British demonstrators simultaneously unfurled protest banners in the capitals of each of the Warsaw Pact countries that had contributed forces to the invasion, and began distributing leaflets, until they all got themselves simultaneously expelled. One of Randle's colleagues in that action, who both knew and heartily disapproved of his role in the Blake affair (among those few in the peace movement who did know of it, several had similarly queasy feelings), now happened to hear how Kavan was bumping around aimlessly, looking for a smuggler—and she put the two of them together.

They became fast pals, although Randle insists that he at no time gave Kavan any indication of his involvement in the Blake escape and Kavan likewise claims to have been unaware of it. They procured a secondhand Volkswagen camper, which they refitted along lines roughly similar to Randle's earlier version, with a principal hiding place under the bed behind the drawers, although others were liberally salted about the cabin as well. In January 1971, Randle himself made the van's first experimental run—again with his wife and two small kids—ferrying a stash of banned books into Brno. Everything went smoothly, so they decided to go ahead and send the duplicating machine in on the next run, a few months later. That duplicating machine was soon to play a key role in the opposition's first concerted action, the clandestine printing and sudden distribution, on November 8, 1971, of over 70,000 pamphlets urging Czechs to boycott the regime's upcoming electoral farce, its first since 1968.

Rosemary, too, took part in that action. Alone now in Prague (her other son, Zdenek, having likewise gone into exile in Britain, though he was pursuing a more conventional academic career), she had independently made contact with the underground. This didn't take much doing; many of its members, veterans of the Kavan Commune, continued traipsing through her kitchen on their regular visits to Prague. She began typing multiple carbon

---

out by readily admitting to every detail in the prosecution's reconstruction of the crime; they then tried to convey their moral reasons for having perpetrated it. The judge, in his final summation, threw out the entire second half of their defense as entirely irrelevant and virtually ordered the jury to find them guilty. But it took the jury only three hours to return a verdict of not guilty. Randle and Pottle thereupon traveled to Moscow, where they met with Blake, who in the meantime had become an enthusiastic proponent of glasnost and one of Boris Yeltsin's most ardent supporters. "Yeah," Randle laughed as he subsequently told me all this. "Incredible . . . incredible . . . it's such an incredible world."

copies of Müller's twelve-page clandestine monthly, *Facts, Comments, and Events,* ten copies at a time, muffling her typewriter for fear of arousing her neighbors' suspicion. After the duplicator arrived, she was one of those enlisted to distribute leaflets in the dead of night (dressed as an old hag). She'd dodge random searches, stare down more focused interrogations—and then would head out once again, collecting and distributing yet another batch of contraband. Following the November 1971 action, however, the noose began to tighten. Müller and several of the others involved in that action looked to be on the verge of arrest, and indications such as the denial of a temporary exit visa to go visit her sons made it clear that Rosemary too was in danger. With profound misgivings she sent Jan a prearranged signal, and within days he'd managed to have her spirited out of the country. A few days following her escape, the police swooped down upon the fledgling underground movement with a devastating series of arrests. In the show trials that followed, Müller, for one, received a five-and-a-half-year sentence.

In London, Jan now redoubled his efforts, simultaneously trying to interest the ever more jaded international mass media in the ongoing fate of his persecuted comrades ("The bloody massacre in Bangladesh," Milan Kundera subsequently wrote of this very period, "quickly covered over the memory of the Russian invasion of Czechoslovakia, the assassination of Allende drowned out the groans of Bangladesh, the war in the Sinai Desert made people forget about Allende, the Cambodian massacre made people forget about Sinai, and so on and so forth, until ultimately everyone lets everything be forgotten") and to fashion fresh links and channels for his smuggling operation. Throughout its existence, Kavan today claims, that operation owed its success to its very narrowness. He alone on the outside knew all the details of what was going in—when and where and how. And although he was feeding and receiving from an elaborate network on the inside, during any given period he himself was dealing with only a single individual. Between 1970 and 1972, that person was Jiri Müller. Following Müller's incarceration, the task fell to Petr Pithart, the law professor at Charles University whose vigorous support of the 1967–68 student movement there had cost him his job after the Soviet invasion. In 1977, Pithart decided to take on a more public role as one of the first signatories of Charter 77. (Following the Velvet Revolution, his signal contributions to the movement would be honored through his selection as the first post-Communist president of the Czech half of the Czechoslovak Republic.) His role in the Kavan channel was now taken over by Jirina Siklowa, the sociologist whom Kavan had likewise befriended during his own radical student days at Charles University (she in turn agreed to relegate herself to a less public role in the dissident struggle so as better to fulfill her crucial function as the focal point for Kavan's entire smuggling operation).

In each instance, the interior contact person was responsible for collecting the vast quantities of material to be shipped out—raw manuscripts, copies of samizdat journals, documentation of human rights violations, personal letters, grant applications, financial records, photos, videos, and so forth—and depositing them all at a safe house in preparation for pick-up. That person was also responsible for distributing the vast quantities of material Kavan had smuggled in: books and journals (including current technical digests for professionally disbarred activists), exile literature, specifically requested medicines, duplicating machines, cameras, and, a little later, video cameras and computers as well).

Kavan's was by no means the only such operation going, but through the 1970s it was easily the biggest and most significant. It was a principal channel, for example, for Pavel Tigrid's Paris-based *Svedectvi* journal, Jiri Pelikan's Rome-based *Listy,* and Josef Skvorecky's Toronto-based '68 Publishers. Kavan had individual couriers streaming in and out of the country on a regular basis, and in addition he managed to pull off forty consecutive van penetrations, one every three or four months, each one loaded down with more than a thousand pounds of contraband—all utterly undetected. Or so everyone assumed at the time, and many still assume, though others now cite Kavan's very success against him. How could it possibly have all run so smoothly, they wonder, unless Kavan was in fact working with the StB all along?

"Trots," Kavan told me recently, laughing. "That was the key. I used a variety of drivers in a succession of refitted vans, but the Trotskyists were generally the best. I often found communication with them a bit difficult for ideological reasons, but I admired their courage and discipline and efficiency. They never talked, they didn't seem to feel the need to brag. You could tell them, 'You'll go here, you'll hand the stuff over, you'll come back the next day, you'll behave like tourists the whole time.' And they'd do exactly that." (For their part, the Trotskyists got to include samples of their own literature in each new shipment, which apparently was all they required, along with the satisfaction of helping to undermine Czech neo-Stalinism.)

Meanwhile, Kavan launched the Palach Press Agency as a vehicle for disseminating the information he was amassing. He endlessly berated journalists (I was one) for not paying more attention to Czechoslovakia. What was wrong with them? Couldn't they grasp its importance?

By all accounts he worked relentlessly—perhaps more so than he needed. His operation was chaotic—he was, one person told me, the sort of worker capable of putting in thirty-six hours straight, without sleep or even food, in order to meet a deadline he could have met days earlier, without much effort, had he been more organized. He ruined his health—and back in Czechoslovakia, nothing changed.

LATE IN HER difficult life, Rosemary found true love—with an Australian painter who maintained a studio in Positano, Italy. She joined him there, though she regularly returned to London to help her son. In the last pages of her autobiography, she marveled at his persistence: "For Jan—even more than for Pavel—nothing is lost simply because it is 100% hopeless. There is always the million-to-one chance that it will succeed. Even with a rope round his neck, he would believe in reprieve or rescue. But I haven't got the nerves for it. . . . I shall never be free of the extraordinarily close bond I have with him. When I'm in Positano I resent the fact that I am not in London helping him and the Czech cause. When I'm in London I find I can't any longer stand the strain of constant let-downs and disappointments for more than a week or so."

And then, in late April 1981, disaster struck. The Czech authorities stopped one of Kavan's vans as it was entering the country. The two French drivers, Trotskyists disguising themselves as a husband and wife on a camping vacation, managed to swallow the personal letters they were carrying, but the customs people soon uncovered the rest of their cache, which included several hundred copies of *Svedectvi*. Within a couple of weeks, the StB, using the incident as a pretext, launched a major crackdown on a significant segment of the Czech oppositionist underground. Among those arrested was Jirina Siklova, the woman who had been serving as Kavan's principal conduit. Many of her domestic contacts—including such veteran oppositionists as Jiri Ruml and his son Jan; Jiri Hajek; Havel's wife, Olga, and brother Ivan; Jiri Müller; and Karel Kyncl—were detained as well, some briefly, others for a more indeterminate time.

As the Czech propaganda machine began gearing up for what had all the makings of a major show trial, Kavan, back in London, grew increasingly frantic. He had been trying for some time to interest a young British television reporter named Julian Manyon in doing a story on his Czech colleagues. Following the van's capture, Manyon, taken with the entire sweep of the story, and especially with its aspects of clandestine derring-do, agreed to undertake the report. He traveled to Prague for some on-scene reporting (and surreptitious filming) and then persuaded Kavan—actually, who persuaded whom to do what became one of the many disputed aspects of this whole affair—to allow himself to be filmed flying to Paris, arriving at Charles de Gaulle Airport, and reenacting his original contact with his drivers. The result of all this was a half-hour program broadcast by Thames Television on June 25, 1981, under the title "The Last Roundup?" The program, which sympathetically evoked the desperate situation of the Czech prisoners, made for compelling viewing. However, partway through the program, in a voice-over narration that, according to Kavan, strayed from a previously reviewed text, Manyon declared in passing that the French drivers had "carried with them the names and addresses of people inside Czechoslovakia, contacts for Jan Kavan's secret organization"—going on to state that these details had now fallen into the hands of the Czech police, giving them "enough evidence to begin the wave of arrests that they had been itching to carry out."

Kavan erupted in fury. No such list or inventory of names had ever been in the van, he insisted, if for no other reason than that no such list existed, or could exist, since, as mentioned earlier, the key to the security of his operation was that he always dealt with a single exclusive contact and himself had no idea who constituted the rest of the distribution network. For good measure, Kavan swore that no lists whatever, no uncoded names of any kind, had been in the van. He said that any statement to the contrary not only maligned him personally—making it seem as if his carelessness had been responsible for the ensuing series of arrests—but also recklessly jeopardized his imprisoned colleagues, since the Czech regime would now be able to manufacture such lists out of thin air and invoke no less an authority than British television as a source regarding their authenticity.

Kavan's British friends urged him to let the matter drop. Yes, they conceded, some damage may have been done, but perhaps not as much as he feared, and, in any case, the documentary had done a lot of good as well. Yet Kavan could not be assuaged. (In retrospect, perhaps the fact that his beloved mother was suddenly dying of cancer, and that this entire fiasco would come to constitute the last light in which she would see him, contributed to his tenacity.) He took his grievance to the *Sunday Times,* and in November the paper ran a banner story headlined "TV LIE," savaging both Manyon's documentary and his reputation. Then Kavan registered a formal complaint with the quasi-official watchdog Broadcasting Complaints Commission, or BCC. That suit, in turn, complicated matters for all kinds of people, including Pavel Tigrid, who knew that there *had* been at least one list in the van—a fact that he himself was already furious about. "I'd *told* Kavan," Tigrid subsequently told me. "I'd *told* him not to include the address labels of the *Svedectvi* subscribers with the magazines themselves—to send them in separately, by courier. But he hadn't listened—you could never get Kavan to listen—so *that* list probably had been confiscated off the van."

Tigrid's knowledge put him in an especially difficult position when Manyon's lawyers came to him in Paris and pleaded that he provide an affidavit to the BCC in Manyon's behalf. He squirmed out of the jam by declining, as a friend of the family and a French resident, to testify at all, but he resented having been put in the position. Tigrid, for his part, is convinced that the main reason Kavan pursued the case was that he had a "megalomaniacal" need to be the center of attention. "Honza worked like a dog and accomplished a tremendous amount," Tigrid told me, employing the diminutive of "Jan." "But the trouble with him—I've often told him as much. 'Honza,' I've said, 'your problem is that you want both to be the world's greatest conspirator and to be *famous* for being the world's greatest conspirator.'"

As it happened, the show trials in Czechoslovakia never took place, the last of the van-case prisoners having been released within a year, with Kavan himself cleared of any responsibility for the fiasco in the opinion of those in Prague most directly affected.

Nevertheless, four years after all the van-case defendants had been released, Kavan was still pressing his case before the BCC. And, thanks in part to his adamant, sworn (and at the time irrefutable) insistence that there had been no lists of any sort in the van, the BCC in 1985 did find in Kavan's favor, noting that Thames Television and Manyon had now conceded having made an "error of judgment." It would prove a Pyrrhic victory at best, for in the process Kavan had managed to make for himself a formidable enemy.

The rest of 1981 would prove no less dreadful for Kavan. By the end of the year, martial law had been declared in Poland, momentarily dashing his hopes for any general opening in Eastern Europe. (Ironically, this very event may have contributed to the early release, within a year, of all the Ruml et al. prisoners; perhaps the Czech authorities no longer felt as immediately threatened and therefore no longer required the domestic propaganda benefits of a drawn-out show trial.) And shortly thereafter, Rosemary died. Four years later, when he finally got her autobiography published, he contributed an epilogue, lamenting the fact that "there is no day in my life when I don't think of my mother and don't painfully feel her loss. I wish she was with me when I'm overwhelmed with problems, sad at being let down by those I trusted, or simply too exhausted to go on."

Still, he did go on. Gradually, painstakingly, he reestablished his channel, this time with Daniel Kummerman as his principal contact, though he could never again achieve the volume of smuggled material that had characterized his pre-1981 transports. He started a dialogue between Western antinuclear peace activists and Eastern European dissidents—two groups that hadn't previously had much use for each other and continued to eye each other warily. There are Czechs today who find *that* involvement highly suspicious. In addition, he focused particular energy on forging links between the otherwise isolated dissident movements from each of the countries of Eastern Europe. There are Poles today who are incredulous about the charges against Kavan because they know him as one of the principal conduits in arranging a highly secret series of meetings between Charter 77 and Solidarity leaders in a remote stretch of the Tatra Mountains deep in the craw of martial law. The security apparatuses of either country would have given anything to know about those meetings in advance so as to upend them and bag the participants—but they never had a clue. Just as, apparently, they never had a clue about so much else that Kavan was doing.

Kavan had frequent recourse, throughout his twenty-year exile, to his deed poll subterfuge as a way of amassing fresh British passports under continually changing identities, so as to facilitate clandestine travels throughout Eastern Europe (by 1989, he'd collected ten separate such identities). He says he used these trips to garner fresh contacts and information for his Palach Press Agency and to help forge those links between the different oppositionist movements. But he steadfastly steered clear of Czechoslovakia —such a visit would have been far too dangerous, both to himself and to his friends there—until Christmas 1987, when he, or rather one I. M. James, suddenly appeared on the streets of Prague. He made two more such visits, in the spring of 1988 and again at Christmas. Some people in Prague today, still solidly in Kavan's corner, can't understand the recklessness of those trips. Others think that his ability to get away with them at all affords yet further proof that he must have been working with the StB all along.

DURING THE LATTER HALF of the 1980s, history seemed to be repeating itself in Czechoslovakia. Just as in the late fifties and early sixties a neo-Stalinist regime in Prague maintained its obdurate hard line for years after most of the Communist world, and particularly the Soviet Union itself, had yielded to de-Stalinization, so now, across the latter half of the eighties, another hard-line Prague regime was refusing even to acknowledge the astonishing liberalizing transformations sweeping its neighbors. When Mikhail Gorbachev visited Prague in March 1987, vast expectations were roused that the Husak regime's embedded rigidities would now begin to give way. But half a year later, when Husak finally resigned as Party general secretary owing to age and ill health, he was replaced by somebody who was, if anything, even more hard-line than he himself—Milos Jakes, one of the foremost architects of the post-1968 purges.

On August 21, 1988, ten thousand people took part in a Prague demonstration commemorating the twentieth anniversary of the Warsaw Pact invasion, the biggest of its kind since 1969. In January 1989, spontaneous mass demonstrations marked the twentieth anniversary of Jan Palach's self-immolation. The Jakes regime responded by promulgating legislation dramatically increasing penalties for "disturbing the peace." On June 4, the Polish Solidarity movement trounced its Communist opponents in that country's first semi-free elections in over forty years. On June 16, Imre Nagy, the martyred leader of Hungary's 1956 rebellion, was officially reburied during a massively attended ceremony in Budapest. At the end of the month, some Czech oppositionists began circulating a petition, modestly entitled "A Few Sentences," which called for the introjection of some of that free-floating redemocratization into Czechoslovakia as well. The Jakes regime responded by stepping up its repressive intimidations—thousands were dragged in for questioning, hundreds arrested. (In London, Kavan was busier than he'd been in years, tracking and publicizing the increasingly embattled fate of Czechoslovakia's oppositionists.) As late as September 1989, the Czech Communist Party's principal ideologist was railing against "the excesses of glasnost." By then things were beginning to move even in stolid East Germany. The biggest demonstration in that country's history took place in Leipzig on September 25; by November 9, the Berlin Wall and the regime it had buttressed for so long were both crumbling. Czechoslovakia's masters simply stiffened further: they would not be swayed, they fully intended to stay the course.

But how could they deny students the right to demonstrate on November 17—the fiftieth anniversary of those Nazi raids on Charles University which culminated in the murder of Jan Opeltal, a day that Czech Communists, among them Pavel Kavan, had themselves been so instrumental in immortalizing as International Students Day? In short, they couldn't. Over one hundred thousand young Czechs showed up for demonstrations, which had in fact been officially sanctioned.

Precisely what happened next remains mired in controversy to this day. Perhaps the officials panicked. Perhaps some elements of the regime intentionally launched a provocation to undermine intraparty rivals. Perhaps—as some suspect—it was a case of the StB itself endeavoring to bring down the ancien régime in an effort to hijack the inevitable. Whatever the reason, security forces now turned viciously on the peaceful marchers, funneling them into a trap in which thousands were compelled to run a gauntlet of truncheon-wielding policemen. Hundreds were injured and some were even reported (erroneously, though perhaps intentionally so) to have been killed.

And now suddenly, a Czech population that for twenty years had been generally cowed into submission reared up in near unanimous revulsion. The Jakes regime's dread authority dematerialized across the course of the ensuing week. Students mobilized throughout the country, calling for a general strike on November 27. Two days after the police riot, Civic Forum was founded and soon took up residence at the Magic Lantern Theater. During the next several days, one hundred thousand, three hundred thousand, half a million converged on Wenceslaus Square to cheer Vaclav Havel and presently Alexander Dubcek as well. Jakes resigned, and though he was initially replaced by another hardliner, Karel Urbanek, by November 25 Urbanek was reluctantly announcing the government's willingness to enter into negotiations with the opposition.

Back in London, Kavan couldn't stand being stuck there as his life's universe was being transfigured in his homeland. On November 25, brandishing the most current of his passports, he boarded a jet for Prague.

And so it was that he arrived at the Prague airport—or, rather, I. M. James arrived. Only this time, according to Kavan, the phony passport set off alarm bells. Customs officials called the Interior Ministry downtown, which dispatched a pair of agents who undertook more than twelve hours of strenuous interrogation (during which, among other things, they established Kavan's true identity), before grudgingly allowing him into the country at three o'clock the following morning. They warned him that they'd likely be picking him up again. And, indeed, three days later (the morning after a successful one-hour general strike, as the regime's leaders were already deep into the negotiations that would quickly lead to their supersession), they once again nabbed Kavan, this time taking him out to an elegant villa in one of the city's leafier districts.

And here's where things get really fuzzy, here's where things turn truly odd. Because two years later, after Kavan had been officially denounced as an StB collaborator and he'd launched an international campaign to clear his name, his parliamentary opponents illegally leaked a videotape of that second interrogation or, rather, portions of it. It didn't seem like an interrogation at all. Its tone was disconcertingly cordial, and, at one point, Jan Kavan and his StB interlocutors were even seen to be toasting each other with champagne.

II

There was a simple explanation, Kavan would insist at that point two years later, when the video leaked—whereupon he'd launch into quite a convoluted one. Nothing was ever simple in the life of Jan Kavan.

But that was still well off in the future, those glorious velvet days of November 1989. Jan joined his friends in the Magic Theater, scaling the balcony each afternoon for the mammoth rallies; spearheading foreign press relations throughout the sleepless, ebullient nights; gazing on in flabbergasted astonishment as the regime's long-dread authority now seemed to melt inexorably into thin air. (Who cared any longer about the StB—with what harm could its agents possibly threaten anyone anymore?) And meanwhile, as the weeks passed, Jan fell in love and rose into parliament, growing ever more fulfilled and content. If only his mother, alas, could have lived to see it. . . .

The trouble, however, was that the StB hadn't just disappeared. It had persisted, like a bad dream from which the country was having a terrible time trying to awaken. People started looking back at those miraculous days of November 1989, when what had started as a simple student demonstration managed, within weeks, to upend an entire era of totalitarian domination, and a worm of suspicion began to eat at the core of their cherished common memory: how could it all have happened so effortlessly, almost as if it had all been planned? Maybe it had all been planned. It *had* to have been planned. The StB itself—rumors were now running rampant—must surely have orchestrated the whole thing, starting with the conspicuously, needlessly bloody suppression of that student demonstration on November 17, which proved to be the catalyst for the entire uprising, and which now, in retrospect, took on all the earmarks of a classic provocation, with one wing of the ancien régime (the omnipresent security apparatus, the StB) arranging to wrest power from the hapless other. Maybe everything else had merely been a shadow play.

A fifteen-member parliamentary commission was impaneled to investigate the origins of the supposed new order, and was named the November 17th Commission. As it launched its inquiry into the events of 1989, rumors continued to proliferate. Not only had the StB staged those seminal events, people were now saying, but it had also succeeded in loading the new Parliament with its former agents and informants—people who were either organizationally or ideologically committed to following the ongoing secret edicts of its hidden High Command, or else people who could be blackmailed into doing so. The new Parliament went through a sudden crisis of legitimacy, and, as a result, on January 18, 1991, an overwhelming majority passed a resolution empowering the November 17th Commission to vet the entire body; that is, to delve into the sealed files and registries of the StB and to identify any former agents or informers who were now members of the Parliament. Such individuals were to be confronted privately with the charges against them and allowed quietly to resign or else within fifteen days be subject to public denunciation. Kavan may have had some mild civil-liberties reservations about the resolution, but, on the other hand, as he said at the time, "I didn't want to sit in the same room with people who were guilty of denouncing my friends."

A month later, on February 22, 1991, Kavan was himself summoned to the commission's offices. Four of the panel's members were seated stiffly behind an oblong desk, and one of them—Stanislav Devaty, a man for whom Kavan had organized several emergency campaigns throughout the eighties, and whom Kavan regarded as a friend—informed him that his name had shown up in the files, along with a code name (Kato) and a sheaf of incriminating evidence, and that he was therefore being given fifteen days in which to resign.

Actually, Devaty told him, only a small part of his file still existed, though it was plenty damning, documenting Kavan's initial recruitment in the weeks after Palach's suicide in January 1969 by the StB operative Stanislav Patejdl (code name "Pavlasek") and his close collaboration in the months thereafter with Patejdl's London deputy Frantisek Zajicek (code name "Zachystal"). Over the next year or so, Devaty insisted that the files irrefutably proved that

Jan had reported to Zajicek frequently (over forty meetings were listed) and thoroughly, providing detailed information on both his student contacts and the opposition's principal British allies, including such figures as the noted author and journalist William Shawcross and the student leader Richard Molineux. In addition, he had repeatedly acted to mute and, where possible, to subvert public demonstrations in Britain against the growing constrictions back in Prague. After the summer of 1970, the file petered out—nobody could say what he had done after that—but this, he was told, was all that the commission needed: his guilt had been established.

Kavan demanded to see the evidence and was told absolutely not—the files were confidential. He asked what sort of appeals process he would be afforded, and he was told none—the law made no such provision. He was simply being given fifteen days within which to resign quietly; otherwise his name would be read out publicly before the Parliament and the entire nation.

Dumbfounded but denying virtually everything, Kavan left the building and began calling friends. One, his fellow deputy Petr Uhl (a longtime dissident colleague of Jan's and now director of the Czechoslovakian News Agency as well), immediately launched a discreet investigation of his own. It turned out that the case against Kavan was nowhere near as cut-and-dried as Devaty and the others had led him to believe. The files of the Second Directorate—the domestic division of the StB—were in good order, and a fairly complete master registry of names existed in which individuals were relatively clearly identified as either agents or informers or subjects of investigation or, indeed, enemies of the state. (Whether such listings were accurate, what they were based upon, and what, specifically, they connoted—those were all other questions.) Parliamentary instructions implied that the November 17th Commission should focus its inquiry on the archives of the Second Directorate alone, and those archives included no file on Kavan. The commission's members, however, acting on their own, had expanded their mandate to include the papers of the First Directorate, the StB's foreign division, whose files were not nearly as straightforward. There was no master registry, and the individual files were peppered with mysterious abbreviations. In the Kavan file that they found there, for example, the designation "DS" had been written in beside the name "Kato," and nobody knew what that meant. The file itself was highly ambiguous: if it was read one way, it appeared that Kavan could not possibly have had any idea of Patejdl's or Zajicek's true identity; if it was read another way, it appeared that he would have had to know.

The commission had apparently assumed that when Kavan was confronted with the charges he would simply fold and slink away. When he refused to do so, the commission was thrown into consternation. For a month, in high secrecy and with increasing urgency, the commission's members and Kavan and his trusted allies struggled over how to proceed. By March 16, the day of Kavan's wedding, it looked as if the commission had decided not to denounce him after all. On March 18, he was at last allowed to examine selected portions of the file—sixty pages out of five hundred—on the condition that he leave the door ajar and not make any copies. On March 21, the commission debated the case until well past midnight; it finally decided, by a vote of six to five (with four members absent), to denounce Kavan.

The next day, Kavan's name was the fifth one on a list of ten names of unmasked agents read out to the Parliament by the commission's spokesman, Petr Toman. A few minutes later, Kavan approached the speaker's stand to deliver a speech, which was being broadcast live to a nationwide television audience. "I do fervently hope that at least some of you will be able to listen in good faith to what I have to say," he began—at which point thirty-five members of Parliament stalked out of the chamber. He then continued, "I am not being condemned to eight weeks' or eight years' imprisonment but am being branded a secret-police collaborator for the rest of my life."

Kavan was almost forty-five years old—the very age his father had been when he died of a heart attack, directly brought on by the legacy of a remarkably similar series of charges of high treachery.

"SOMEONE must have been telling lies about Jan K, because without having done anything wrong he was arrested one fine morning." Thus did I begin an op-ed piece on Kavan's situation, a few months later. I was not alone in making the Kafka allusion, and I certainly wasn't alone in writing an op-ed piece. One of Kavan's first moves following his public denunciation was to tap into the international network of contacts that he had painstakingly cultivated during his Palach Press years. If there was one thing that Kavan definitely knew how to do, it was send out an SOS. He's a veritable Horowitz of the fax machine, and within days he had compiled dozens of testimonials from prominent foreign journalists and parliamentarians, who pointed to their own experience of his passionate effectiveness: the journalists Edward Mortimer, Neal Ascherson, Christopher Hitchens, and William Shawcross (all of whom also wrote about Kavan's situation in the press); and, among countless foreign dignitaries, Senator Paul Simon and Ken Coates, the chairman of the European Parliament's Subcommittee on Human Rights. I hadn't known

Kavan nearly as well as many of these had, but I had frequently relied on the Palach Press Agency's dispatches in my own work (they invariably checked out), and I, too, had in the past been the object of his occasional emergency harangues. (Most recently, it occurred to me, in the matter of two of Stanislav Devaty's hunger strikes, early in 1989.) Why, Kavan would typically demand, *why wasn't I paying attention?*

In April of 1991, Kavan visited the United States briefly and called on me at my office in order to bring me up to date on the latest developments in his case. He was, as ever, a short, mildly pudgy fellow, with a pear-shaped body and an oversized egg-shaped head, partly bald—slightly nebbishy—who somehow manages to present an aspect that is simultaneously sloppy and fastidious. He started out by recalling for me his vertiginous sensation upon first being confronted with the commission's accusation: "Suddenly, they were reeling off all these names. I recognized many of the English ones—these were my friends and allies—but most of the Czechs they mentioned I'd long forgotten, if I'd ever known them at all. Patejdl, for instance—I had a vague recollection of someone of that name identifying himself as from the Foreign Ministry who got in touch with me around the time my passport was confiscated, in January of 1969. But I spoke with a *lot* of people at the time, and I certainly didn't make any sort of deal with him, nor did I have to. The situation was resolving itself of its own accord. As for Zajicek, his was a name I did remember." He went on to recall his contacts with the London embassy's education attaché on behalf of the Student Union, adamantly insisting, however, that he never divulged any privileged information about any of his contacts. "And anyway," he went on, "how was I supposed to know he was recording everything I said for transmittal back to the StB, sometimes with considerable embellishment?"

Kavan declared that he wasn't expecting anyone to credit his protestations of innocence on the basis of his word alone. All he wanted, he said, was some sort of due process, a forum in which he could prove his innocence by calling witnesses and cross-examining his accusers. He said he was trying to get the entire file released to the public, on condition that the release be accompanied by his own point-by-point commentary. But the authorities were pleading the sacrosanct confidentiality of the files—all the while allowing out-of-context leaks of their own that were sometimes quite damaging. (All three hundred members of Parliament had now been granted free access to the entire file.) As his only apparent legal recourse, Kavan had launched a defamation suit in Prague Civil Court against the Interior Ministry, but the case had bogged down in the chaotic post-Communist judicial system. It was commonly being asserted that the only reason he was refusing to resign was sheer greed for his parliamentary salary, so he ostentatiously renounced that salary for the duration—a noble gesture but a relatively disastrous one for somebody in his situation, with a wife and infant daughter, no savings, and no independent income. He had begun receiving hate mail—most disconcerting of all (he pulled out some samples) crude anti-Semitic slurs and sketches. Moreover, he said, some of his onetime allies, even people who professed to still believe in his innocence, were now advising him to resign.

"This whole StB de-Communization business is now becoming terribly politicized," Kavan told me. He was pale and trembling as he talked. "The country seems to be heading toward a crackup. The Czech lands have made a clear break with their prior Communist *nomenklatura*—or, anyway, are trying to—while in the Slovak region the old apparatchiks, many of them truly terrible and corrupt people, have gained a new lease on life by recasting themselves as fierce nationalist defenders of various supposed Slovak prerogatives. Inside the Federal Parliament and the Slovak regional assembly, these people are hanging on and messing things up for everybody else. Nothing is getting done—and that is precisely their intention. It's an awful situation, and there are good people, some of them old friends of mine, who feel that the only way to break the logjam is to expose the long-standing ties of many of those Slovak politicians, say, with the StB—for many of them do have such histories. Some people even think their leader, Vladimir Meciar, does, though I have my doubts. But, anyway, it's a key part of their counterstrategy.

"And here I am desperately claiming that the process behind such exposures is seriously flawed. So these good people come up to me, with great circumspection, and say, 'Listen, we realize that there has been some terrible mistake in your personal case, but can't you just let it be, can't you just quietly take the fall, *for the greater good of the country?*' And for me the terrible thing in such suggestions is that those were precisely the kinds of arguments that his interrogators tried to use on my father during his incarceration—how, yes, he'd obviously been a dedicated Communist, but how he should still sign this confession, *for the greater good of the Party*. And I just won't have it!"

Presently, Kavan returned to Prague. I wrote the op-ed piece, placed it in the *Washington Post,* and turned to other concerns. Calamitous though Kavan's situation appeared to be, it also seemed somewhat ludicrous. Surely there had been some mistake; surely tempers would cool, and the mistake would become obvious to everyone. The fever would subside, and Kavan would be allowed to resume his well-earned career. But that didn't happen. A full year passed—I heard occasional updates—and, if anything, Kavan's situation seemed to be growing even more dire. There was obviously something here I wasn't getting, so I decided to go to London and Prague.

AT THE TIME, I was open to surprise, but I wasn't really expecting it. My expectations were upended almost from the very start, however, for it quickly became apparent that Kavan was a much more complicated individual than I had supposed—or, at any rate, one who provoked an incredibly complex range of emotions in those he came in contact with. His activities in 1969 and 1970 were the least of it; the very substance of his character, the entire arc of his career, seemed to be up for grabs.

It wasn't that he lacked for friends and supporters—particularly among those he had supposedly been informing on in 1969 and 1970—many of whom (including Mortimer and Shawcross) found the current charges against him preposterous.

"Let's put it this way," William Shawcross told me. "Maybe Kavan was working for the StB all along. But, if so, then all you can say is that the StB itself would have to have been running one of the operations most significantly responsible for the eventual downfall of Communism in Czechoslovakia."

But, even while praising Kavan, people often portrayed his operation as spectacularly chaotic, and Kavan himself as cantankerous and difficult—at times, very difficult. "He had an uncanny ability to complicate and confuse," John Keane, a professor of politics at the University of Westminster, said bemusedly. "You're never going to be able to counter all the current unfair ad hominem attacks on Jan with the simple claim that he was an all-around nice guy."

"He worked so hard that he resented it when others didn't, and he would always find something wrong," Joanne Landy, the executive director of the New York–based Campaign for Peace and Democracy, told me. "He was tremendously effective, but he was both relentless and ungrateful. And I *agreed* with his politics. Imagine if I didn't!"

A good deal of the resentment against Kavan, both in London and Prague, had to do with those politics—the way, for instance, he'd tried to forge links between the Western antinuclear peace movements and Eastern European dissidents. "I was suspicious of him from quite early on," Roger Scruton, the conservative political theorist, told me in his office at the University of London. (Scruton had a long history of pro-Czech activism through the Jan Hus Foundation.) "I never really thought of him as an agent, maybe because he looked so much like one and behaved so much like one, and, with his family's Communist past and all, it would have been too obvious. But his association with the peace movement never felt right to me. He would have had to know how it was linked with the KGB and how furthering it here was furthering their goal." Kavan, of course, argued just the opposite—that only by uniting dissident movements on both sides of the divide could the mutually reinforcing cycle of arms race and totalitarian repression be broken. But his was a decidedly minority position among Czechs, both at home and in exile, and it made him few friends.

Kavan was portrayed to me as intensely competitive, and even vindictive, and almost maniacally secretive. The scene was littered with people who used to work with him but finally couldn't take it anymore. One of them, George Joffe, who had actively collaborated with him between 1973 and 1976, serving both as an organizer and as a frequent courier during the early days of the Palach Press, said, "Jan had an uncanny ability at making enemies. He could never tolerate others' knowing more than he did; simply because someone knew too much, he would begin to distrust, to offend, to conceal, until, finally, inevitably, there'd be some sort of explosion."

Several people I spoke with described Kavan as a pathological liar, and these were usually people who at one time had revered him. Jirina Siklova, the Prague sociologist who for years in the late seventies and early eighties served as the principal contact for Kavan's distribution network inside Czechoslovakia, told me that the Czech dissidents had always had a problem with Kavan. "He was doing terribly important work for us, but we'd get these horrendous reports about his operating style," Siklova said. "Whenever new people were getting set to emigrate, we'd urge them to get in touch with Kavan, saying that we knew he was difficult, but, still, what he was doing was so valuable and he was obviously overworked. And invariably the same thing happened. Everyone who went West from here would immediately fall madly in love with him. 'How could you claim he was so difficult?' they would write us angrily. 'He's wonderful!' But within six months they'd be writing, just as angrily, 'Why didn't you warn us? He's a monster, completely impossible!' I had the same experience with his lovers. He had an incredibly chaotic personal life. He'd send his girlfriends in as couriers, and then he'd get rid of them, but in the meantime they'd have fallen in love with

Czechoslovakia, and they'd keep coming back. I had a room here that I called my private psychological counseling room for the former girlfriends of Jan Kavan—and, my God, the passions, the torments! And it was funny, because at times I'd find myself thinking, My God, what do they all see in him?"

One of his former girlfriends told me, "He had this helpless act—how he was so overworked, and he needed you, and you alone could help him accomplish this great thing, whatever it was. You couldn't help wanting to shelter and protect him. But then little inconsistencies would emerge, for no reason—stories of those who had fallen out with him and how it was all their fault. And then you'd just catch him in the most blatant lies, until you began to suspect everything. Some of that was unique to Kavan, but over the years I've come to realize that a lot of it is typical of Czech men generally. Milan Kundera got it exactly right—his blending of the personal and the political is the purest reporting. Theirs is a culture of compulsive compartmentalization and lying."

"Compartmentalization" was a word I often heard in connection with Kavan. He seemed to have dozens of schemes going simultaneously. The chaos extended to his financial affairs: his smuggling operation was continually on the brink of economic collapse, which he always seemed to avert by the narrowest of margins, and often in highly questionable fashion. For example, one disillusioned former coworker told me that somebody once donated a duplicating machine for shipment into Czechoslovakia, and somebody else donated money to buy a duplicating machine for shipment, and Kavan simply "bought" the donated machine and pocketed the money. This sort of thing happened all the time, the coworker said.

In all this, Jan Kavan resembled nobody, perhaps, as much as his father, Pavel—or, at least, the Pavel portrayed in Rosemary Kavan's autobiography, where one reads of a man who was likewise a curt, peremptory, ungrateful, and compulsively secretive workaholic (though not a womanizer). I tried this notion out on Eduard Goldstücker, an old friend and colleague of Pavel's, and he agreed that there was something to it, except that Pavel had been a milder case. "He didn't make these bitter, bitter enemies, the way Jan does," Goldstücker said. "With him, the pattern tended to get laughed off more often: 'Oh, that's Kavan for you—what do you want?' But I think there is something to this feeling you have about Jan, and it applies to many of the other children of that Slansky generation—they feel the need to somehow live out the interrupted lives of their idealized fathers. But they idealize the father out of all proportion, so that with Jan, for example, you get his father's deviousness wed to a scale of ambition that far exceeds anything his father ever aspired to—this sense of being a man of destiny, which is so much more explosive and dangerous."

George Joffe made a similar point: "I think Jan's case is all tied to this business of a young boy's enormously idealized father who, when he finally did emerge from prison, turned out to be quite cutting and dismissive, always belittling the boy as inadequate and a failure—as not living up to *his* own idealization of his son while he was in prison—and who then died suddenly. He accomplished so very much—but there was always a desperation in Jan. A frantic edge, as if he were always trying to prove to his father that he wasn't the failure his father had imagined him to be."

Kenneth Roth, the deputy director of Human Rights Watch, once remarked to me, "Kavan has alienated so many in the human-rights community by being such a cowboy—for instance, all those forays behind the Iron Curtain. On the other hand, perhaps you had to be such a cowboy to get such good stuff."

As my conversation with Joffe ended, he asked to make one final point. "Although I fell out with Jan and felt very, very bitter toward him for a long time—and, in fact, haven't spoken with him for years—still, I never suspected him of any of the sorts of things he's being accused of nowadays," he said. "He seemed to operate out of a complex set of psychological motives—almost as if he needed to make a sacrifice of himself. There's no way I can see that he was playing a complicated, cynical double game with the Czech secret police." He paused and then added, "Though he may have been playing one with himself."

OF ALL THE PEOPLE I spoke with in London, prior to my visit to Prague, perhaps the one least reconciled to Kavan's maddening complications was Julian Manyon, the TV reporter whose reputation he'd so badly smeared with that dubious BCC suit. Indeed, almost a decade after Thames Television's original airing of the disputed documentary, and six years after the BCC's finding against them, Manyon was still resolutely determined to clear his own name. As Kavan himself now came under suspicion in Prague, Manyon rushed to the scene and apparently developed contacts inside the Czech government, such that his lawyers had now been able to get the case reopened before the

BCC, in part on the basis of freshly uncovered material from the original 1981 Interior Ministry investigation—records that included the *Svedectvi* list along with several uncoded, plainly addressed letters to various dissident figures.

When I reached Manyon, he told me that his documentary had been "a model of fairness and accuracy," adding that Kavan was "a liar, a malicious liar who caused both me and Thames Television truly grievous harm over the years." He went on, "He accused me not only of being a bad reporter but also of jeopardizing the safety of good dissidents in the process. Those are serious charges, among the most painful that can be leveled against any journalist, especially when he *knows* them to be false but at the time just can't prove it." Manyon cited Kavan's original letter of complaint to the BCC, which had concluded with the statement "If Julian Manyon was employed by the Czech Secret Service, he could not have done a better job," as particularly ironic in the light of Kavan's current difficulties. But then he doubled back, wanting to make it clear that the two questions—Kavan's role in the matter of the BCC complaint and the question of his possible StB involvement—were unrelated. He might be "a liar of Munchausen proportions, which he demonstrably is," and nevertheless be innocent of these other charges, he said. But that was his problem, wasn't it?

DURING MY FIRST conversation with Kavan in Prague, I quickly brought up the question of the Manyon suit. Why had he felt it necessary to dissemble before the BCC by stating flatly that there had been no lists in the van? He replied that the gist of his complaint to the BCC had been accurate, as his lawyers had once again told the BCC during the most recent hearings. (The lawyers had in the meantime acknowledged the existence of the *Svedectvi* list.) Manyon *had* got the story wrong, Kavan continued to insist— whatever names had been seized off the van hadn't been those of "contacts" of any "secret organization"—and his lawyers were trying to get the BCC to revisit the case on that basis. He repeated his claim that he had been forced to behave as he did in order to protect the prisoners themselves, so that the regime wouldn't be able to bandy the *Svedectvi* list about as if it *were* a list of "Kavan's secret organization," and cite Thames Television as its authority. Fine, I said, but why had he continued to pursue the case after the prisoners had been released? "Because they could have been rearrested at any time," he said. "We needed that finding on the record. Beyond that, it's always difficult to drop such a proceeding halfway." And why had he put the list in the van in the first place, against Tigrid's advice? "It was easy for Tigrid to offer advice like that," Kavan said. "But that list—twenty-four pages of labels—was incredibly bulky. You couldn't just send it in by courier; it had to be hidden in a safe shipment."

We were meeting in the cafeteria in the Parliament building. We didn't need to talk quietly, because others kept their distance, with many of Kavan's fellow deputies occasionally glaring at him across the divide. I asked him about the financial irregularities I had heard of in his operation—for example, the matter of the double-billing on the duplicating machine.

Kavan screwed up his face in distaste and seemed to squirm. "It's true that bookkeeping and accounting are things I dislike and have no propensity for," he said. "This specific thing about the duplicating machine—I really don't recall it. I don't think it's true. But I would regularly move funds from one project to another—I was always scrambling. You see, unlike Tigrid or some of the other active émigrés, I was refusing to accept any foreign governmental or intelligence funding, and as a result my circumstances were always desperate. People were always wanting to contribute toward a specific item—the purchase of a duplicating machine, say—so they could get all the credit, but no one wanted to contribute to the entire operation's overhead, which was considerable. There was the purchase and refitting and storage of the vans, the drivers' expenses, the cost of specifically requested medicines or technical manuals, and so forth. So that, yes, I can see how somebody looking at all this scrambling around from the outside might have grown suspicious. On the other hand, everybody knows how I lived in those years, the physical conditions I endured—and still do. I doubt if anybody seriously imagines I was profiteering for my own benefit."

I asked Kavan about his "cowboy" reputation, and, specifically, about his repeated breachings of the Iron Curtain.

"There's nothing mysterious about it," he said. "I needed to travel, regularly, to keep up my contacts with the various clandestine movements and to effect linkages between those movements, to develop sources for the Palach Press Agency, and generally to gauge for myself how things were evolving on the ground. And it happened that traveling wasn't all that difficult." He described his deed-poll method, whereupon he reached into his satchel and pulled out ten passports with ten different but technically legal names, with pictures showing Kavan in various bearded disguises. "This is how I traveled for nineteen years," he continued. "Now, for seventeen of those years, I didn't return to Czechoslovakia—I didn't dare to risk either their security or my own—but, as you can see, I went just about everywhere else."

We leafed through the passports, noting the visas and the stamps: Warsaw, Budapest, Bucharest, East Berlin, Sofia. "By Christmas of 1987, however, I was having an increasingly hard time withstanding the homesickness and the sense of separation, and I was feeling an incredible need to come back, if only for a visit," Kavan went on. "There were, of course, legitimate reasons as well—things I needed to discuss in person with my colleagues here. There's only so much you can do through couriers. I don't know—maybe it was the fact that my mother had died, and her mother as well, to whom I was also very close. No one was around anymore who would have been personally crushed if I were to be captured and thrown in jail. I didn't intend to get captured, and took enormous precautions, both then and on two subsequent trips, in 1988, the last of which I made with this passport here, under the name I. M. James, and on none of which was there any trouble. It was only after the last of those trips—at the end of 1988—that a slight hitch developed, after the fact: somebody let something slip during questioning on some other matter, and I was warned not to attempt to enter the country under the same name again. I'd been intending to go through a new deed-poll procedure, but, though easy, it does take several weeks, and then everything started happening so quickly, such that at the end of November, 1989, I decided to risk it, I came back as I. M. James, and sure enough, for the first time, they caught me."

The passports lay fanned out on the table before us. What was it about him, I finally asked—this talent for endless complication? And not just that but the whole pattern of seduction and disappointment that seemed to run through his life, his apparent genius for arousing suspicion and making enemies?

Kavan grew quiet and gazed around the cafeteria, and then, his countenance darkening, he said, "Of course I'm aware of all that. I'd hoped that I had inherited enough from my mother to combat it, but it's true that I seem repeatedly to exhibit patterns of my father's which I never liked. He, too, had a tremendous ability to lose friends."

I was reminded of that passage from Rosemary's autobiography: "Pavel's voice and Pavel's question." After which she'd gone on to note: "Genetics had done a good job. Poor Jan, he was only partly to blame. . . . His organism had reacted to Pavel's imprisonment with severe headaches. Psychologically he had adapted to continuing tension, but once the pattern had been set, he seemed compelled to create unending stress situations."

Kavan's fingers tapped on the tabletop. I asked him how the defamation suit he had filed against the Interior Ministry was going.

"Incredibly slowly," he replied. "The court meets, raises interminable technical complications, recesses for months at a time. I don't hold out much hope of ever achieving satisfaction there. That's one of the reasons I decided to have myself lustrated."

III

Being lustrated, as various observers have noted, is every bit as painful as it sounds. The word "lustration" derives from the Latin *lustratio,* which means purification by sacrifice. Czechoslovakia's 1991 lustration law, which established the basic ground rules for the country's political-purification rituals, derived from the Czech public's rapidly evolving attitude toward the country's immediate past. On New Year's Day of 1990, shortly after becoming Czechoslovakia's president, Vaclav Havel gave an address in which he spoke of a "decayed moral environment" as being one of the country's principal legacies from its Communist past, but he was careful not to assign blame too narrowly. In a passage that in many ways epitomized the velvetness of the Velvet Revolution he noted, "When I talk about a decayed moral environment . . . I mean all of us, because all of us became accustomed to the totalitarian system, accepted it as an unalterable fact, and thereby kept it running. . . . None of us is merely victim of it, because all of us helped to create it together. . . . We cannot lay all the blame on those who ruled us before, not only because this would not be true but also because it could detract from the responsibility each of us now faces—the responsibility to act on our own initiative, freely, sensibly, and quickly."

This attitude, at once expansive, forward-looking, and scrupulously lucid, typified much of the thinking at the top of the new government, including such veteran oppositionists as the Czech premier Petr Pithart, and the foreign minister, Jiri Dienstbier. As had happened earlier in Poland, a decision was made that there would be no easy scapegoats. In part (again as in Poland), this decision grew out of the very way in which the final transfer of power had been effected—through negotiations, without violence. One just didn't turn around and arrest the very people whose hands one had been shaking on occasions of high solemnity only a few weeks earlier. In the Czech case, however, the forbearance was taken to such an extreme that for the first six months of the new order the StB was left largely to its own devices; it is partly for that reason that so many of the key files were subsequently found to be missing. And that forbearance was in turn partly responsible for aggravating the growing public feeling that the entire transition must have been one big fix.

During any extended period of totalitarian governance, terrible things happen to good people and wonderful things happen to bad ones. And during any transition from such a period of unjust governance a principal challenge is that both those legacies must be addressed. One problem with Havel's magnanimous initial position was that it addressed neither. There were many people—and not just dissidents—who had suffered grievously under the previous regime, and many other people who had inflicted much of that suffering. As upset as Czechs were by the continuing plight of the victims, they were even more galled by the seemingly blithe impunity being lavished upon the perpetrators. Unpunished, these earlier winners were quickly turning their advantages of position to more purely financial advantage, and thus setting themselves up to emerge as the new winners. Furthermore, many people felt that as long as those minions of the prior system continued to retain their positions of authority they would inevitably sabotage all attempts to set up a new dispensation, either intentionally (and maybe even systematically) or else through sheer incompetence and ineptitude. As months passed, the calls for a more thoroughgoing housecleaning became increasingly insistent, and as those calls began to be answered by ad hoc improvisations, differing radically from one region or ministry or industry to another, pressure grew for the central government to arrive at some unified policy on the matter.

Rightwing parliamentarians, in particular, were clamoring for a bill that would simply prohibit all former Communists above a certain level, all military officers above a certain rank, and all security agents and their collaborators from holding any positions of authority—fairly broadly defined—within the state. While Havel and his allies now acknowledged the validity of some of the thinking behind that impulse, they nevertheless objected to its basic premise of collective guilt—the theory that individuals ought to be punished for mere membership in a group, regardless of personal culpability for the evils perpetrated by that group. A draft bill that the government presented to Parliament in early September of 1991 required that whatever purging eventually took place be limited to those members of the previously delineated categories who could themselves be shown to have participated in "suppressing human rights," with the burden of proof falling on the government, and the accused guaranteed a certain minimal due process and right of appeal. The rightist parliamentarians objected that such a standard would have the opposite effect of insulating most of the malefactors, since it would be virtually impossible to prove any given individual's participation in suppressing human rights. The debate seemed to settle into a shrill impasse, but then, in October, in the immediate aftermath of the scare caused by the failed hardliners' coup against Gorbachev back in Moscow, the rightists were suddenly able to force through a bill largely along the lines they had originally favored.

Once the bill had passed, Havel faced a new signing drama, in many ways more subtle and complex than any he had confronted or written about during his simple days as a dissident: whether or not to affix his signature to a bill many of whose provisions he disdained. There were, however, powerful practical reasons in favor of signing, not the least of which was the challenge of those obstructionist former Communists in Slovakia who had recast themselves as nationalists and, as such, were threatening the very survival of the Czecho-Slovak union. Eventually, he did sign the bill, while simultaneously submitting proposed revisions for consideration by the Parliament—a moot gesture, since the revisions were of precisely the sort that the Parliament had rejected in approving the bill.

Havel's behavior with regard to Kavan's case was remarkably similar: notwithstanding the fact that for years, during his English exile, Kavan had been responsible for smuggling and distributing many of Havel's principal texts, still, after his denunciation, Havel, as president, declined to inject himself into the controversy in any public, active way. In part, perhaps, this may have been because he harbored doubts of his own (Kavan *was* a controversial figure even in oppositionist circles), but mainly, it seems, it was because he was attempting to keep his office above the fray so as to be better able to wield his influence in the more important struggles of the day, notably his attempt to keep the country from breaking up. Whenever he was directly asked about Kavan, he would speak in a general way about his pain at the potential injustices inherent in the procedures and their lack of due process. He did eventually find a way to express a bit more solidarity on a personal basis, however, agreeing to meet informally one afternoon with Kavan and Petr Uhl in a very public setting, the Hlavkova café, from where he presumably could be sure word of the meeting would quickly spread throughout the city.

The new law applied to both current and prospective holders of more than two hundred thousand government positions. (Kavan was able to bring about his lustration merely by applying for one of those jobs.) Its operation in the matter of senior Party or military or security-service officials was more or less straightforward: if you had been above a certain rank, you were fired or, at any rate, had to accept a lower position. When it came to former collaborators with the secret police (informers and the like), the secrecy of the collaboration rendered the situation far more complex. Anybody could have been a collaborator, and many people had been.

Indeed, grasping the extent of the StB's penetration of Czech society requires an understanding of how the StB operated. In part thanks to the dramas of Vaclav Havel himself, people in the West are fairly familiar with the classic totalitarian quandary of whether or not to sign the petition—the decent, if somewhat weak, man faced with the terrible dilemma of whether to risk his livelihood and his family's well-being by finally taking a principled stand in opposition to some particular state travesty. The tattered page before him, his trembling hand: to sign or not to sign? But we are perhaps not as aware of another sort of signing drama—this first one's eerie obverse —that was continually occurring inside Czechoslovakia, as in the other Communist countries, all through those years. For the secret police there demanded more than mere conformity; they craved collusion. They would set their sights on a given individual, and through artful blends of threat and seduction, of extortion and bribery, they would endeavor to get that person to cross over to their side, to join their ranks. And this dance always culminated—for theirs was a bureaucratic culture par excellence—in the proffering of a form, a mere sheet of paper, and the request for a signature. A pact with the devil, and again the same barbed question: to sign or not to sign? Sometimes, all that was being asked for was that signature; sometimes, more would be required. Sometimes, that signature connoted the commitment to do considerably more, sometimes nothing more than solemnly to promise never to speak to anyone else of these dark contacts (an odd agreement, that: "Sign here your confirmation that we never met"). The StB agents were under considerable pressure continually to extend their web of complicity, to recruit more informers, to collect more signatures. They got bonuses: three more signatures, a television set! Sometimes, as is now known, they fabricated signatures, although not people: the people were real, the signatures were faked.

("We're not talking Kafka here," as one observer noted. "This was Gogol, or Graham Greene: 'Our Man in Prague.'") All the signatures gravitated toward the center and got entered into the registry, a master list, which also included the names of mere subjects of investigation, or even of established enemies of the state. Sometimes it was easy to tell the difference, but often it was not.

At any rate, this master registry became the focal point for the lustration process as it related to the security services. The drama of signing would now be turned inside out—into a drama of naming. According to the new law, every state employee or applicant for state employment above a certain defined level would be required to have himself lustrated; that is, his name would be submitted to a panel at the Interior Ministry, and the panel would consult the registry and, within sixty days, issue a certificate declaring the person "StB positive" or "StB negative." If the applicant turned up negative, he would present that certificate to his superior and retain his job. If he came out positive, the best thing for him to do would be to resign quietly.

AS THE LUSTRATION campaign began to kick into high gear, it aroused concern among several international monitoring organizations, ranging from the International Labor Organization, in Geneva, to Helsinki Watch, in New York. Serious questions were raised about the principle of collective guilt, the reliability of the StB registry, the failure to distinguish between levels of culpability within that registry, the lack of due-process safeguards (including a misplaced burden of proof and a too limited right of appeal), and the imminent likelihood that the campaign would break out of its current high-governmental context.

Jeri Laber, the director of Helsinki Watch and a veteran defender of Charter 77 and other Czech causes, summarized many of these concerns in an article that the *New York Review of Books* published in its April 23, 1992, issue, under the headline "WITCH HUNT IN PRAGUE." Many of the people I spoke with, both in London and in Prague, were angry about that piece, and angriest of all, perhaps, about its title, with its implication that things were getting out of hand in Czechoslovakia—indeed, that the place had already descended into a McCarthyite hysteria. Two confederates of Roger Scruton's, Christine Stone and Mark Almond, writing under the letterhead of the British Helsinki Human Rights Group, composed a letter to the *New York Review*'s editor, in which they noted, "Although Ms. Laber mentions meeting various well-known figures in Prague she does not seem to have discussed the lustration law with Jaroslav Basta, the chairman of the Independent Commission implementing it. Had she spoken with Mr. Basta, Ms. Laber's fears might have been laid to rest. He is an eloquent advocate of the right of all individuals to the presumption of innocence until guilt is proven beyond reasonable doubt. His Commission's use of forensic analysis to date and authenticate secret police documents, and its unwillingness to rely on the testimony of former StB agents, refute Ms. Laber's assertion that the secret police 'still rule, reaching out from the grave.'"

Partly with this letter in mind, I made a point of visiting Mr. Basta at his office when I went to Prague, and I indeed found him both eloquent and manifestly decent.

Basta is a relatively young man—roughly Kavan's age. He had known and worked with Kavan when both were student radicals. Basta was an archeologist by training, but after being arrested, in 1970, for "subversive activities" and serving a subsequent two-and-a-half-year sentence in prison he had been blocked from pursuing his chosen profession—officially, at least. He had been consigned to work in construction thereafter, yet he nevertheless managed to pursue his real vocation in his spare time, composing dozens of highly regarded papers on the prehistory of Western Bohemia. In our conversation he acknowledged that many of the skills he had honed in those studies were of considerable value in his current work, which consisted of sifting through reams of ambiguous data in search of plausible accounts of the prehistory of various fairly or unfairly accused individuals, and our talk turned to the archeology of collaboration.

"I feel I've seen it all by this time," Basta said, with a deep sigh. One of the first signers of Charter 77, Basta was one of the first delegates that the Civic Forum finally posted to the Interior Ministry, and he had held various positions there and in its successors. "I've scoured hundreds of files," he went on. "There were so many different kinds of collaboration and reasons for collaborating. Some people informed for the StB out of ideological conviction—though, actually, surprisingly few. With some, the motivation was petty jealousy or small-time revenge. Some were just born informers; in many ways, those were the worst—the twisted ones. Some collaborated for material gain, or to advance their careers—so as to be able to travel abroad, for instance—or not to have their careers dashed. There were some who were blackmailed into collaborating: the StB was regularly on the lookout for people's weaknesses, and it would exploit every lapse, every vulnerability. I've heard horrible stories. Some people were put under terrible pressure while serving jail sentences for various political crimes—or, threatened with jail, they were unable to withstand that pressure—and signed on. Some did it out of love—so as not to blight a child's education, or so as to be able finally to visit a family member stranded abroad. Some who signed went on to do terrible damage to the lives of their neighbors or coworkers. Others signed and did virtually nothing, offering no information of any import whatever. Still others signed and almost immediately thought better of it; racked by guilt, they may have collaborated for a few weeks and never again. Some of those then joined—or rejoined—the dissident movement and subsequently put in years of solid, important work."

And was that his job, I interjected—to sort out all those gradations and evaluate all those mitigating factors?

"Oh, no," he replied. "The great majority of those people I can't help at all. The law makes no provision for any such mitigating circumstances. If you ever signed—if you're listed in the registry under Category A or B, which means that your signature is on file—that's it: you're StB positive, and there's no appeal. You're lustrated. No, our commission is empowered under the law to handle only the appeals of people in the borderline so-called Category C, which is a very narrow category—maybe only two thousand cases. We can examine the entire files of those people, subpoena witnesses and enforce testimony under oath, and then render a binding verdict. When it comes to those people, we do have the authority to clear their names. But everybody else . . . " He shrugged, paused, and went on, "I've considered this law for a long time, and I have to tell you I don't think much either of it or of the people who initiated it."

THERE WERE all kinds of arguments both in favor of and opposed to lustration, some more convincing than others, but it seemed to me that the real sources of the passion swirling around the issue ran deeper than mere argumentation. This was particularly evident, I came to feel, with regard to two types of support that the campaign was garnering.

The first involved former dissident activists who were vehement proponents of lustration. They were a small minority. In general, you could almost take it as a rule: go through Amnesty International's old Czechoslovak files, and you'd find that the more severely persecuted an oppositionist had been under the old regime, the less adamant he was likely to be today about lustration. Nevertheless, its enthusiastic advocates did include some distinguished longtime oppositionists, and I had a lengthy conversation with one of these: Pavel Bratinka, a leading Catholic radical free marketeer, who had become one of the guiding lights of the relatively small but remarkably dynamic new ODA (Civic Democratic Alliance) political party. At one point in our discussion, I brought up a couple of Basta's examples—people who had been blackmailed into signing, or those who had signed out of love, out of a wish to be able to visit a daughter abroad, say—and I asked Bratinka whether he felt that such cases might not rate some special dispensation.

His lips curling with disgust, he said, "If they were blackmailable before, who's to say they wouldn't be blackmailable again? The people have a right to protect themselves from those who enslaved them; of course such people should be lustrated. The point is that these acts of cowardice of theirs had consequences. There were people who didn't sign, who retained their dignity and didn't get to go see their daughter. If a man admits that he was nothing but a weakling—and that is what his having signed those papers proves—why shouldn't people have the right to know he was a weakling? And why should society have to endure the continued presence of such weaklings in positions of authority? I am a solid-state physicist, but for eight years, because I refused to sign, I was forced to work as a street-cleaner and a stoker. Everybody could earn a living honestly during those years in this country. And those who failed to showed a bizarre lack of moral conscience. Why should they be spared the publication of that truth now?"

Many of Bratinka's former allies in the dissident struggle recoiled at such expressions of self-righteous vindictiveness. "Savonarola" was one formula I frequently heard to characterize the attitude. The self-righteously vindictive theme, however, amounted to only a trickle in the pro-lustration flood, perhaps because only a small number of lustration's supporters had any claim to feelings of self-righteous purity. For the fact is—and this was a key part of the Czech reality and, indeed, the principal source of lustration's main tributary of support—that hardly anybody in Czechoslovakia ever did actively oppose the regime. Unlike the situation in Poland, for example, where millions took an active role in the 1980–81 Solidarity movement—the movement that both prefigured and provoked the collapse of Communism—the post-1968 opposition in Czechoslovakia was never able to claim more than a few thousand active members. For example, Charter 77, for all its moral weight and historic import, garnered only 1,864 signatures. As late as the summer of 1989, well after the Soviets had clearly signaled that they would no longer be coming to the assistance of any floundering fraternal allies, that Czech "A Few Sentences" petition was able to secure only thirty-nine thousand signatures out of a total population of more than fifteen million.

"THAT SILENCE was what mattered, not any individual bastards," Jan Urban, a journalist, who was one of the bravest and most dynamic opposition activists during the eighties, told me. "And all the current noise surrounding lustration is simply a way of keeping silent about that silence."

"There is an old Czech proverb," a young veteran dissident named Vaclav Trojan told me in Prague. "'The robber always cries "Stop, thief!"' The fact is that a lot of people did benefit under the previous system. They attended the May Day parades, joined the requisite organizations, kept the Party posters in their storefront windows, as in Havel's famous example. And, in exchange, they enjoyed their petty prosperities and got to build and stock their summer houses." These summer houses were an important part of Husak's post-1968 strategy of normalization. During the seventies and eighties, the residents of Prague, for example, embarked upon a vast program of constructing small summer shacks and cabins in the hills and valleys surrounding the city. Within the boundaries of their little summer plots, they were allowed virtually complete freedom—just as long as they didn't try to extend that freedom an inch beyond those boundaries. As time passed, one of the most effective threats the regime was able to wield was precisely the enforced forfeiture of such summer amenities.

Jaroslav Basta told me during our conversation, "You may have noticed how the countries having the most trouble with issues of the lustration sort are those where the transition was the most abrupt—Czechoslovakia and East Germany, for example, as opposed to Poland and Hungary. I see this as a delayed reaction to the *way* we did away with Communism. People found that if they just went into the streets en masse for a few days, jangling their key rings, the whole regime would crumble—and after a few weeks of merriment they began asking themselves, somewhat sheepishly, 'Well, why didn't we do it sooner if it was all so easy?' And they answered themselves, 'Because we were afraid.' But of what? The thought that there may have been nothing to be afraid of would be very unpleasant to accept. That's why it became better to speak of this demonic, omnipresent StB apparatus, with its treacherous agents everywhere who held us all down and now needed to be revealed and expunged—better that than admitting the truth, which was one's own lack of courage."

Zdenek Kavan, Jan's brother, who himself largely steered clear of oppositional politics during the decades of his own British exile, and instead became a lecturer in international relations at the University of Sussex, pointed out to me that the current purge storm in Czechoslovakia was hardly unique. "It saddens me, of course, but in general terms I anticipated something like this—it was bound to happen, especially in Czechoslovakia," he said. "After all, we're speaking of a small nation in the middle of Europe which has been trying to assert its independence while being regularly overrun, either occupied by or subsumed under the control of its vastly more powerful neighbors—a place where individual survival has necessarily entailed varying degrees of collaboration over long periods. Czech history over the past century constitutes a series of harrowing switchbacks: 1918, 1938, 1945, 1948, 1968, 1989—major upheavals followed by purifying purges, and never enough time between upheavals to settle into any lasting pattern of stability or to develop ordinary rules for managing disagreement. The common thread running through this entire history is an allergy against accepting degrees of ambiguity, layers of personal responsibility. It is those who never lifted a finger to oppose the old regime who are pushing for these purges, demanding the publication of all those lists. The nice thing about a list is that if you're not on it you can consider yourself pure."

Jiri Hajek, Dubcek's foreign minister and one of Charter 77's leading spokesmen, commented bitterly, "Those who considered us pointlessly quixotic and never deigned to assist us in any way—now, suddenly, they're all so fiercely courageous!"

And matters were even more perverse: it wasn't just who got to purify himself; there was also the question "At whose expense?" Though the lustration law cited various categories of lustratable offenders—officials of the Communist Party above a certain rank, members of the People's Militia, and so forth—it was principally the informers on the StB registry who most seemed to capture the public imagination and to provoke the greatest ire. And this was no accident.

Jana Frankova, a well-connected interpreter, told me, "The terrible thing is that those most likely to arouse the notice of the StB in the first place and hence to get dragged in for questioning—whether or not they subsequently succumbed to its pressures or seductions and thus ended up being placed, rightly or wrongly, on the registry list—were those who had been showing their opposition to the regime in some active way. With a few exceptions, one can see in retrospect how that was the organizing principle behind all those lists."

Someone else recalled for me the once common aspersion "Oh, he's so stupid not even the StB would care about him." And that was precisely the attraction of the StB-informants list as a principal vehicle for purification: by definition, the resolutely stupid and the deliberately disengaged were not likely to be on it. On the contrary, and not by coincidence, it was former activists—and in significant numbers—who were likely to be making appearances on that list, right alongside the authentically reprehensible.

"People now realize that it was possible to live differently, not just in silence," commented Jirina Siklova. (She has written extensively on the so-called gray zone, the class of surly managers and bureaucrats and academics who, despising the regime all the while, never did a thing to oppose it.) "The dissidents persist as a kind of living guilty conscience. That's why there's so much resentment directed against the old dissidents, Havel excepted, and why they hold very few of the major posts. People hate themselves and project that hate upon the StB or onto the dissidents. And whenever it becomes possible to imagine that the StB and the dissidents were somehow collaborating all along—well, that's enormously satisfying to people. 'See?' they can tell themselves. 'The dissident movement *was* completely infiltrated and controlled by the StB, just the way I always figured!'" (A few days later, I heard a variant of this formulation from the mouths of organizers of the Anti-Communist Alliance, an extremist wing of the purifying crusade. "The other day, there was a Charter 77 reunion," one of them told me. "Jesus, I've never seen so many StB agents in one place." He paused, and then added confidentially, "You know, we have evidence that fully one-third of the Charter 77 members were StB agents.") "'See?'" Siklova continued her encapsulation of the majority temper. "'I was *right* not to get involved in their silly games. The *smart* thing to do was to keep quiet.'"

This attitude was not merely a vague temper permeating Czech culture as a whole: it was the quite specific program of one of the country's most successful political parties—the ODS (Civic Democratic Party), headed by the charismatic finance minister, Vaclav Klaus. Klaus was perhaps Czechoslovakia's most articulate and compelling advocate of the fastest possible conversion to the most extreme free-market economy as the ideal solution for all the woes of post-Communism. As such, he and his party were leading contenders in the coming parliamentary elections. The trouble was that his résumé could not boast a single anti-Communist credential before November of 1989. A quintessential inhabitant of Siklova's gray zone, Klaus had maintained a cushy sinecure at the Economic Institute of the Academy of Sciences, where, shielded by a boss who was a member of the Communist Party, he hadn't had to sully himself personally with Party membership. Nor, on the other hand, had he ever sullied himself with anti-Party activism. People say that as late as 1989 he declined to sign a petition protesting Havel's most recent imprisonment.

The ODS's problem was that there were other free marketeers (including many of those grouped around Pavel Bratinka's ODA), and also politicians who were by no means as sanguine about the prospects for a full-bore conversion to untrammeled capitalism (including many of those grouped around Foreign Minister Jiri Dienstbier's OH, or Civic Movement) and who could claim far better oppositionist pedigrees, as veterans of either Charter 77 or the original 1968 upsurge, or of both. And so the ODS strategy was, in effect, to undercut the authority of Charter 77 through tarrings with the StB brush, while downgrading the Dubcekite achievement to the level of mere intra-Party wranglings involving Communists of varying stripes.

Frankly, I was astonished at how successfully this revisionist perspective on the events of 1968 had taken root, and how thoroughly Dubcek was held in contempt by many of the people I spoke with. It looked as though, under the provisions of the lustration law, Dubcek himself, once his term as chairman of the Federal Assembly was over, wouldn't even be allowed to return to his internal exile as a desk clerk in the Forestry Ministry—the job to which the Communists had long since remanded him. (There was a good deal of ludicrous historical revisionism on both sides of the divide. While the members of the generation of '68 were by no means the vile Communist toadies they were being portrayed as, neither was the stunning current transformation "precisely what we'd had in mind all along," even though that's what many of their number had taken to proclaiming.) At any rate, Kavan, as both a veteran '68er and a prominent Charter 77 supporter, offered a perfect foil for this crucial campaign of de-legitimation, and ODS-allied journals often tended to lead the charge against him.*

*The lustration law's defenders regularly pointed to its rigorous provisions delimiting applicability (to only those 200,000 "top" state jobs) and guaranteeing absolute confidentiality. By the winter of 1992, however, with the country in growing thrall to the coming parliamentary elections, both claims had utterly fallen by the wayside. Head cooks at local elementary schools were being lustrated ("This is not exactly in harmony with the law," the education minister

This was the backdrop against which Kavan was endeavoring to press his case. On February 25, 1992, when the Interior Ministry finally ruled on Jan Kavan's lustration application, the determination, to everyone's astonishment, came back StB negative. When Kavan, accompanied by Petr Uhl, went to the Ministry to pick up his certificate—in effect a conclusively clean bill of health—he says, a woman there told them that for the past two weeks the employees there had been talking of little else. They had twice been ordered by their superiors to recheck the registry, the master list, to make sure Kavan's name wasn't on it, she told him, but it wasn't—he was clean.

No sooner had Kavan begun exulting over such sweet vindication, however, than, just two days later, on February 27, Interior Minister Jan Langos, obviously flustered, called a news conference to announce that there had been a terrible mistake—that Kavan was StB positive after all, under Category C. The evidence, he said, wasn't contained on the list so much as in the file itself. Supposedly, they'd finally cracked the "DS" code, and it stood for *duverny styk,* which translated as "a secret collaborator/confidential contact." Langos also said that the head of the committee that had mistakenly ruled otherwise had already been fired.

In the days that followed, Langos offered several contradictory accounts

---

acknowledged, "but it answers pressure from the public"), and in any case, the lists themselves were leaking wildly, with hundreds, even thousands of names scrolling down the pages of rightist tabloids in inky fine print, utterly unvetted and without the slightest standards of accountability. People were being fired (including even the deputy editor of one of the journals that published the lists) or blacklisted, with no right of appeal (since no official action had in any case been taken).

As one such victim, a famous photographer from the generation of 1968 named Antonin Novy, told me when I asked him who he held responsible for the whole lustration fever, "Either it's the old mafia trying to unsettle and destabilize the country so as to cover their own tracks, or it's the new politicians trying to distract the country from serious economic problems and to open a space and gain some short-term advantage for themselves. Or it's a combination of the two." He paused and then added, as if as an afterthought, "And really they're the same thing."

For a more detailed discussion of this aspect of Prague's lustration fever, see my original Kavan piece in the *New Yorker,* October 19, 1992, pp. 85–87. Also see Tina Rosenberg's treatment of the entire Czech lustration drama in the first third of her book *The Haunted Land: Facing Europe's Ghosts after Communism* (Random House, 1995).

I should perhaps note here in passing how much my own feelings about the free ventilation of security lists during moments of democratic transition have changed since I first began of how such a monumental foul-up could possibly have happened. Kavan, meanwhile, became the first Czech to possess two separate, equally binding lustration certificates—one vouching him to be StB negative, the other StB positive. (It occurred to me that Kafka was no longer the operative metaphor for Kavan's situation, so much as Dreyfus, with the state beginning to turn itself inside out trying to sustain an increasingly dubious fiat.)

Kavan, for his part, immediately appealed his StB-positive reclassification to Basta's Independent Commission. It turned out that his case had now joined that narrow band of cases over which the commission was empowered to rule. Among other things, Kavan would cite new evidence to the effect that the category "secret collaborator/confidential contact" didn't even exist in the StB lexicon during the period 1969–70, having come into use, if at all, only during the eighties. He also began mobilizing a string of witnesses on his behalf, both for his civil suit and for the Independent Commission hearing, including Shawcross, who, according to the file, had been one of the main subjects of Kavan's supposed informing but was still eager to testify on his behalf. Though both processes were likely to prove long and drawn-out, Kavan nevertheless remained grimly hopeful that his reputation might yet be redeemed.

Kavan's enemies, meanwhile, had clearly been spooked by his recent near-escape, and they prepared to launch a counter-offensive. They were immea-

---

covering such situations of transitional justice over a decade ago in Latin America. Or not changed, exactly: complexified. In my book *A Miracle, a Universe: Settling Accounts with Torturers* (Pantheon 1990 and forthcoming from the University of Chicago Press), I chronicle, among other things, the adventures of a group of Brazilian victims of state torture who, in the wake of the blanket amnesty the state lavished on their onetime tormentors, in 1980, concocted an extremely dangerous, top-secret, long-term conspiracy to get even with those tormentors by sneaking into the military's own archives and, over a period of months and years, on a night-by-night basis, photocopying the entire universe of documents to be found therein. They subsequently ordered all that material—over a million pages—into seventeen volumes of charts and databases, including exhaustive lists of torturers and victims, sites and types of torture, collaborating doctors and judges, and so forth. They then synthesized all of that material into a single volume, *Brasil: Nunca Mais,* which they released to the public in 1985 and which went on to become the bestselling volume of nonfiction in the history of Brazilian publishing.

At the time, the unimpeachable reliability and authenticity of those lists seemed guaranteed by the fact that they were based, after all, on the regime's *own* files. It seemed a simple matter: the forces of common decency and transparency winning out over evil and obfuscation. After covering parallel developments in Eastern Europe, however—here in Czechoslovakia, but in East Germany and Romania and Poland as well—I'm no longer so blithe in my certainties.

surably aided in this endeavor by the serendipitous fact that just a week later, on March 5, back in London, the Broadcasting Complaints Commission did officially overturn part of its own 1985 finding in Kavan's favor in his complaint against Manyon and Thames Television—the first such action in its history. The new finding was relatively narrow in scope. Noting that even Kavan himself now admitted having been less than entirely forthright with the BCC in his submissions during the original proceeding and specifically declining to accept "his explanation that he was justified in withholding this information by reason of the need to protect others," it annulled its anti-Manyon adjudication, which had been based in part on those submissions. As for Kavan's wider claims, the commissioners declined to revisit the case, in part because so much time had passed but mainly because Kavan had "already once, from whatever motive, misled the Commission."

Manyon was delighted with the outcome, which he saw as a vindication of his original report. He assured me that the language in the BCC's finding was by no means casual but had been based on voluminous submissions, including proof that there had indeed been a "secret organization," a fund-raising and channel-overseeing entity jointly headed by, among others, Kavan and Tigrid, with members both in and outside the country, many of whose names and addresses had indeed been on the captured *Svedectvi* list or in the uncoded letters—although not *as such*, not as contacts of the organization. Still, whether or not Kavan himself knew the specific details of his own distribution channel, this was the "organization" to which Manyon maintained he had been referring all along, and its members the "contacts" in question. "One might hope that this finding would put an end to matters once and for all," Manyon told me, "but I doubt it. Dealing with Kavan is like being confronted with one of those matryoshka dolls: every time you break through a layer of falsehood, there, underneath it, is another bright, shining lie—which may be smaller than the previous lie, but it's still a lie. The question is whether anyone can ultimately be bothered to get through to the last doll and see what's there." To some extent, it seemed to me, the whole painful, messy business was beginning to turn on a question of semantics—just what either of them had meant, implied, or imagined might be inferred, over ten years ago, from such terms as "secret organization" or "contact."

At any rate, back in Prague, Benjamin Kuras was now able to lead one of two scathing pieces he published in the March 9 issue of the rightist weekly *Respekt* with the sensational (and misleading) statement that in London the

BCC had just found Kavan "guilty of perjury." (Among the problems with this claim—which quickly assumed the status of established truth in most Prague circles—was that, as merely a quasi-judicial panel, the BCC was in no position to find anybody "guilty of perjury," besides which their actual finding in the recent Kavan-Manyon case had been considerably more circumspect.)

Kavan suddenly found himself in a desperate trap, at least partly of his own making. Manyon and Thames had been able to use the possibly false accusation of Kavan's StB collaboration, back in Prague, as a part of their campaign to get the BCC case reopened in London. And now it was going to be possible for Kavan's Prague enemies to use the BCC's inaccurately reported finding against him, to devastating effect. From here on, whenever Kavan tried to contest the charges of StB collaboration against him, his enemies would crow that "even the British courts" had declared him a liar, so why should anyone bother listening to him? It was an unmitigated mess—yet it was one that even Kavan's friends, shaking their heads in amazement, described as "quintessentially Kavanian."

Nor was that all. With Kavan thus hobbled, a ferocious campaign of press vilification was launched simultaneously in London and Prague. "WAS CZECH DISSIDENT SECRET POLICE INFORMER?" asked a banner headline above an article by John Sweeney in the March 8 Sunday *Observer*. ("File shows generation of UK radicals hoodwinked," the subhead replied.) Although Sweeney's article started out more or less judiciously, citing a few steadfast testimonials, it quickly abandoned that dispassionate tone. "Balanced against this sympathy for Kavan are hundreds of pages of raw detail in the Source Kato file—number 11777/307, later renumbered as 12402/332—which the *Observer* has seen," Sweeney wrote. Sweeney went on to offer several quite damaging details, such as the fact that the file included at least one receipt, actually signed by Kavan, for "30 pounds sterling" ("a figure with Biblical resonance," Sweeney insinuated darkly).

Most damning of all, perhaps, Sweeney reported the existence of "a video recording, taken in late November 1989, just after the Velvet Revolution," which "shows Kavan with two StB officers who he appeared to be acquainted with," continuing, "Kavan had just come from a meeting of Civic Forum, the dissidents' grouping. He talked, over a bottle of champagne, of hotel bookings: one of the secret policemen says: 'Let us say that we shall reserve accommodation for you for the next time. . . . On the 18th, then?' Kavan replies, 'Sometime after.'" Sweeney acknowledged that Kavan was claiming that "this, too, was a frame-up," but went on, in his final paragraph, to cite the BCC's adjudication "last week," quashing its original adjudication on the ground that Kavan had withheld information and misled the commission.

Kuras's *Respekt* piece covered much the same ground, though in considerably greater detail. (The *Respekt* and *Observer* pieces were so similar, in fact, that most assumed them to be part of a coordinated campaign. As to whose, journalists in London noted that Sweeney had once worked for Thames Television, while several witnesses in Prague claimed that Ben Kuras and Manyon were known to have been working together.) The file on which both Kuras and Sweeney had based most of their reporting was still supposed to be secret, its confidentiality sacrosanct (its leaking had technically constituted a crime, in fact, and Kavan himself still didn't have a complete copy), but this did not prevent others from selectively mining its contents. (One observer pointed out that the StB archives seemed to be becoming "a veritable lending library" for certain well-connected, politically correct journalists.) When I asked a lustration supporter about the propriety of such leaks, he explained that the state had to defend itself against the claims of all those unjustly protesting their innocence.

Although the *Observer* did eventually print a rebuttal letter by Kavan, only two Czech papers, the English-language *Prague Post* and the ex-Communist *Rude Pravo,* made more than the briefest reference to his continuing protestations. "Why should we?" I was challenged on more than one occasion. "He's a proven perjurer." Perhaps even more disconcerting, not a single Czech paper—once again with the exception of the *Post* and *Rude Pravo*—gave any substantial attention to a dramatic move in Kavan's defense that occurred on March 18: the release of a petition, signed by twenty-five top former dissidents, angrily protesting "the current media campaign" against him and pronouncing it "incompatible with the principles of civic and journalistic ethics and law."

The campaign was proving dauntingly effective. Kavan's entire life was being splayed open and combed for intimations of treachery. The trouble was that, while much of this coverage was manifestly unfair, some of the revelations were profoundly disquieting, even to many of Kavan's most fervent supporters. A third- or fourth-generation copy of that video excerpt from the "champagne interrogation" was making the rounds—I, too, got a chance to see it—and, though the sound quality was poor, the scene itself was sickening, and, frankly, I found it difficult to square with any simple account of Kavan's innocence.

I WENT BACK to talk to Kavan, this time at his office. I wanted to explore a couple of the more damning allegations in the recent flood—for starters, the question of the receipts in his 1969–70 file.

"Does anybody seriously believe that I would have betrayed my friends, my ideals, the memory of my father, for 'thirty pounds sterling,' as Sweeney puts it?" Kavan said. "I mean, obviously there are people who do believe it, or who infer that there must have been other payments, even though there are only two such receipts in the whole file. Again, I was meeting with my Embassy's education attaché. I was head of the Union of Czech Students and had certain legitimate expenses—the rental of a meeting hall, for example—for which I applied for reimbursement. Regarding that specific receipt, it happens that Mr. Zajicek has testified about it in open court. He finally did testify in my sporadically ongoing civil case, by the way—a fact that was nowhere reflected in this recent spate of articles."

Kavan slid open a desk drawer, riffled through some papers, and extracted a transcript of Zajicek's testimony. "It happens his memory differs from mine. He says that that receipt covered expenses related to a news bulletin I was preparing on Palach's then recent suicide and funeral. That would be even better for me, but I think he's mistaken. Unlike me, he didn't have access to the file, and, after all, it has been twenty-three years. In this particular instance, I believe I was being partly reimbursed for some of the money that had been improperly confiscated from me several months earlier, when I was attempting to leave Czechoslovakia for my second term at Oxford. But the key passage in his testimony is here. 'In conclusion,' he says, 'I would like to add that I did not at any time try to recruit Mr. Kavan for any collaboration with the secret police, either verbally or in written form. I never mentioned to him during our meetings anything about my other [StB] role in the Embassy. Indeed, I couldn't have done so without risking not only disciplinary but also criminal sanction.' And there is this other passage here, incidentally, where he explains aspects of the StB's internal record-keeping system. 'Files starting with the number one,' he says, 'refer to "objects of interest," whereas files starting with the number four refer to agents. As you can see, Mr. Kavan's file started with a one. By the way, I already explained this to the people at the November 17th Commission,' he says, 'and they chose to ignore it.' So did all the recent so-called journalists, including Sweeney. Of course, my enemies will simply claim that as an StB agent Zajicek is now trying to protect his old colleague. But this *was* public testimony, under oath."

And what of the famous videotape of his own interrogation by the StB in November of 1989? I told him that I had seen it, and had found it deeply distressing.

"First off, when I arrived, I was not whisked past the regular customs control at the airport by happily expectant StB officers, as some of the reports now have it," he began. "I happen to have a witness, a British journalist who was standing in line right in front of me right up to the moment I presented my passport, apparently setting off alarm bells, and was then shunted aside. Second, the ensuing twelve hours of interrogation was videotaped in its entirety. And what I'd like to know is: Where is *that* videotape? If they have the one, they must have the other, and why don't they release *it,* too? The tenor of that interrogation, believe me, was much more tense and confrontational. At the end of it, as they decided to let me into the country after all, they instructed me not to mention our conversation to anyone—instructions I broke the following day, telling Petr Uhl about it right away as we embraced. He remembers my doing so, although, as he says, it was the least of his concerns at that euphoric moment, as was my question of how I ought to proceed if I were to be picked up again, as indeed I was. *Not,* as Mr. Sweeney has it, having 'just come from a meeting of Civic Forum.' I was dragged out of bed at 7 A.M. at my hotel—again, I have a witness, the hotel's desk clerk—escorted out to a waiting car, and driven to a villa in Prague 6. There I was questioned by three men, one of whom, just as Sweeney says, I 'appeared to be acquainted with': he'd been one of the guys at the airport. The senior official, who did most of the talking, I'd never met before.

"They had me sit at a particular spot on the sofa—so, I now realize, I'd be facing their hidden camera. Has anyone figured out why they were bothering to videotape me if I was such a trusted collaborator of theirs? Anyway, this time the tone was much friendlier, almost cordial. Things had already proceeded well along in the outside world, and this almost had the feel of a conversation among generals after battle, as the saying goes. The main guy had a thick file in front of him—presumably the one that has now disappeared—and he leafed through it, periodically asking questions about my finances, for instance, and mainly, it seemed, trying to impress me with how much they knew about me, although almost all their information could be accounted for in various after-the-fact ways. At one point, however, they did make reference to something that had happened in London which really surprised me—I couldn't figure out how they knew, whom they could have got it from.

"Anyway, halfway through, the one guy says, 'Do you want whiskey or champagne?'—like that. I could have kicked, made a fuss. I didn't. But I didn't see any reason to be confrontational, and why not accept a glass of champagne? At some point, one of them made a casual toast—'To the future,' or something. I didn't think much about it: the future *was* on all our minds. Conversation turned to my own future plans. I said I had to go back to London briefly but would be returning. They became very solicitous, offering me accommodations. I played along—in part because they still did control the border and I was worried they wouldn't let me back in, but also because I had this silly idea that I might be able to get them to reveal their London contact if I asked how they were going to get word to me in London about any eventual accommodations. I was stupid. But one of my fellow oppositionists recently commented on how he and the others were also always doing the same sort of thing—playing games with them during the interrogations. Anyway, nothing came of it."

Kavan went on, "The video of the entire session was in the safe at the November 17th Commission, but it was only that one short section—the part that casts me in the most awkward light—that got leaked. There are members of Parliament who have seen the whole thing, however—Petr Uhl, for one—and he tells me that at a certain point on the tape I get up and go to the bathroom and the two StB guys are talking to each other, evaluating my performance, and one of them says something like 'In any case, he's still lying to us.' And what I want to know is: Why didn't they leak *that* passage? It's all so preposterous."

ON ONE OF MY last days in Prague, I visited the Interior Ministry headquarters, a dour modern white edifice on the outskirts of the town's central district. Langos himself was declining all interviews in the run-up to the coming elections, but the deputy minister, Jan Ruml, indicated that he would be willing to see me. Ruml—the son of the veteran dissident Jiri Ruml, who had chaired the November 17th Commission—was himself a veteran oppositionist. In fact, he had been a key link in Kavan's secret distribution network, and, as such, had been one of the principal figures ensnared by the StB as a result of the notorious 1981 van incident. He ended up serving a year in jail on account of it. It was going to be interesting to see to what extent, if any, he retrospectively held Kavan responsible for that ordeal.

The waiting room outside Ruml's office was decorated in the standard-issue mid-Communist-era manner—thick Naugahyde-padded door, blond wood sofas with orange foam cushions. The tall young man who presently emerged from the inner office, however, his shoulders stooped, his manner soft and deferential, was anything but standard issue. Nor could I imagine the inner offices of any other high security-service official anywhere in the world done up with quite the same brio. Large, bold, vigorously colorful abstract canvases graced each of Ruml's walls. ("My old friends used to come visit me during my first days here," he explained, smiling, "and they'd see how depressed I was, how depressing this place is, and they launched a campaign to rescue my spirits.") Ruml, who was wearing a rumpled green jacket over a black T-shirt and sported a full, bearish brown beard, would, it seemed to me, have looked more at home in Greenwich Village. (His boss, Langos, with his black stringy hair cascading messily down below his shoulders, for his part looked as if he might have come tumbling straight out of Woodstock or the Haight.) On second thought, maybe this *was* the new standard in Eastern Europe—apparent hippies heading Interior Ministries. Still, one could easily be fooled by appearances, for these same hippies almost invariably turned out to be ardent fans of Reagan and Thatcher, their discourse festooned with references to Hayek and Friedman. Ruml would soon be quitting his Interior Ministry post to take up a prominent slot on the electoral slate of Klaus's ODS party.

I asked him what it had been like when he first arrived in this office. "It was terrible," he said. "This was April of 1990—up to then, for the first six months of the Velvet Revolution, the old StB had continued to have pretty much free run of the place, and you could still feel the ruling spirit. In fact, most of the old people were still here. And it was my first task to dissolve the StB as an organization. During the past two and a half years, we've released eight thousand of the old employees."

This meant that he had been one of the people who uncovered, collected, and secured the surviving StB registries and files. That, too, he said, had been an excruciating experience—repeatedly coming upon the names of trusted old friends in the various registries. "It was always the same," Ruml recalled. "I would confront them privately, and invariably they'd deny it. I'd dig deeper into the files, pulling up their personal records, and there you'd find all the evidence—the signed documents, the receipts, and so forth—and I'd confront them again, and they'd break down crying, admitting it, offering up their various excuses. It was all very painful. I even found out the name of the man who was responsible for betraying our operation back in 1981 and sending me to prison."

Kavan?

"Oh, no, no, there's no evidence that Kavan was working for them at that time. No. The fellow who betrayed us was one of our most trusted collaborators here inside the country, a Charter signatory who'd spent four years in prison—that's probably where they got to him somehow. In fact, it turns out he was working for the Soviets, for the KGB—some of the key documents in his file were signed in Russian—and he'd been assigned specifically to infiltrate and upend our distribution channel. He was in Parliament at the time we made the discovery, and when we confronted him he resigned and quietly slipped into private life. It was all very painful, as I say, but also a relief, because up to then we still hadn't been able to figure out what had happened, how our security had been breached."

What about Kavan?

"Kavan was a person who for a long period, especially before 1981, helped us very much in keeping up contact with the world outside—both the world of exile and the world of our potential international sympathizers. At the same time, he was a very contradictory person."

Although Ruml had disapproved of Kavan's secret trips to Czechoslovakia in the later eighties, he didn't seem to feel that either they or the StB video of his November 1989 interrogation constituted serious evidence of Kavan's latter-day collusion with the StB. He didn't understand or approve of Kavan's politics—but that was not the issue. He had worked successfully with others whose politics he disdained. No, as far as this top security official was concerned—a man who, after all, had had open access to all the files and data involved—the case against Kavan largely boiled down to the question of his behavior during 1969 and 1970. "And, having carefully reviewed the files, I've made a determination that Kavan must have known that he was dealing with an StB agent in 1969–70, during those contacts with the Embassy's education officer," Ruml concluded. "I don't think he would have continued much longer, no matter what—as you know, the education officer was himself recalled to Prague by late summer of 1970—and maybe he just imagined himself to be playing some kind of game, thinking he could outsmart or manipulate them, or something. I've seen hundreds of cases like that. In fact, that's maybe the most frequent motive."

And ought that to be cause enough for lustration?

"He was labeled a person who knew he was collaborating with the StB," Ruml declared, stiffening noticeably. "I myself would not have been terribly concerned about this, especially in Kavan's case. According to the file, he did not offer them any substantive information, or anything that could have harmed others. But the November 17th Commission came to the conclusion that he collaborated knowingly, and if he says he did not, then he's lying, and *that's* why he shouldn't be in Parliament." Ruml seemed very pleased with that formulation.

But, I persisted, if all he was doing was playing games. . . .

"I believe that those who knowingly collaborated, even if they did nothing harmful, even if they were just playing games, should be lustrated. It's difficult for you in the States to understand this—you didn't live for forty years under Communist rule. This regime destroyed all of us; we have all been to a greater or lesser extent tainted—even those of us in the opposition. We are attempting some kind of moral cleanup here, to clean the society of those who morally compromised themselves. And one of the criteria we're using is that people not have knowingly collaborated with the StB—it's as simple as that. Kavan did, and if he says he didn't then he's lying, and, furthermore, by taking his case internationally, the way he's doing, he's undermining the reputation of the country, and that's another reason he deserves to be lustrated."

"THAT'S NONSENSE," Zuzana Blüh declared, with utter finality, as I began to relate one of several theories I had heard about Kavan's possible motives in collaborating with Zajicek, the London Embassy's StB operative, back in 1969. Blüh was serving as Petr Uhl's deputy at the Czechoslovak News Agency, and we were meeting in her office. A stylish woman with a helmet of thick black hair, black squarish glasses, a black-and-white plaid jacket over a black dress, and a broad, easy smile, she went on to say that the reason Kavan had had anything at all to do with Zajicek was quite simple: he had been ordered to. As the only SVS student-union officer resident in Britain, he had been empowered by the SVS executive board in Prague to represent Czechoslovak students stranded after the invasion. And the reason she knew this for certain was that she was the one who had delivered the mandate.

"It was 1969, and the situation was getting more critical," she recalled.

"The SVS had moved into open opposition against the regime, and the regime was moving to have us banished—things were very tense. At the same time, we *were* a student union, and we were supposed to be representing students in their everyday interests. And so—I remember it vividly, spring of 1969, because it was my first trip West—I arrived with power of attorney for our man, Jan Kavan, and instructions for him to found a branch of our union there. Identical things were happening in other places. I was present at the meeting of Czech students where he was elected chairman. And I remember telling him afterward to go to the Embassy—that it would now be one of his responsibilities to serve as liaison for all these students with the education officer there. Luckily, I didn't have time to go there myself that day, or I'm sure I'd have got listed as a collaborator as well. But he came back, he told me about this sympathetic diplomat he had met there who seemed to share many of our views. And so, over the months ahead, he opened up to him a bit. Big deal."

Had she read the Kavan file?

"Aha!" she exclaimed. "This I want *on the record.*" Up to then we'd been weaving in and out, onto and off the record. "*This* I want on the record," she repeated. "Three hundred members of Parliament have had access to that file, a copy is circulating in Britain, other copies are circulating among journalists here, totally illegally. And I was told by somebody who saw the file—and, incidentally, was breaking the official-secrets act even telling me this much—that it looks as follows. It has an index at the front, and my name figures third in the number of references. You see, it's not simply his file, as such; there are subfiles folded into it on various contacts of his, such as me. There's a whole subfile on me—whom I met, what I ate, whom I allegedly slept with. There are reports by all sorts of agents, and analyses by other agents. And a minimum of three hundred people—most of whom I don't know, and many of whom I don't trust in the least—are pawing over this material, titillating themselves. And me, I don't even get to read it at all, the law denies me any access—that is, until suddenly I'm reading all about myself, totally out of context, without explanation, in the pages of *Respekt.*"

Shaking her head, she said, "It's amazing. Amazing. Disgusting. And, on top of everything else, they got it all wrong. Every single detail about my alleged love life they got wrong. If the rest of the file is anywhere near as reliable as what they had to say about my love life—well, then . . . "

Her voice trailed off. "And this is what gets treated as holy writ in this country," she resumed. "Agents speculating and cross-analyzing the prurient speculations of other agents. This is what gets treated as unshakable, unquestionable truth—this, this garbage. This is what we're doing to ourselves in this country with this crazy lustration process."

ON MY LAST evening in Prague, I was talking with Helena Klimova, a psychotherapist (and incidentally the wife of the novelist Ivan Klima), in her consulting office, and I asked her about Kavan, whom she, too, had known in his days as a student radical.

"I don't think he's anywhere near as bad as he often gets portrayed here nowadays," she began. "I think he was really very efficient—he did a tremendous amount. At the same time, though, he regularly made tremendous mistakes. In part, this is understandable, in that he was doing a very difficult and dangerous job, with no prior experience or training. People forget that: he had no one to teach him how to do all those things; most of the people he was collaborating with, his friends, were back here, so he was largely on his own. But, at the same time, there was this other aspect of the matter, in that he is not too stable psychologically—in part owing to the legacy of his father's terrible persecution. I think that in a sense he felt compelled to continue in the steps of this father he had idealized enormously. He did his best, but no one could have lived up to such an ideal—still, he'd take bigger and bigger risks trying to do so. So he became capable of both heroic things and terrible mistakes—a very risky personality."

She went on, "Even back in our student days, he seemed consumed by this inner turmoil, and he's the kind of person who tends to project his personal chaos onto the society around him, the society at large. And maybe the reason his case is causing so many difficulties in Czechoslovakia these days is that Czech society is currently manifestly irrational itself."

I asked Klimova what she thought of the lustration process generally in this context.

"Its initial motivation was a healthy one, it seems to me, this need for a sense of justice," she replied. "Only, we missed the opportunity for real justice, and lustration now serves as a kind of facsimile. At the very outset, you see, there was this consensus: we wanted justice, but we didn't want to be like them. What we really wanted to hear from the Communists was an expression of sorrow or contrition, some kind of confession, after which we'd have been prepared to forgive. We wanted to forgive, I think. But the forgiveness came too soon. There was anxiety at the very top, among people like Havel and Czech Premier Pithart and Foreign Minister Dienstbier. They stopped various attempts at wholesale purges: *we weren't going to be like them*. And then the Communists stopped confessing before they even started. Instead, they became all puffed up with their success—their economic success, for example. They were shameless, and people got angry, and that's when the cry for punishment began to be heard."

The room was darkening. I could hardly see her anymore in the gloom.

"What happened then is comparable to obsessive neurotic behavior in individuals," she went on. "Such patterns usually start when a person has an aim that for some reason can't be reached, and instead you get a series of ersatz fulfillments of that aim, as in bulimia, for instance. In our case, we binge on these lists the tabloids have started publishing, ever larger lists—only, they are hollow, because what can you say about these supposed master lists of informers? Isn't the whole point that the masters of the list aren't on the master list? It's all phony. The impulse is authentic, it needs to be addressed. But the execution in this instance is empty, the justice is ersatz."

The room had gone completely dark. Outside, meager street lamps were flickering feebly to life.

"And in the middle of all this you have Kavan," Klimova concluded. "Kavan, with his propensity for complication and self-destructiveness. It's as if Kavan and the society were feeding on each other." She sighed, collecting her thoughts. "Still, maybe Kavan shouldn't be in politics. I know, it's a terrible thing to say—almost tragic, in a way—because politics has been the basis of his whole life. But maybe he should not try to be in public life."

IT WAS a moot point. Kavan wasn't going to be in politics much longer in any case. No party invited him onto its list in the coming election. None could afford to: it was generally assumed that Kavan's inclusion on any party's slate would doom that party's entire list. He sat out the campaign grimly.

Lists continued leaking, ever more "complete" versions—until finally over a hundred and fifty thousand names were in circulation. Kavan's was emblematic of a plethora of national dramas—by no means an isolated case. In Slovakia, the lustration strategy was proving decidedly ineffectual. During the later stages of the campaign, it seemed, the more his opponents asserted Vladimir Meciar's alleged former ties to the StB, the more popular he became among a Slovak population tired of being bullied by its Czech counterpart, and eventually his forces there triumphed overwhelmingly. On the other hand, back in the Czech lands the lustration strategy proved astonishingly effective. Virtually none of the former dissidents made it back into the new

Parliament. The moderate social-democratic OH faction, led by Dienstbier and Pithart (and sentimentally favored, it was thought, by the officially neutral Havel), failed even to clear the 5-percent-minimum threshold required for any sort of inclusion in the Parliament. But that threshold also eluded Pavel Bratinka's right-wing ODA faction: here it wasn't so much that he had been tarred with the StB brush as that his distinguished career in the oppositionist underground no longer counted for anything; it had been bled of its authority, in part through the very lustration campaign with which he'd colluded. If people were going to vote for full-throttle capitalism, they would rather have the charismatic Klaus's ODS version, his indifferent prior career notwithstanding. Furthermore, in the end the growing support for Klaus and Meciar in their respective polities seemed to have a reciprocal effect: the stronger Meciar seemed to grow in Slovakia, the more Klaus was able to cast himself as that particular bogeyman's only truly credible opponent, and vice versa. By the time of the election, June 5 and 6, Klaus and Meciar, with their diametrically opposed visions of the country's future, emerged as the two big winners. And after that the country itself began to fracture. Unable to avert disunion, Havel resigned as president; and Klaus and Meciar now entered into edgy negotiations aiming at a January 1993 divorce of their two polities. (Havel subsequently reemerged as president of the newly truncated Czech Republic.) Meciar largely suspended the lustration program in Slovakia. Klaus's ODS, meanwhile, quickly moved to consolidate its hegemony over the Czech side of the divide: Petr Uhl was fired as director general of the Czechoslovak News Agency; Jan Ruml was appointed interior minister; the publisher Miroslav Macek, one of the leading purveyors of the free-floating lists, was named federal deputy prime minister and quickly became embroiled in a front-page scandal amid allegations that he was exploiting his government position for personal financial gain.

Kavan, for his part, continued his personal crusade, trying to clear his name. I received regular updates—insanely detailed faxes analyzing each new turn in his elusive quest for vindication, which is to say that he was now lavishing upon his own case the same care and thoroughness that he used to expend on all the others. And of course, it suddenly occurred to me, that was probably at least part of the whole idea all along: his enemies had effectively neutralized him. The civil-court case seemed to have become permanently bogged down in judicial evasions regarding standing, venue, precedent, and the like. So, increasingly, Kavan was pinning his hopes on Basta's Independent Commission. But even there—and despite the fact that regulations provided for conclusive judgment one way or the other within sixty days—closure was being endlessly deferred. Basta personally subpoenaed key records from the Interior Ministry, but the records never materialized.

Finally, on September 15, 1992, Kavan himself was invited to present a defense before the commission—his first such opportunity in any quasi-judicial setting. He prepared tirelessly for the occasion, arriving, as ordered, at 8:30 A.M. But the commissioners themselves failed to show up—or enough of them, anyway. For this hearing, on what was easily the most controversial such case in the entire country, Basta found himself falling one short of the required quorum. Finally, just before eleven, a tardy commissioner wandered in. Kavan immediately launched into his defense, but before he could complete it another of the commission's members announced that he had to leave, and the whole proceeding had to be adjourned.

Basta himself clearly seemed to have come to a determination that Kavan was innocent (for one thing, he noted, Kavan's was proving to be the *only* file in the entire archive with the mysterious "DS" designation, so that it couldn't even be considered an authentic category, whatever it was). With increasing exasperation, Basta tried to explain to several of the commission's younger members the subtleties of oppositional life in 1969 and 1970—but they were having none of it. For them, it was cut and dried: by even having allowed himself to be in the same room as the Communist education attaché, Kavan had proved his guilt, as far as they were concerned. The question seemed hopelessly politicized, and the commissioners, at least in this instance, seemed anything but independent.

Kavan was describing all this to me over the phone one day, and he seemed forlorn. At one point, I asked him why he even bothered anymore. Why keep bashing his head against that wall?

I heard him sigh—a sigh, it seemed, from way back. "My passion to clear my name is at this point very much for my children's sake," he finally said. "For my newborn baby daughter, Monika, and also for Caroline, my seventeen-year-old daughter back in England, and for my eleven-year-old son, Michael, here in Prague. Their opinion matters enormously to me. And, while I do not think they could ever believe that I ever served as an informer, some of their friends might, and they could be made to feel uncomfortable. You see, that's something I know all about. I'm not so much battling for their hearts or their minds as for their peace of mind."

Incredibly, Kavan's case dragged on for months, and even years.

Following the fiasco of the September 15 session of Basta's so-called Independent Commission, a new hearing was slated for October 16 at which Kavan was assured he'd at last be allowed to complete his opening statement and present his evidence, including a string of witnesses. He and his allies arrived promptly that afternoon, only to be informed that their presence would no longer be required after all: the commission had already reached its verdict, which was that Kavan had indeed been guilty of being a "conscious collaborator" with the StB. (Basta, who'd dissented from the ruling, subsequently told Kavan that "other factors besides an unbiased evaluation of the available facts had played a role," but he did not elaborate.)

Kavan was told curtly that he could appeal the commission's ruling to the Prague Municipal Court, which is to say back to Kafkaland—the very miasma from which he'd been trying to escape when he appealed to the Independent Commission in the first place. There, for example, one of the Interior Ministry's first gambits when faced with Kavan's renewed suit was to declare it entirely bereft of legal substance on the grounds that the country of Czechoslovakia having in the meantime broken in two, the Interior Ministry of the Czech half could no longer be held accountable for cases growing out of its earlier incarnation. It took the better part of a year for Kavan and his lawyers to slash their way through that particular thicket. (It should be remembered that throughout these travails, his thirty pounds sterling notwithstanding, Kavan was facing desperate financial pressures that further undercut his ability to sustain an effective legal challenge.)

Admittedly, Kavan was not the only person facing such tribulations. (To cite but one further example: Since the early seventies, from their exile in Toronto, the Czech novelist Josef Skvorecky and his wife, Zdena, had been running 68 Publishers, perhaps the foremost publisher of authentic Czech literature anywhere in the world. Their authors included Milan Kundera, Vaclav Havel, Ivan Klima, Jaroslav Seifert, and countless others. One day early in the summer of 1992, they were shocked to discover that Zdena's name, too, had surfaced on one of those toxic free-floating lists of StB informers—an utterly preposterous stigma, yet one that, as in Kavan's case, was proving almost impossible to remove through any sort of appeal. Skvorecky himself began taking to quoting Joseph Conrad, that other great Eastern European exile, on the subject of revolutions: "The scrupulous and the just, the noble, humane, and devoted natures; the unselfish and the intelligent may begin a movement—but it passes away from them. . . . Afterward comes the turn of all the pretentious intellectual failures of the time.") Still, Kavan was probably the most notorious of the breed, and undoubtedly the most tenacious.

Finally, in September 1994, his dogged persistence began paying off: after a thorough review of the files, the Prague District Court concluded that there was no evidence whatsoever that Kavan had ever consciously collaborated with, passed information on to, or fulfilled tasks assigned him by the StB. Kavan, however, wasn't given much time to savor that victory either. Almost immediately, utterly unbowed, the Interior Ministry appealed the ruling, hinting darkly at the existence of further even more damning "evidence." So for yet another year Kavan had to endure a campaign of media leaks and libels, perhaps the most disfiguring yet. In November 1995, having thus far failed to deliver any new evidence whatsoever, the Interior Ministry applied for—and was granted—a continuance. But apparently even the courts of Kafka's Prague have their eventual limits, for finally, on January 16, 1996, an exasperated Appeals Court ruled decisively against the Interior Ministry, reaffirming the District Court's vindication of Kavan's name and specifically forbidding the ministry from filing any further appeals.

Probably no one was more relieved about this outcome than Kavan's doctors, who'd been urging him for years to return to Britain for vitally needed heart surgery. Now, at last, perhaps he'd allow himself to do so.

Except that, of course, he wouldn't. Instead he threw himself back into politics in an attempt to reclaim his parliamentary seat in the upcoming elections, scheduled for later in the year. Conditions proved somewhat more favorable this time around. Klaus's ODS coalition had been wracked by financial scandals (the free-market transition had proved a bit more problematic than promised), and there'd been other sorts of scandals as well: for instance, Klaus's new head of state security services, Stanislav Devaty (Kavan's onetime dissident client and subsequent nemesis as chair of the parliament's November 17th Commission), was forced to resign following allegations that his agents had taken to spying on the agriculture minister.

At any rate, to the astonishment of his many enemies, Kavan did triumph at the polls and was able to return once again to the Senate.

And meanwhile his wife gave birth to a second child, another daughter—one hopes the first Kavan in three generations who will be allowed to grow up under not the slightest cloud.

For an additional postscript to the Jan Kavan saga, as of 1999, see page 195.

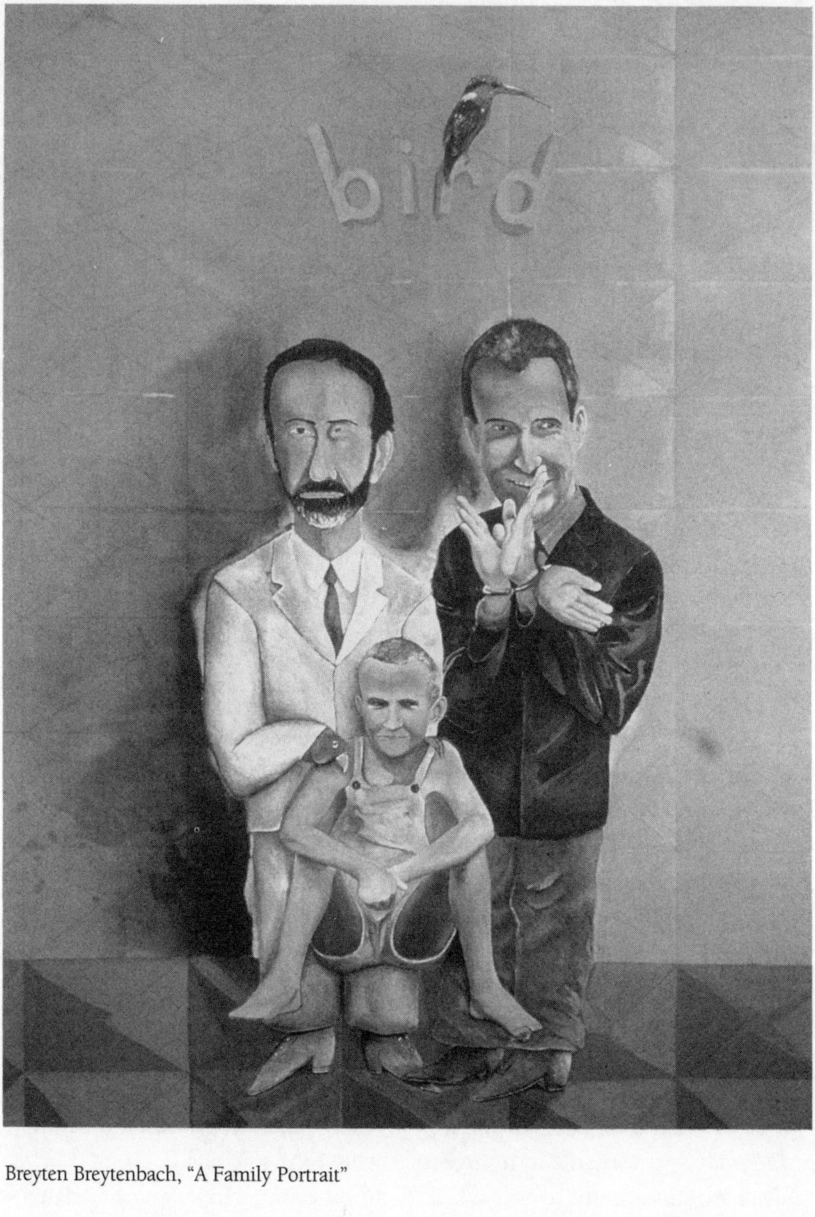

Breyten Breytenbach, "A Family Portrait"

A Horrible Face, But One's Own

Breyten Breytenbach in and out of South Africa

1993

I once asked Breyten Breytenbach, the exiled South African poet and painter, why, in his opinion, after the fiasco of his clandestine return to his homeland in 1975 (traveling incognito as a would-be revolutionary organizer), the calamity of his arrest (his cover having likely been blown before he even entered the country, such that not only was he arrested but virtually everyone he'd contacted was arrested as well), the debacle of his trial (his appalling, groveling breakdown, his operatic recantations and expressions of contrition, all to no avail), after his being sentenced to nine years' hard time in the country's notorious penal system, why, I asked him, had the authorities who allowed him to go on writing in prison nevertheless forbidden him to paint?

At the time, we were sitting in Breytenbach's airy, light-drenched studio, in Paris. (He had been released in 1982, a year and a half short of the completion of his nine-year term, and had immediately returned to his Paris exile.) We had been looking through a life's worth of canvases, dazzlingly colorful paintings with surreal images by turns lyrical and profoundly unsettling. He paused for a moment to think about the question, then said, "They weren't stupid. I think they must have realized that for me an empty canvas would have been an open field of freedom—and they weren't going to allow me that."

They wouldn't let him paint, and for years they barely allowed him even to see any colors. This quintessential colorist had fallen into a nightmare universe of monochrome grays and browns and goose-shit greens. ("*Caca d'oie,*"

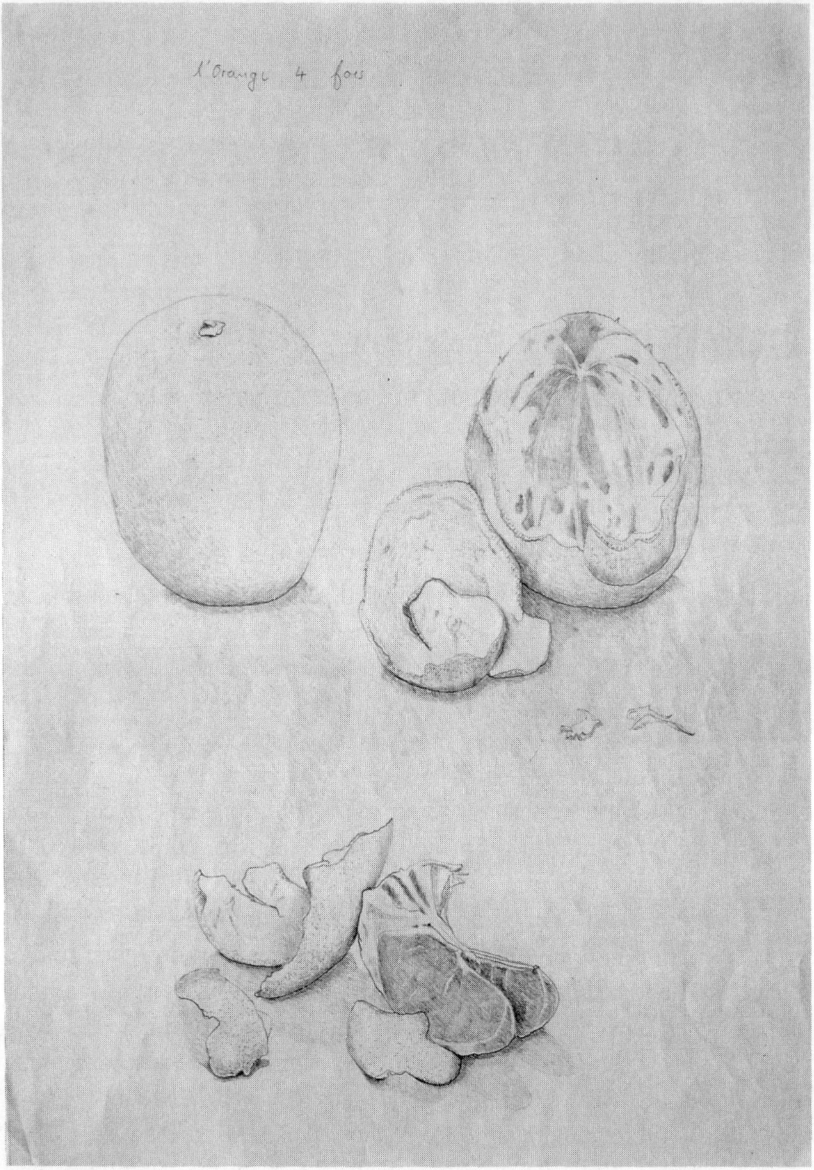

Breyten Breytenbach, "The Orange, Four Times"

he had commented earlier. "That's the term the French have for the predominant color of prison life.") The pressure within him to paint—or to create images, at least—had become almost overwhelming, and finally he had managed to create and smuggle out to his wife, in Paris, a few dozen drawings. She had preserved them, and some of them were among the pictures we'd been looking at. Several seemed to derive from the tumultuous cauldron of his interior life—images of decapitation, copulation, mutilation, and confinement—but others, almost as if in compensation, seemed to be exercises in minute observation: a scuffed shoe, a folded blanket, a draped jacket, a burned note and the extinguished match. Somehow, these modest images were more affecting than the imagined ones, and perhaps the most haunting of all was a drawing entitled "The Orange, Four Times," which portrayed, first, an orange whole (its very *orangeness,* shining through the pencil gray, in some ways seeming to be the drawing's incantatory subtext), then the orange partly peeled, then the orange three-quarters eaten (that is, with just a few last sections to be seen), and then—well, nothing (empty air, the orange consumed).

That drawing reminded me of a painting we had been looking at earlier—one of a series that Breytenbach completed during the first years after his release. Against a lush orange-colored background Breytenbach had created what he was calling "A Family Portrait," which was in fact a group self-portrait, three images of himself at different ages all grouped together under the sign of the Bird (birds being frequent self-tropes in his poetry: birds of passage, birds of prey, lovebirds, birds unhindered in their movement, migrating birds, caged birds, jailbirds): as a poor young farm boy, a mischievous glint in his eye; as a clean-shaven, manacled prisoner in a blue jacket, putting on a brave face for the photographers at his first trial; and as he saw himself at the moment of painting—squinting through crossed eyes, prematurely aged (at least in his own mind), his black beard frosted with gray. Breyten, I found myself thinking, *Breyten, Four Times.*

I

I'd first met Breyten Breytenbach in January 1986 in New York City at the International PEN Club's annual congress, which was taking place that year at the St. Moritz Hotel. This was barely three years after his release and a year since I myself had first encountered his writing, through the publication of his extraordinary memoir of prison and calamity, *The True Confessions of an*

Albino Terrorist (the middle volume, as it would turn out, of a trilogy launched in 1974 with *A Season in Paradise* and concluded in 1993 with *Return to Paradise*).

Over the years I've occasionally reminisced about those days at the PEN congress with others who were present, and time and again, Breytenbach's name has come up, unbidden, as one of the event's most forceful presences: his mordant and self-deflating opening statement on the conference's main theme, "The Writer and the State"; a memorably sharp exchange between him and the already rightwardly zagging Mario Vargas Llosa; his especially evocative participation in a panel on the challenge of translation. (Breytenbach, naturally, has acquired a considerable fluency in the paradoxes of translation: nowadays, he composes his poetry in Afrikaans, his prose—essays, tales, and novels—increasingly in English; his painterly base is in Holland, and his Dutch is virtually indistinguishable from a native speaker's, as is his French, as well as his Spanish—he spends increasing amounts of time in the snug little farmhouse he and his wife have managed to procure in the countryside north of Barcelona.)

I made a date with Breyten for immediately after the PEN congress was over, hoping to pursue some of the themes he'd raised, but by the time we got together, he was almost all talked out. "Too much, too much," he pleaded, "I'm getting bilious at my own thoughts." So instead we set off for a walk through the park (it was a brisk, clear midwinter's morning) over to the Metropolitan Museum. There we meandered aimlessly and mostly silently through the halls, until we drifted into the room with the Vermeers, where Breytenbach came to a sudden halt before the one of the woman in the blue dress, her hand poised upon a silver pitcher. Maybe she's pregnant, but it's hard to tell. On the wall behind her hangs an unfurled map. Light pours in from the window, the very essence of lucid grace and tranquillity. Breytenbach gazed silently at the image for a long time, finally letting out a deep sigh. "Look at the date," he said (1660). "It's hard to believe that from all that serenity . . . emerges the *Boer*. Look," he continued, a finger stabbing at the map in the background—a map, one suddenly realized, of the coast of Holland, tiny boats bobbing off the shore—*"that's them leaving right now!"*

OVER THE YEARS (for we subsequently entered into a sort of far-flung friendship, meeting now and again, here and there, in Paris, in New York, in Spain, in Dakar, and finally in South Africa, where I joined him for a brief tour of his old haunts) that moment in front of the Vermeer often returned to me, in part because it proved so anomalous. Breytenbach tends to downplay the European roots of contemporary Afrikaner culture, emphasizing instead its African or, at any rate, mongrel origins. Once I asked him when his people had first set foot in Africa. "Oh, millions of years ago," he replied, smiling, "just like yours." After a bit more prodding, he conceded that the first appearance of the name "Breytenbach" in the Cape's historical record occurs in 1656, just four years after the Dutch East India Company founded its small colony on the sheltered slopes of Table Mountain, in the form of one "Coenrad Breytenbach," who was immortalized as a minor military figure sent out to retrieve some wayward cattle. To the extent it's been possible to trace that branch of the family line farther back, it appears if anything to have been German or Alsatian, perhaps Belgian, rather than Dutch in origin.

Breytenbach's mother's family, the Cloetes, were for their part originally French or Flemish. They arrived very early on in the history of the Cape Colony, probably in flight from religious persecution, and their name was associated with the colony's first vineyard. The "Cloete" name quickly became a very common one in the Cape, denoting both rich landowners and the mostly East Asian slaves they imported (and to whom they assigned their own name); and it's by no means obvious from which side of the divide Breyten's mother's Cloetes derive. Nor, for that matter, was the divide itself all that clear-cut in the olden days. Subsequent Afrikaner fantasies of racial purity notwithstanding ("Mongrels often have a big hang-up about identity," Breyten notes, "and precious little tolerance for ambiguity"), there was a good deal of racial intermixing in the early Cape ("It's a shame they didn't just keep on interbreeding like that," Breyten muses, "it would have saved us all a lot of trouble down the line"). The very term "Afrikaner" originally connoted not "white" or "European" but rather the product of such mixed liaisons.

As for the Afrikaner language, Breytenbach likewise insists on its creole essence. Its richness, at any rate, can hardly be subsumed, as some Afrikaners contend, under the simple rubric of "a daughter-language of Dutch." It's precisely "kitchen-Dutch," the language that arose in the space between the original colonists and their imported slaves, and its riches—the very splendors in which Breyten's poetry so continuously revels—are largely slave riches.

Not that his own family spent much time thinking about such things as he was growing up. Despite what one sometimes reads about Breytenbach (for example on the jacket notes accompanying some of the American editions of his own books), his family was not particularly "distinguished" in lineage and certainly not in worldly station. If anything—Breyten was born in 1939 into a South Africa still mired in the worldwide depression—one might more plausibly describe his family's status as a bare rung or two above a South African version of "poor white trash." Breyten was the third son, born seven years after the first, Jan, and six after the second, Cloete. (He was a twin, but the other twin died at birth. A fourth brother and a sister eventually rounded out the family.) Jan and Cloete can still recall their father's labors as an itinerant worker, scraping together a subsistence living on a crew digging an irrigation canal while they and their mother pitched a tent each night in nearby fields.

During Breyten's own early years, his father did manage to acquire a succession of small farms in the Boland region, east of Cape Town, but he must have been having a hard go of it (Breyten recalls that his father was drinking a good deal in those days), and presently he had to give up farming and move back closer to Cape Town—to the small town of Wellington. There the family ran a combination general store and boardinghouse called Grevilleas, just on the wrong side of the tracks (most of the customers at the general store were "colored"), prophetically situated between a library and a police station.

Breyten never laments the circumstances of his upbringing. ("For one thing, we were all—everybody in that region—poor in those days," he says.) On the contrary, he seems to cherish every moment of it, and those memories feed the wellspring of his creativity in painting, poetry, and prose. The paintings one just needs to see for oneself; the poetry, in the sheer density of its embeddedness, is almost untranslatable (I once asked Breyten what gets lost in the translation, and he replied, "Oh, nothing much; just the poem"). But a fine sense of how those memories get filtered through the medium of Breytenbach's sensibility can be gauged, for example, in some of the early rhapsodic pages from *A Season in Paradise,* which in turn read like a Southern-hemispheric version of the prologue to James Agee's *A Death in the Family,* as reconceived, perhaps, by García Márquez. Thus, for example, he recalls his family's old blue Mercury, with its rumble seat, and how, one evening, returning from a band concert, "I tumbled out of my little seat just like a ball of dung released by a horse in full gallop, and broke my neck in two places." The account goes on, "In the dark, no one had noticed my fall, and when they found me three days later, I was already dead and decaying and with the baby Jesus. My mother was very sad." In case the reader thinks that he may have misread this passage, the very next page describes a resurrected Breyten playing in a neighboring professor's yard, falling into a fishpond, and being nibbled into oblivion by a swarm of ravenous goldfish; and a few pages after that, young Breyten gets sliced and diced by a passing plow ("So that my head was just left lying there loose to one side. Thus my bloodsoaked little body was decapitated, lifeless"). Of course, one of the things that make these darkly whimsical pirouettes so affecting is the way they seem retrospectively prophetic of—almost rehearsals for—the real-life disaster and ensuing entombment the author was so relentlessly approaching.

But there are other passages in this book as well, passages of unalloyed lyricism, as for example, his recollection of a pear tree in the backyard at Grevilleas:

And under that pear tree I first discovered love. She was seventeen and an operator at the local exchange. In the evenings, around dusk, she would lift me onto her lap and hold me tightly, and I smelled the pear tree. There were other smells: the small fires beginning to crackle everywhere to cook supper, the lawns and flowers newly watered, the oil under Pa's Mercury, Dawid's working clothes, and my sweetheart's milkplump breasts. And sounds: the chirr-chirr of grasshoppers between lawn and hibiscus tree, dogs in the neighborhood barking at the smoke, the prayer meeting bell and the sexton's boots on the gravel path when he has emptied the bell of its peals, my mother puttering in the kitchen, the sucking and groaning as my father removes his Wellingtons, and my sweetheart's heart beneath my ears thud-thud-thud-thud, just like the gurgling when my father secretly opens the sluiceways out of turn, or just like the plop-sounds of the frog.

And the sky is the color of mother-of-pearl like the palm of one's hand when one has spent a long time in the sea. That pear tree will never stop flowering again.

Perhaps I'm reading too much into that last passage, but I suspect Breytenbach has embedded a pun—it would be just like him—in that Wellington, where he spent his adolescence, is just a few kilometers away from Paarl, a town that is cherished in Afrikaner iconography as the birthplace of "the Taal," the Afrikaans language itself; and some people argue that Breytenbach's special feeling for Afrikaans arises, in part, from the fact of his having been brought up in the language's very cradle. Breytenbach himself cites other inspirations for his literary vocation—specifically, his mother. Although the Breytenbach family was run, in typical Afrikaner fashion, as a patriarchy, it was the mother who seems to have left the greater impression on the children—or, at least, on Breyten. She was, he has told me, "intensely uncomplicated." While his father was dour and somber, occasionally almost despondent, she immersed their modest digs in color and systematically refused to get depressed: difficulties simply had to be solvable—often through cooking (in later years, as family get-togethers became increasingly contentious, it was she who would invariably impose order: "Enough! Let's eat!"), or else through music. But mainly she liked to talk. (Breyten's brother Cloete once told me, "That woman, let's face it, the lady suffered from verbal diarrhea. I tell you, her whole family, they'd get together and yak and yak, play their music, and yak some more, all bloody day.") When Breyten cites his mother as an influence, he is probably referring to the specific quality of that jabber: its wildly leaping, continually unexpected free-associative character, and its tendency to fill a space—qualities that also apply to Breytenbach's poetics.

Even if the Breytenbach clan wasn't exactly "distinguished" in terms of its circumstances, it proved immensely accomplished, certainly in terms of Breyten's own generation, among whose members Breyten was by no means the only standout. Cloete, the second son, became a widely published photojournalist, who specialized in scenes of war carnage and devastation, ranging from Vietnam through the Yom Kippur War, but most often across the African continent. Over and over, people I met in South Africa assured me that Cloete's reach was so wide and so seemingly effortless that he *had* to be some kind of government security agent—a charge he explicitly denies—or at least a close collaborator with the propaganda services, another charge he denies, as he denies any paid relationship of any sort with the apartheid regime. (He claims not to have supported apartheid, but then, as he says, he doesn't think the Swiss should bar Italians either: "Prejudice should be personal," he says, "not institutional.") Such avowals notwithstanding, he certainly projects an aura: his second wife was the niece of General H. J. van den Bergh, the head of the state security service, and at least two former parliamentarians (and countless others) described Cloete to me as "a shadowy figure" or "a spooky guy" ("You just kept very quiet when he was around," said one, "you watched your tongue, because you just sensed everything you said was being reported back"). His production often dovetailed nicely with the regime's current line, as, for example, in the case of a striking book of photographs entitled *Savimbi's Angola* (1980), celebrating the apartheid regime's stalking horse in that particular civil war. He was and in a sense remains a true believer in the apartheid regime's 1970s doctrine of the "total onslaught" (the existence of a worldwide Communist conspiracy aimed at bringing the South African government down through both internal subterfuge and revolutionary upheaval in all the neighboring countries), which in turn justified a totalizing response. He readily acknowledges his close ties to sources inside the South African military, though he insists that these were like any other journalist's—he was just good at what he did.

Still, what ties! For the oldest Breytenbach brother, Jan, just happens to have been the most decorated soldier in the history of the contemporary South African Defense Force. Wounded in battle seven times, he fought all over Africa—in Biafra and Rhodesia and Mozambique, and especially in Angola and Namibia—and not only fought but created entire fighting units. He founded the SADF's first reconnaissance, or special-forces, unit; he also created the SADF's most highly celebrated and deeply feared parachute brigade, the Forty-fourth; and, in between—and most famous of all, perhaps—during the mid-seventies he fashioned almost single-handedly the fearsome 32 Battalion, also known as the Buffalo Battalion, forging it, for the most part, out of the suddenly disenfranchised black irregulars, former collaborators, or partisans from defeated factions, all left over following Portugal's colonial collapse in Angola. In *They Live by the Sword,* one of Jan's two books chronicling the history of that battalion, he is quite frank about the rationale for creating such a force: "It was politically far more expedient for a foreign black Angolan to be killed in a battle defending South Africa than it was for a white national serviceman to die." And yet he goes on to maintain that the blacks in 32 Battalion were not considered mere cannon fodder, at least by him, and it is true that the unit was renowned for the tendency of its white leaders to fight alongside their black troops at the forefront of any battle, in the process sustaining far higher casualty rates among white officers than other such units in the SADF.

Jan Breytenbach figured prominently in many of the most famous battles in South Africa's cross-border campaigns—great victories, to hear the South Africans tell it, or "appalling massacres," to hear the verdict of many of the regime's opponents (and of such independent watchdogs as the World Council of Churches, the United Nations Office of High Commissioner for Refugees, and the World Health Organization)—and yet he himself was no enthusiastic Afrikaner nationalist. Early in his career, he enlisted in the air wing of Britain's Royal Navy (a decidedly un-Boerish thing to do), was present at Suez and served during "the Malay Emergency," returning to South Africa only in 1961 (with a British wife), after the Republic of South Africa decided to sever its ties with the British Commonwealth. As his South African military career advanced, he declined repeated invitations to join the Broederbond, the secret society of Afrikaner business and governing elite, refusals that many military observers speculate must account for his otherwise inexplicable failure ever to have been promoted above the rank of colonel. He often claimed to despise the apartheid system, and maintained that race consciousness had no place in his own units. But he hated Communism even more than apartheid, and, buttressed by such ironclad certainty, he may have done as much as any other one person to assure the prolongation of apartheid.

And yet Breyten, for his part, doesn't buy the anti-Communist rationale —or, anyway, doesn't see it as his brother's fundamental motivation. "The anti-Communist stuff came later, and really just served as a kind of overlay," he says. Rather, Breyten looks upon Jan's development as more of a generational matter—a romantic dreamer of a child in thrall to news accounts of the Second World War. (Montgomery was Jan's first hero, and tanks were his first passion.) "He lost himself in fantasies of the military life—the manliness of it, its physical and spiritual demands, its glorification of an élite that was at the same time an élite of rogues, the lonely ones, those highly trained, wild-eyed, long-haired killers. There's a deep Christian side to his makeup, but alongside it as well there's a nihilistic, almost death-seeking or anyway death-fascinated aspect. A love of being wild and being in the wild. I think that if he had come to maturity just a bit later he might have become a game warden; a big set piece in his legend has to do with his having personally tamed three lions and a leopard."

NOT THAT THE emergence of a political firebrand like Breyten Breytenbach from such an environment makes much more sense. Actually, Breyten's eventual opposition to apartheid and his general propensity for radical political engagement might well be understood—as in the case of his brother—as an overlay on previous tendencies. In Breyten's case, at least as he now understands himself, the artistic impulse preceded the political.

Like most Afrikaner youths, Breyten regularly attended church—of the Dutch Reformed hellfire-and-damnation variety (his father served as an elder)—and though he always enjoyed the stories (the imagery still permeates his work), and easily grasped the social value in attending (church was the heart of the community's social life, "the only way to court a girl"), he gradually fell away. "God just didn't talk to me," he says. What did speak to him, and overwhelmingly, was art—poetry, painting, and music. "And in that kind of macho environment those were simply interests you weren't supposed to have if you were a boy, if you wanted to become a man," he once said to me. "I began to feel increasingly marginalized. And from feeling oneself marginalized it's only a small step to beginning to question the values of your society. I mean, nobody at that age is going to accept himself as a marginal case. There must be something wrong with the society when it puts you on the sidelines like that."

Marginal though Breyten may have been, he excelled as a student, graduating as valedictorian from Wellington's Hugenoot High School. He would be the first in his family line to attend university, and yet, shockingly, he declined a full fellowship to the "Afrikaner Oxford," the University of Stellenbosch, opting instead to attend the Michaelis School of Art, at the English-speaking University of Cape Town. He enrolled there in 1958, and found himself one of the very few Afrikaners in his class.

Invigorating as art school proved to be, Breyten was even more entranced by Cape Town itself. "How alive the Mother City used to be before fascist political engineers and other black-shoed Broederbond planners destroyed it," he recalls of those days, the late fifties, in *Return to Paradise,* going on to cite the exuberantly cosmopolitan and pluralistic makeup of this "Alexandria in the Southern Atlantic": the Muslim Malay community; the Central European refugees; "black laborers and trade unionists and intellectuals; effete Britishers looking for sun and a tax-haven; brown families from St. Helena; dispossessed barons and shady war criminals; painters with little goatees and doe eyes and funny accents walking like ducks; Portuguese greengrocers and Indian tailors and Chinese launderers; long-legged, barefoot beauties from up-country farms; *dagga*-smokers and antique dealers and Trotskyists and mad versifiers and nudist nature lovers and magicians and textile workers and jazz musicians and degenerates and creators and ascetics." And on and on. And Breyten drank it all in, unquenched. Evenings he spent in jazz clubs, listening to the likes of Dollar Brand (Abdullah Ibrahim), or else tracking down such luminaries of an earlier generation of Afrikaans poets as Uys Kriege and Jan Rabie. He steeped himself in Kafka and Kierkegaard, in Frazer and Graves, but especially in the new Beat literature (Kerouac and Ginsberg, for example, were just emerging) and in works on Eastern mysticism.

If 1958 in Wellington was perhaps not all that distinguishable from 1928 there, 1958 in Cape Town (just sixty kilometers away) was not all that different from 1958 in New York City: the offshore breeze was wafting in the first intimations of the turbulent decade to come. Breyten studied art, painted canvases, painted the walls of his room black and spread his mattress on the floor, got stoned and got laid. "Like a head of cabbage, I grew rapidly," Breyten subsequently recalled of that year. "But, like a head of cabbage in shallow earth, I, too, was probably more air than leaf."

Airily though it may have been, Breyten now began to get politicized. In a sense, living in the countryside of the Boland, Breyten had been shielded from the harshest realities of the developing apartheid order: for one thing, there were virtually no blacks in that area (there were, of course, "coloreds," descendants of the region's original Khoikhoi inhabitants or else of the imported East Asian slaves, but few of the sorts of black Africans who'd borne so much of the brunt of the exploitation further north). In addition, racist feelings among Boland Afrikaners were somewhat less pronounced than among their Transvaal counterparts: these, after all, were the Afrikaners who'd elected to stay behind during the trekker days, the ones who hadn't been so bothered by the creeping English hegemony. But now, in Cape Town, Breyten was simultaneously encountering a sizable black population and a central government hellbent on its subjugation (for 1958–59 was also the year the National Party regime, now firmly ensconced after a decade in power, began to apply the screws of its apartheid policies to the country's universities, expelling all blacks from majority-white institutions (they'd previously constituted 12 percent of the student body at the University of Cape Town). Breyten joined campus protests against the expulsions, spent late nights parsing the situations with his housemates, began receiving visits from the police.

The politics of his homeland were drawing him in, but they weren't the only draw. The more worldly his exposures became, the more he longed for exposure to the rest of the world. After a year and a half, Breyten dropped out of school and, without seeking his parents' approval (he knew they would never give it) or saying so much as a goodbye, he booked a fourth-class passage on a Portuguese cattle boat. Rucksack on his back and twenty pounds in his pocket, he headed north for Europe, and specifically for what he called "the honey pot" of Paris.

BREYTEN ARRIVED in Paris in the winter of 1961. It was a difficult arrival. "My efforts at making money, as events in later life were to bear out, could not be described as being particularly successful," he told the court at his trial, in 1975, "and it goes without saying that I immediately started yearning for the fleshpots of South Africa." After a year of bumming around, spending nights in fleabag hotels or under bridges, rushing to London to catch up on events back home (the Sharpeville massacre), teaching English in Norway and playing street artist in Cannes, he'd probably have returned home as he'd originally intended, except that he met Yolande.

Ngo Thi Hoâng Liên Yolande Bubi was the beautiful nineteen-year-old daughter of a Vietnamese widow who had brought her entire family to Paris soon after the Second World War so that they could benefit from a classic French education. Yolande was four at the time—and, like Breyten, the middle child in a swarm of siblings—and the family was among the first Vietnamese to live in the capital. When she and Breyten met, in 1962, she was still living at home. On the streets of Paris and in the classrooms of the Sorbonne, her life was entirely French and cosmopolitan, while at home it was entirely Vietnamese and traditional. Yolande and Breyten have different versions of their meeting and courtship—differing principally on who fell first and hardest for whom—but within three months, despite her mother's initial misgivings, they were wed. "I suppose it was unusual to marry that young," Yolande recalls. "Breyten for his part was only twenty-two—yes, it *was* unusual. When he first proposed, I said, 'But why? It's only a piece of paper.' Still, he persisted and I finally agreed. I suppose it just shows that Breyten wasn't quite such a bohemian as all that."

Breyten's youngest sibling, Rachel, was still living at home, back in Wellington, when the family received word of the marriage in a letter. "Father was initially quite upset," she recalls. "He kept grumbling about how this was no good, it would dilute the white race, and so forth, and Mother just cut him short: 'I absolutely will not stand for that kind of talk. He has found the woman he intends to share his life with, and you have no *right* to second-guess him.'" From the very start, Breyten's mother would include little notes in English to Yolande at the bottom of her letters to Breyten ("It was only much later," Yolande avers, "that I came to appreciate how truly radical that was"). As the years passed, both Breyten's parents grew to treasure Yolande (and, for that matter, Yolande's mother grew to love Breyten).

The couple moved into a tiny two-room flat on the Left Bank. Breyten converted one room into a painting studio, and Yolande headed off each morning to an office job to support his art. (Of his many commitments, Yolande has always most championed the painting.) Had Bosch or Breughel bored a wormhole through to the twentieth century and then, turning hard left ("Look, that's them leaving *right now!*"), tunneled deep south to Africa, or at least, to the Mediterranean, they too might have started producing the sorts of images Breyten was now creating: perverse, fetoid northern imagery in lavish Matissean colors. By turns dreamlike or fevered, whimsical or crass, involuted or blatant (strange doings in cramped spaces), his work began to garner a certain reputation in Paris, but even more of one in Amsterdam, where the Dutch sensed a distant kinship with the Afrikaner and saw an affinity between his work and the then-reigning COBRA surreal-expressionist sensibility.

Meanwhile, he was writing as well—"Constantly," Yolande recalls, "across every stray scrap of paper"—poetry and brief, surreal prose narratives, in Afrikaans. One day, he showed a few samples to a visiting Afrikaner poet, and the poet insisted on taking them back to South Africa. Within a year after that—in 1964, at age twenty-five—Breyten was making a dazzling double début with a book of poetry and another of short prose pieces.

From the beginning, his voice was both startlingly assured and oddly self-alienated. The first poem in his first book begins with an almost Brechtian displacement. It is dedicated "For B. Breytenbach," and, in the translation of Denis Hirson, it launches out (in Breyten's italics):

> *Ladies and Gentlemen, allow me to introduce you to Breyten Breytenbach,*
> *the lean man in the green sweater; he is devout*
> *and braces and hammers his oblong head*
> *to fabricate a poem for you*   *for example . . .*

And then, out of italics:

> I am scared to close my eyes
> I don't want to live in the dark *and* see what goes on

Continuing on like that for several stanzas. And then, just as suddenly, it's all over:

> *Look he is harmless, have mercy on him*

In other translations, the key word in that last line is rendered as "blameless." Either way, Breyten's debatable harmlessness or blamelessness would become the leitmotiv and animating engine of the rest of his life, but at that early stage the Afrikaner reading public was more than merciful; it was ecstatic, and within months the young poet received word that he had been awarded the Afrikaner Press Corporation Prize, the first of five major Afrikaner literary prizes he would receive in the coming decade. With the prize money on its way, he immediately began making arrangements to travel to South Africa with Yolande to receive the award in person, but, to his horror—and, he says, to his complete surprise—he was told that Yolande would not be granted a visa: the apartheid state simply refused to recognize the validity of their manifestly illegal interracial marriage, in effect condemning Breyten to a life of exile. Breyten got truly angry. In an open letter to a Cape Town newspaper he declared, "If I could give up my Afrikanerhood today, I would. I am ashamed of my people. I am shamed by the humiliation of my wife, my family and friends, and her family. . . . I hate and abhor apartheid with all its implications, and if it is representative of Afrikanerdom, if the two cannot be separated, then I see no future for the Afrikaner in our beautiful country."

The breach was complete. (Yolande, curiously, never took the prohibition to heart; she never felt "humiliated," always feeling, as she says, that it was their problem, not hers.) With the passing months, Breyten's rage became more and more pronounced, and he poured it into his poetry: "I have rooted out the gods of my youth / it was like poison." And: "To the best of my powers, I oppose my people: cave dwellers." And the craziness of it all was that the more he excoriated his countrymen, the more they—or, at any rate, the reading élite, whose comfortable liberalism he savaged no less thoroughly—adored him for it: never before had the language been made to sing like this. Afrikaner self-identity was deeply tied up in an almost idolatrous glorification, an exaltation of the Afrikaans language itself—as distinct from both English and the surrounding African tongues—and poets generally had thus long held a uniquely prized station in both the society and its ideology. And here was Breyten, ever more obviously the greatest poet of his generation, taking the Afrikaans language places it had never been, breaking it down, breaking it open, opening it out. Ryk Hattingh, a young writer of the next generation, characterized Breytenbach for me as an Afrikaner Dante: "Dante did exactly the same thing, a political exile undermining the home regime by hijacking its vernacular, its very language." And the younger generation was the most captivated, the most subverted—not only by the power of Breyten's poetry but by the image of the poet himself, this thrilling Beat rebel living free, snarling and singing, in Paris.

There were layers upon layers of oddity here. One after another, his publishers dropped him, furiously protesting that this time he had gone too far, but no sooner was he dropped than he garnered another prize. For vituperation was by no means Breytenbach's only chord. There was also a pervasive homesickness, a deep, deep love of home and homeland coursing right alongside all the bitterness, and a heartrending sense of exile and remove:

ma
I've been thinking
if I ever come home
it will be without warning towards daybreak . . . there's still a
    blueness on the world
sht—softly I open the backyard gate.

And so forth. The Afrikaners loved this stuff, its uncanny specificity; it was almost worth keeping him in exile just to keep getting more of it. (His descriptions of the physical beauty of the Boland at times verge on the hallucinatory.) And then there was the love poetry: supple, sensuous erotic verse whose like the language had never seen; poetry stripped of any sense of political subtext except for the outrage of its very existence—the never-ending scandal that the finest love poetry in the Afrikaans language was being written in celebration of a "colored" woman, who, furthermore, couldn't even read it. (So who was he writing it *for?*)

On top of everything else, there was the psychodrama of it all, the eerie sense of a writer almost sleepwalking toward his own doom, fully conscious, utterly unaware. In the poem "breyten prays for himself" he pleads,

Keep Pain far from Me o Lord
That others may bear it
Be taken into custody, Shattered
    Stoned
    Hanged
    Lashed
    Used
    Tortured
    Crucified
    Interrogated
    Placed under house arrest
    Made to slave their guts out
Banished to obscure islands till the end of their days
Wasting in damp pits down to slimy green imploring bones
Worms in their stomachs heads full of nails

But not *Me*
Never give us Pain or complain.

This in 1964, in his very first book, and already it's as if he can see it coming. Simultaneously, in the book of prose pieces he includes a dreamlike scene of himself on the beach with his parents, only his father has been struck mysteriously dumb and his mother is gravely ill: she tries to tell him something, but he cannot hear, and as he bends closer she dies. He is overwhelmed, because he knows that "my mother has died of heartbreak on account of me." This foreshadows almost exactly what is going to happen some fifteen years down the line. Such moments of dark premonition—visions of hypnotic intensity—occur again and again, and they render the poetry all the more compelling. The entire oeuvre becomes like a car wreck, a head-on collision, rendered in excruciating slow motion.

BREYTENBACH wrote continuously, and yet he increasingly came to doubt the efficacy of writing—or, at any rate, of writing only. Though he remained in exile, he was still a leading member of the so-called Sestigers, or Sixties, movement in new Afrikaans writing, but he came to feel alienated from what he saw as the merely cultural posturings of its members, their willingness to remain confined within the laager of Afrikanerdom (even if, through their writing, they saw themselves as incrementally expanding its boundaries from within) when he felt that what was needed was a razing of the laager itself. By the mid-sixties, Breyten was anxiously trawling for some as yet undefined but decidedly more engaged alternative.

In Paris, he began seeking out the company of more activist-oriented South African exiles. Paris itself, meanwhile, was about to erupt in a political drama of its own—in May of 1968, surging students and workers and artists almost succeeded in toppling the sclerotic administration of Charles de Gaulle. Militance was rampant—some nonviolent and some less so. "Direct action"—which is to say, activism several degrees beyond Gandhi's—was a particularly bracing slogan.

Breytenbach observed and participated and drew his lessons. Like many young radicals of that era, he grew contemptuous of the depleted institutions of the old left—especially the French Communist Party, which played a particularly regressive and disreputable role during May of 1968. A few months later, as Soviet-led tanks crushed the Prague Spring, the French Party was one of the world's first Communist parties to extend its heartiest congratulations to the Old Guard in the Kremlin. The South African Communist Party, or SACP, was *the* first—and therein lay a huge dilemma for Breyten and many of the other young, ardent South African exiles and would-be activists. For the SACP had a lock on the executive organs of the African National Congress in exile during those years: it controlled the ANC's finances and security and communications; and even non-SACP leaders, such as the ANC's chairman, Oliver Tambo, were effectively surrounded by SACP cadres. Breyten objected to the SACP's style, which he considered Stalinist —that is, both doctrinaire and rigidly hierarchical—and he also objected to its long-term gradualist and racially oblivious strategy.

Breyten was by no means alone in these misgivings. In fact, the ANC in exile was itself rent by internal battles along the same lines. The London ANC was under the domination of the SACP, and worked closely with the French Communist Party to impose its control over the French anti-apartheid movement; the Algerian outpost of the ANC, by contrast, was in the hands of so-called Africanists, members of a movement that (like Breyten) was less in thrall to Moscow and favored a more militant and race-conscious approach. And they, too, were grappling for control in Paris.

Johnny Makathini, a lifelong activist, militant, exile, and insomniac conspirator (a character pitched, as it were, at the crossroads of Fanon and Dostoyevski), was the chief representative of the Algerian ANC, and he now began courting Breyten in a serious way. In 1969, he recruited him to work with a clandestine leftist organization called Solidarité, an outgrowth of the wartime French Resistance that had become a sort of servicing agency and clearing house for anti-imperialist liberation movements the Third World over. Its leader, a mysterious Egyptian Jew named Henri Couriel who'd somehow earned the particular enmity of the Israeli Mossad (he was always extra cautious lest they nail him; years later, they apparently did), now took a special, almost paternal interest in Breyten, seeing to his training in the techniques of conspiracy, smuggling, and subterfuge. Makathini, meanwhile, helped to put together a small secret organization of non-Communist white South African exiles—called Atlas originally, and later Okhela—with the approval, he assured its members, of top elements in the ANC, though Okhela's people were never to mention the organization's existence to any ordinary activists. (At one point, however, Tambo himself came to address them secretly.)

Curiously, during this same period (which was also, for him, a period of considerable painterly and literary productivity), Breyten was immersing himself in a discipline of an altogether different sort: he had joined a Zen center to which he repaired early each morning for a few hours of silent meditation. "I know, I know," he once acknowledged to me, smiling. "To be a Zen Communist seems a contradiction, or at any rate peculiar—I believe I was the only clandestine activist in my dojo, I know I was the only Zen student in Okhela. But it's not such a contradiction as all that. The concreteness, shying away from abstractions, not manipulating facts or other people, forswearing personal ambition, attentiveness, *awareness*—all these are functional political precepts as well."

The Zen influence—the evenness, the tolerance for incompatibles, the way of seeing—was making itself increasingly felt in Breyten's painting, but the poetry was becoming more and more overtly political, most notably in a new volume of poems published in Holland in 1972 under the title *Skryt*—another quintessentially Breytenbachian construction, which, as the critic Peter Dreyer has noted, melds the Afrikaans words for scream (*skreeu*), cry (*kryt*), shit (*skyt*), and write (*skryf*), among others. But this time, he'd really gone too far for the Boer censors, and the book soon became the first piece of Afrikaans literature ever to come under South African government proscription. The ban was hardly surprising, since the volume included the instantaneously notorious poem "Letter from Abroad to Butcher," dedicated to "Balthazar," which is to say to Prime Minister Balthazar John Vorster. In one stanza, the poem adopted the agonized viewpoint of a political prisoner, but in the next the poet addressed the prime minister directly:

and you, butcher,
you who are entrusted with the security of the state
what do you think of when the night reveals her
framework
and the first babbling shriek is squeezed out
of the prisoner
as in a birth
with the fluids of parturition? . . .
does your heart also stiffen in your throat
when you touch the extinguished limbs
with the same hands that will fondle your wife's
mysteries?

The poem was said to have enraged Vorster—and antipathy for the insolent poet thereafter became a private obsession of the prime minister.

LATER THAT YEAR, bafflingly, Yolande received an approval on her regularly proffered and regularly denied visa application. (Had strings been pulled somewhere? By Cloete? By Jan?) She and Breyten were granted permission for a ninety-day visit, on condition that they agree to keep it strictly private, quiet, and nonpolitical.

A strictly private, quiet, and nonpolitical visit was not in the cards, however. From the moment of their arrival, the last week in December of 1972, their every move was dogged by journalists ("whornalusts," as Breyten called them) and bannered in the news media. The public attention was by no means all negative. On the contrary, as the novelist André Brink subsequently recalled, the great poet "was swept through the country in a wave of near-hysterical adulation, even in the most conservative circles." If the Afrikaners were momentarily ravished by the human—the positively *charming*—face of their fire-breathing, previously demonized exiled prophet (for no matter how bitter or angry his writings and pronouncements, Breyten has almost always come across in person as gentle, wry, self-mocking, eminently delightful and delightable), he was no less overwhelmed, all over again, by the natural warmth and vitality of many of the Afrikaners he was seeing. By that, and by the sheer physical splendor of the place—its light and its vistas. And by the grace, at long last, of being able to linger for hours and days at a time, in the presence of his parents, in the coziness of their Wellington home, and to show Yolande off and show her around. (Yolande was spending hours exchanging recipes and gardening lore with his mother.) All the things, in short, that he had been dreaming about longingly for more than a decade in the cold, gray north. Though the title of the memoir he would write about that trip, *A Season in Paradise,* was obviously ironical, it wasn't entirely so, for he was continuously experiencing South Africa, with the fiercest intensity, as *both* heaven and hell.

It happened that the University of Cape Town summer school had already scheduled a weeklong conference—a sort of ten-year retrospective—on the Sestigers movement for the last week in January, and now that Breytenbach, one of the movement's preeminent masters, was actually in the country he was, of course, invited to take part. Breyten delivered a scalding address. "Mine will be a funeral oration," he began, elaborating, a few moments later: "Together all of us have industriously and blindly as ants, dragged this country to the last abyss before hell." It quickly became clear that he no longer put much stock in literature as a transformative agent. Yes, he acknowledged, "Afrikaans writers occupy a privileged if unenviable position in the tribe, even if only by virtue of the fuss made about them, because so many of that tribe's aspirations pass for cultural aspirations." Still, "I contend that our literature, no matter how clever sometimes, is largely a product of our stagnation and our alienation, and that it cannot be anything else, given the framework within which it originates."

Bewailing the way that racism had become like a poison flowing "deeply in our veins, even in our language, our beautiful language, our wonderful vehicle," to the point where "ours [has become] a fecal language," he concluded that only "by taking cognizance of the nature of the struggle we are involved in and share, by making that struggle clearer—and even more: *by taking a stand based on that knowledge*—[can] we expand our humanity and our language. Then only will we be freed from the trap of Apartaans, will we speak Afrikaans: one of the many languages of Africa!"

The audience's response to Breyten's talk was rapturous—so rapturous that it was by no means clear whether the majority had grasped the implications of what he was saying (which is not to say that *he* had, either). In private, his friends and fellow writers pressed him for specific alternatives and, in turn, tried to press their own misgivings upon him, but he seemed eerily immune to and removed from their entreaties.

Breyten saw hardly anything of Jan on that trip, but he saw a good deal of Cloete, and they spent a lot of time arguing. ("Enough!" his mother repeatedly felt called upon to break in, "Let's eat.") Cloete even accompanied Breyten and Yolande on many of their car excursions (from Cape Town to Johannesburg through the parched Karoo, for example). But Breyten managed to ditch Cloete on occasion to undertake a variety of secret missions for his underground cabal—getting in touch with a new Okhela recruit, for example, and scaring her half to death (or so she later testified at his trial) with requests that she obtain information on how airports and harbors operated, so as to facilitate the possible future importation of arms. (He denies the latter charge.)

One day, late in their trip, while Breyten and Yolande were back in his parents' Wellington home, someone—"let's just say 'an acquaintance'" is how Breyten framed the matter, coyly, in *A Season in Paradise* (in fact, it was Cloete)—called to inform him that two men from Pretoria were insisting on meeting him and taking him out for a private meal in a secluded spot, not even in Johannesburg or Cape Town: they'd come down to see him right there in neighboring Paarl. And he was not to refuse. A few evenings later, without telling either Yolande or his parents, so as not to alarm them, he drove over for the rendezvous. The two Pretorians proved to be top officials from the Bureau of State Security, or BOSS, the apartheid regime's central intelligence agency. (The senior of the two, Jan Vermaak, was one of the bureau's very top people.) The dinner, in the private back room of a hotel restaurant, went on in a spirit of positively creepy politesse, but in the end the gist of his companions' discourse boiled down to this: they knew everything about him, he was on the wrong track, they were all-powerful and could hurt him terribly, but they were still willing to extend their largesse, so how about it—why not cooperate? For the time being, matters were left at that. They had a few drinks at the bar downstairs. ("We are all friends. The cats and the mouse are the best pals on earth," Breyten wrote in *A Season in Paradise*.) He was not to mention this little conversation to anyone, and they would be expecting to hear from him before his departure. After which, he was "allowed to drive home, through the fields of my youth."

Now the ninety days were quickly running down. Yolande and Breyten embarked on a last excursion through the Carlsberg mountains; while there, they received word that Breyten's father had suffered a serious heart attack—he'd survived and was resting in a hospital in Paarl. Breyten immediately blamed himself: "I began to realize how trying it must have been (for both of them) all those years, with what petty-mindedness some neighbors in the village and elsewhere act toward them, for the sole reason that he is my father."

Of course, they wanted to stay on in South Africa, but despite his father's illness they were granted no extension. On March 30, 1973, therefore, they rushed through Jan Smuts Airport, past the ticket counters and customs and passport control. Suddenly, a heavy hand seized Breyten's elbow and an icy voice demanded to know what, exactly, he thought he was doing. Of course, it was Vermaak, with his pal beside him, and this time they were accompanied by another man, identified solely as "Colleague" in Breyten's account of the incident in *Season*, though in fact this was Breyten's oldest brother, Jan. Why, they wanted to know, hadn't he got back in touch? Luckily, Yolande, oblivious of what was happening behind her, was already boarding the plane up ahead. What were they going to do—create a scene right then and there? The grip loosened. Vermaak, smiling, extended his hand for a shake, and, like an idiot, Breyten took it. A blond photographer stepped out from behind a pillar and captured the moment. One can easily imagine the purposes to which such a photo could be put, but Breyten didn't stop to think about them: he was already on his way down the ramp, into the plane, and out of the country.

BREYTEN AND YOLANDE returned to Paris. The contradictions of his various involvements were becoming increasingly untenable. He was spending more and more time in Amsterdam, where other Okhela members—notably including Barend Schuitema, then the secretary of the Dutch Anti-Apartheid Movement—were drafting an Okhela manifesto. Their marriage was suffering: Yolande, who had always been an advocate of Breyten's painting, had never warmed to his political adventurism, and he was having to keep most of it a secret from her. Besides, he was having affairs—this was partly a matter of the times, partly a matter of his bohemian self-image, partly a matter of the clandestine life itself—including a fling with Schuitema's girlfriend, another prominent Dutch anti-apartheid campaigner. His Okhela colleagues were putting him under ever greater pressure to commit to ever more dangerous assignments, and he was feeling increasingly jammed.

Against this backdrop, Breyten was composing *A Season in Paradise,* this text in which it seemed, at times, that he was trying to kiss off the literary option altogether. In passage after passage of exquisitely beautiful writing he questions the utility of writing itself, and the morality of the beautifying impulse. He keeps trying to egg himself into further activism, but at the same time the memoirs are drenched in foreboding: he reports one dream of himself on a train platform, waiting anxiously for a train, the crowd around him staring at him with barely disguised contempt, when he realizes to his horror that he is standing there "*naked* as the dead," the train is pulling out, and "the policemen with the hairy knees [are] approaching unhurriedly"; and another of himself in prison, alongside a group of other prisoners for whose incarceration he feels personally responsible, all of them at the mercy of the Authorities, who "are going to break us like one does with crabs to get to the soft flesh They have the power To break one To a small heap of vomit To make you want to puke out your own brokenness Your desire to go on living." He approaches a final leap and then pulls away, approaches the leap again, hesitates, and then pours contempt upon himself for the entire charade.

Soon after Breyten finished the manuscript of *A Season in Paradise* (though he had not yet seen it through to publication), his Okhela colleagues cornered him into making an insane commitment. This was at the beginning of 1975. They needed to send someone to South Africa to recruit two activists, one white and one black, who would agree to come north to Brussels and man a coordinating office—and then to help spirit them out of the country. (The recruiter would take two blank forged passports down with him.) In addition, he would take along a draft of the Okhela manifesto (complete with its call for developing "all possibilities for defensive and offensive direct action") for comment by potential recruits inside the country. It was going to be an extremely delicate assignment, and, for some reason, the collective chose Breyten.

He was racked by misgivings. (Those last few weeks, he was working on a painting of himself being crucified.) He wrote Yolande a letter in which he acknowledged that things had been going badly but promised that soon he would shed his other commitments and return to her and to his work. He continued to hesitate, but in the end, perhaps out of loyalty to Makathini and Curiel, perhaps out of an exhausted surrender to the fate he had already so clearly envisioned, he agreed to go. ("You have to be careful what you create," he told me years later. "You run the risk of prefiguring your own future—you can confess things into happening. In the future, I'm going to try to write exclusively about taking walks on the beach.") He shaved his beard and adopted a new identity and a new passport (under the name Christian Galaska, an Italian academic on holiday) and headed for Rome. There he applied for a visa and boarded a plane for the flight down.

Sixteen years earlier he'd left South Africa without so much as a word to his parents. Now he'd be heading back, with hardly so much as a word to his wife.

II

It was a botched job from the start, from before the start. Breytenbach subsequently inferred that South African consulates throughout the world, and particularly the one in Rome, had been placed under special instructions to facilitate the visa application of any Christian Galaska who might happen to present himself.

So what had happened? Who had betrayed him? I recently accompanied Breyten on a trip to South Africa, and one evening, over dinner at a restaurant in the Cape Town harbor district, I asked him about his own suspicions.

"I never really found out," he replied, sighing. He went on to list people who would have known of his coming movements—Makathini, Curiel, Schuitema, Schuitema's girlfriend—any of whom might conceivably have been working for BOSS, or, more likely, for the London ANC, which would have had a motive itself to betray this upstart organization of independent anti-apartheid activists to BOSS In the meantime, Makathini, Curiel, and Schuitema had all ended up either dead or unhinged. "I was out of my depth, of course," Breyten said. "But so were we all. And, at least, in the end, I survived." He paused, gazing out over the harbor toward the spangling city, the inky silhouette of Table Mountain slumbering just beyond. "As for the rest, I don't know—and, what's more, I don't want to know. People come up to me every few months with some new piece of information, and I tell them I don't want it. To become wound up in that labyrinth would simply be to let myself be manipulated by it all over again, forever. It's just as well that all those bottomless transferences and fantasies got burned out of me once and for all."

He took a sip of Boland wine. "And who knows? Maybe there weren't *any* finks as such—maybe nobody intentionally betrayed anyone. Maybe they—BOSS and the others—were just damn good at what they do, and had us under good, solid surveillance the entire time. Or maybe we just got sloppy and inadvertently screwed things up. Makathini was screwing up all the time."

But then so was Breyten himself. Ampie Coetzee, who was his publisher for a long time and is still one of his closest friends, throws up his hands in exasperation whenever he approaches the subject. "He was such a bloody fool, such an inept conspirator," Coetzee told me in Cape Town. "He may well have simply tripped himself up—for instance, by being too careless over the phone—or even actively betrayed himself. His whole life, he has practiced a kind of body art—*'allow me to introduce you to the lean man in the green sweater.'* He could easily have written the authorities himself to tell them he was coming. I'm only being half facetious."

André Brink has speculated along similar lines, writing how, "In the mood of a cloak and dagger tale one might say that [Breyten] deliberately made as many stupid mistakes as possible in order to get himself arrested and saved from a political involvement he could no longer handle; saved, above all, from himself."

In *The True Confessions of an Albino Terrorist,* his 1983 memoir of those years, Breytenbach himself candidly acknowledges, "My going there, my being there, was contrary to all principles of underground organization."

This was true in at least two senses. First, by sending in Breytenbach his handlers were sending in a man who was manifestly on the verge of a nervous breakdown before he even entered the country. Second, he was an incredibly famous man on the verge of a nervous breakdown. And, on top of that, he was a poet and a painter, an artist; he had no business trying to be a spy and, as Coetzee says, very little aptitude for it. As Christopher Hope subsequently wrote, in a piece in the *London Magazine*, "He crept about the country in a manner most likely to attract attention. . . . To say he left a trail does not do him justice: he positively blazed one."

As soon as Breyten arrived in the country, for example, he began an affair with one of the stewardesses on the flight down, even though it was known that stewardesses on South African Airways were often BOSS informants; indeed, Breyten believes this one did end up informing on him. A few months later, in any case, she married his newly divorced brother Cloete.

Coetzee was at his university office in Johannesburg one afternoon when he got a mysterious phone call from a woman telling him simply that "Panus wants to meet you at the Rotunda Terminal building" at such-and-such a time. (Panus is a famously recurrent character in Breytenbach's fictions.) Showing up at the grungy terminal at the appointed hour, Coetzee immediately recognized the clean-shaven figure in the dark glasses. "Breyten," he said, "what are *you* doing here?" Breyten was taken aback: "You recognized me?" he stammered. Coetzee laughs merrily as he tells the story. "Breyten swore me to secrecy and then told me of Okhela and showed me this blood-curdling manifesto—I mean, the organization was a good idea, it addressed a real vacuum, but the language of the manifesto seemed way too radical, to me anyway, at that moment. He asked me to help him get in touch with Jerry Marais, who was a leading white student union activist in those days down in the Cape and a possible candidate for this position they were trying to fill—which I did. And then, just before he left for Cape Town, he dropped by my house and gave me a plastic bag full of books, which he asked me to store for him during his travels; I put it in my cupboard and frankly didn't give it a second thought. And then he was off."

Breyten made similar contacts with dozens of individuals during his next few weeks in South Africa. One day, a week or so after arriving in Cape Town, he was driving around with Marais and another student militant, making preparations for a trip to Port Elizabeth, where they hoped to recruit Okhela's first choice for the black activist to be sent north to Europe, an up-and-coming young firebrand named Steven Biko—when they noticed that they were being tailed by a white Ford. The next few days were "like something out of a very corny third rate movie," as Breyten writes in *The True Confessions*. He would lose his tails, they would track him down, he would lose them again. But in any case he had nowhere to go, and he was now terribly exposed—"a bat outside in daylight," he says. Police roadblocks and checkpoints sprang up all around the city, and the airport and the train and bus terminals were swarming with reinforcements. He eventually contrived to catch the night express train to Johannesburg—boarding not at Cape Town Central Station but at its next stop, which happened to be Wellington. He got a friend to drive him there on back roads, passing through Paarl, in the hills above which, just a few weeks earlier, the regime had dedicated a hideous phallic monument to the Taal. (Breyten's interrogators would subsequently seem possessed by the conviction that Breyten had himself attended the dedication ceremonies *disguised as a woman*—they claimed to have photographic proof—and nothing he could say would disabuse them of the notion.) Breyten and his friend drove by Grevilleas, his parents' old boardinghouse (though they had in the meantime retired to Onrus, on the coast); he glimpsed the pear tree in passing, and all the other staging areas of his youth, the tapsprings (*sht—softly*) of his vocation. When the night train finally arrived, he boarded it, and made it to Johannesburg without further incident.

But Breyten had nowhere to go there, either. He couldn't very well look up his previous contacts: he had to assume that they had been compromised, and if they hadn't he certainly didn't want to get them into any trouble. Desperately tired and alone, he ducked into a movie theater, which happened to be showing, as a prelude to the main attraction, a patriotic documentary on the SADF's heroic Recces, the reconnaissance unit founded by his own brother Jan—and, in fact, there Jan was, blazoned across the screen, big as John Wayne, leading his men in parachute jumps and demolition exercises and ferocious impalings of blackened dummies, the audience whooping with excitement. (It so happened that at that very moment, in the middle of August 1975, the real-life Jan Breytenbach was helping to lead a massive, top-secret South African incursion into the midst of the civil war that was rapidly enveloping the neighboring Portuguese colony of Angola as it approached its upcoming independence, scheduled to take effect in November.)

Galaska's visa was now running out. "Everything was coming to a close," as he subsequently wrote in *The True Confessions,* "the various pieces of the jigsaw puzzle were being fitted together and, perhaps fatalistically, I felt that it was no longer possible to fit the odd-shaped blank piece that I am into any other hole than the one that seemed preordained for it." He booked a seat for a flight to Paris, on August 19, and went ("maybe with death already in my soul") to Jan Smuts Airport at the appointed hour. The terminal was like a military camp, bristling with security forces. Something Breyten didn't know at the time (it had been in all the papers, but he hadn't dared to look at a paper in days, for fear of being confronted by the image of his own face) was that later that evening Prime Minister Balthazar John Vorster, the Butcher himself, would be returning from state visits to Uruguay and Paraguay.

Though Breyten assumed that the military saturation was all for his benefit, he checked in and presented his passport. A few moments later, Galaska was being paged, and before he could even approach the information counter a gentleman came up beside him and asked, "Are you Mr. Galaska? Would you mind following me, please?" As he was being led into a small side office, he caught a brief glimpse of his own reflection in a windowpane as he passed.

"Looking into South Africa," he had written, years earlier, "is like looking into the mirror at midnight when one has pulled a face and a train blew its whistle and one's image stayed there, fixed for all eternity. A horrible face, but one's own."

It was just his luck that the case officer on duty that night was the senior BOSS operative, Jan Vermaak. At first, although Vermaak appeared delighted to have nabbed the dreaded Galaska, he didn't seem to recognize him as Breytenbach. Or perhaps he was just playing games. Breyten kept up the charade, protesting his bewildered innocence in Italian, but the questioning grew increasingly tense. Finally, Vermaak peered at Breyten intently, then rose and, pointing squarely between his eyes, growled, in Afrikaans, "Come on, Breyten, the game's up. We know who you are. Do we have to fetch your brother so as to confront you with him? You know he's here at the airport right now."

And indeed he was, for the prime minister's plane had in the meantime landed, and traveling right alongside Vorster throughout the entire trip had been Cloete (officially in his role as a photographer for the newspaper *Beeld*).

"No," Breyten replied, in Afrikaans. "That won't be necessary."

Donald Woods, the South African journalist, was subsequently told by Vorster's justice minister Jimmy Kruger that later that same evening, when Kruger personally informed the prime minister of the capture of his poetic nemesis Breytenbach, Vorster smiled and then instructed him, "Don't tell anyone else, and definitely not the press, not for a while anyway. I want some time to savor this one all to myself."

AS IT HAPPENED, no one on the outside heard anything of Breyten's arrest for a full eight days, until word finally leaked out, apparently inadvertently, in the midst of a triumphalist Transvaal National Party congress. In the meantime, the police had been closing the net over Breyten's entire "organization." Ampie Coetzee, for example, had heard nothing of Breyten for several weeks after the poet's brief stopover at his home on his way out of town, when suddenly one evening two beefy security police agents arrived at his door demanding to be let in. ("I penetrated the premises," is how one of them would eventually describe the scene at Breyten's trial. And then what did he do? "I penetrated *deeper*.") "They said, 'We know Breytenbach has been here,'" Coetzee recalls. "I couldn't deny it. 'And he left a plastic bag here—where'd he put it?' That I denied. 'It's no use denying, we'll just tear your whole house apart looking for it if you don't tell us.' So, okay, I apologized for denying—this bloody Christian upbringing: *apologized!* I mean, why apologize? Jesus!—and led them to the cupboard. Then they took the bag and me downtown to John Vorster, the headquarters building of the security services"—the domestic security services, that is, as opposed to BOSS, which handled external security. "Those guys were really heavy duty, and one grew increasingly anxious in their presence, one's sphincter tightening. So, I asked, have you arrested Breyten then? 'We ask the questions,' they barked. I was taken into the office of the director of the whole operation, Johan Coetzee—same surname, it's true, but we're not related and it did me no good. His shelves were lined with volumes of Lenin, Marx, and Trotsky—he fancied himself an authority on such political deviance. Now *he* was a really scary character—had one blue eye and one gray. 'So,' he says, 'what do you know about this stuff Breyten was involved in?' I denied any knowledge whatsoever—and it was a lucky thing, since in a neighboring room another of our friends was being similarly questioned and he too was denying any knowledge of Okhela or any of that. So Coetzee looks over at the plastic sack, rummages about in it, pulls out a particular book—'Do you know about this?' he asks, and gives me a good long stare . . . those eyes! I don't have a clue, and say so. He pulls a knife out of his desk drawer and proceeds to gut the inside covers of the book, extracting two perfect blank passports—German, as I recall. And he looks over at me again—blue and gray. In retrospect I realize that Breyten must have told them everything about the books in an effort to shield me, assuring them that I didn't know a thing. So then they take me into this small side room and give me some paper and tell me to write down everything I know about Breyten's coming and his visits with me. I do, and an hour or so later, they come back in, take the pages away, give me some more paper, and tell me to do it all over again. Fucking good technique. After about ten hours of this sort of thing, and following a stern warning, they let me go. Others weren't so lucky: Marais and several of the other student union activists ended up being held a good deal longer. It was about a week after my release that the papers exploded with news of Breyten's arrest, with the incriminating details blown way out of proportion—they were now claiming, for instance, that he'd been trying to smuggle in hundreds of false passports."

Breyten's parents in Onrus first heard the news over the radio. His father let out a wail and crumpled onto the bed, moaning repeatedly, "I will not survive this—this I will not survive." That evening, his mother busied herself in the kitchen, resolutely cooking a batch of sausages and eggs and keening, "We must go on, we simply have to go on."

BREYTEN, meanwhile, was in solitary confinement in the maximum-security section of Pretoria Central; in fact, he was on its death row, in a small cell, to which he had been taken soon after his arrest. Nothing in his training—the clandestine political work or the Zen studies—seems to have prepared him for what he was now facing. He was completely out of his element, and he was reeling.

"The actual moment of arrest and the terrifying hours immediately thereafter stripped away any intellectual sense, for example, of Zen-centeredness," he recalled for me in a conversation a few years ago in a Paris café. "All there was was this brutal changeover from having some control over your life, no matter how minimal, to having none whatsoever—to complete impotence—and then the shock at the ferocity of your own urge to survive: the rat scrambling around inside your skull, snarling."

The first phase of Breyten's interrogation lasted forty-eight hours straight, during which he was denied any sleep. He was ordered to write out a statement, the statement was taken away, and he was ordered to write it out again. He was questioned at length, and in relays. In the Paris café, Breyten said, "Nowadays, sure, looking back on my situation then, I'd say, 'Don't talk, just don't talk to them.' At first, I just kept protesting my innocence. 'But if you're innocent,' they'd say, 'write us about your innocence.' And the minute you begin writing—well, then you're fucked. My big mistake, of course, was imagining that since I was so obviously smarter than these lunkheaded interrogators I ought to be able to outsmart them. Which, of course, now I realize is crazy, but I didn't realize it at the time—and I desperately *needed* to outsmart them. There were people I was trying to protect —I needed to get a sense of what they knew. So I would say or write something in an attempt to draw them out. I never gave real names, always used made-up code names. There were certain things one didn't do."

Breyten was silent for a moment, drumming the café table absent-mindedly, momentarily absent. "And then," he said, exhaling deeply, "I mean, I *am* a writer. In a strange, macabre way, it's a fascinating experience to be writing one's confessions to the police. For me, writing has always been a way of better understanding the connections of the world. But, in that situation, to really probe and manipulate those linkages immediately posed, in a very literal way, the life-and-death sorts of issues we writers ordinarily just like to make believe we're confronting. And then, as well, I did feel a need to explain myself, to justify and account for the decisions of my life—to myself as well as to them. And, too, the way in which the whole interrogation was taking place in Afrikaans—the language itself, after all, being at the core of my problem, my sense of complicity, but, also, the hope that it could arouse a feeling of sympathy in them—that too was key."

Although Breyten was not physically tortured—and, of course, during this time there were many who were being horrendously tortured, especially among the black prisoners—the pressures brought to bear on him were singular. He was not just a white Afrikaner political prisoner—a rare enough bird—and hence a traitor over and above any mere subversiveness but also an Afrikaner *writer,* with all that that implied.

During the months that followed, Breyten was passed among a battery of interrogators, but with one such agent—the lead investigator for the domestic-security police, a man named Kalfie (Little Calf) Broodryk—he developed a peculiarly perverse relationship. At a moment when Breyten was exceptionally racked and vulnerable, Broodryk made a personal project of this new prisoner—and Broodryk himself was, as Breyten now says, "really twisted, that guy . . . *really* twisted."

The two of them got into a strange dance, indeed. Broodryk's idea of a good time was to have Breyten summoned from his cell after weeks in solitary and then escorted out of the prison gates to his own personal car, inside which there was a seventeen-year-old girl whom Broodryk introduced as his niece, supposedly studying to be a teacher. "He then left her alone with me. She claimed to be a fan of my poetry, and so emotional did she become at the thought of my plight that she ended up weeping. He was standing a little way off, hands in his pockets. When he'd enjoyed himself enough he came and had me escorted back to my cell." Perhaps Broodryk's most cynical display of power occurred one Saturday morning, when, accompanied only by his son, he came to take Breyten out of solitary and to drive him to his own home, for a walk through his garden, a meal with his family, a bit of badinage with his two young daughters—this was, after all, the foremost poet in the language. He then invited Breyten to make use of his bathroom to wash up, even offered him the use of his own toothbrush, before hurrying him back to prison. But, once there, instead of escorting him immediately to his cell, he led him into a small side office, in the middle of which stood Yolande—the first time they had seen one another since his arrest. And then Broodryk didn't leave the room: he just stood around, savoring a reunion made all the more agonizing by the previous few hours' cleverly choreographed hijinks.

And yet, a few months later, Breyten was dedicating a new book, consisting entirely of poems composed during his imprisonment, to this very Broodryk. Broodryk's interest in allowing Breyten to continue writing such poetry and then in seeing to its publication seemed twofold—in part to further toy with Breyten's mind, and in part to win points with the Afrikaner professoriat, whose cultural validation he appeared to crave. The regime's interest in allowing publication of the book was more convoluted. Many of Breyten's poems included gut-wrenchingly vivid evocations of his actual situation (only one of them was censored outright by the book's editor, the sister-in-law of foreign minister Pik Botha: a poem entitled "Help," which read, in its entirety, "Help!"). The decision to allow them to be published seemed to be another swirl in the Afrikaner pattern of simultaneous revulsion from and idealization of Breyten's poetry—the notion that they could separate the language master from the terrorist. (Even with Breyten in prison, his poems continued to appear in school anthologies, though the box reserved for his photograph was regularly blanked out.)

Why Breyten was allowing the book's publication at all under those conditions—by Perskor-Utigewers, an establishment printing house closely allied to the regime's élite Broederbond—and, more gallingly, with *that* dedication, is another matter. Breyten claims that he was desperate to get out to the wider world a signal, any signal, that he was still alive, and, furthermore, that he hoped that whatever royalties might accrue could be of some help to Yolande. As for the dedication, he says that it was a simple matter of horse-trading, that Broodryk insisted on the dedication in exchange for allowing the book's publication. All of which may be true. But it is also true that by this point a frightening symbiosis between the two had developed, a relationship uncannily captured in one of the collection's poems:

I had dealings with the enemy
my eyes became entangled in the eyes of the enemy
with his eyes he held mine
the better for to stab me in the back

THE ROLE of literary agent in this affair was played by Breyten's brother Cloete. He collaborated closely with the authorities from the earliest days of Breyten's incarceration—even before the arrest was made public. In *The True Confessions* Breyten relates that on the fourth day "my one brother is allowed in to come and see me briefly and in so doing there's this terrible destruction of the love that I had for him as a brother, him, on such close terms with them, him taking exactly the same line they did, doing their talking for them." Cloete would later claim that he was just pulling whatever strings he had at his disposal to rescue Breyten from the mess he had managed to get himself into.

At any rate, it was now Cloete, acting on behalf of the family, who secured Breyten's defense team—two nervous lawyers who apparently had never tried a political case in their lives. And that was the whole idea: the regime was tremendously eager for this case *not* to become a political one, at least from Breyten's side. The regime may have been particularly anxious lest a combative Breytenbach publicly reveal whatever he might happen to know about that SADF incursion into Angola, which, though top secret and emphatically denied, was at that very moment being led by, among others, Breyten's brother Jan.

The original indictment against Breyten was terrifyingly broad. Framed under provisions of the Terrorism Act, it alleged large-scale weapons smuggling, plotting of violent acts of sabotage, and conspiracy to commit still wider crimes—charges that carried the distinct possibility of a capital conviction. It's worth remembering that throughout this period Breyten was being housed on a death row that in those days was witnessing the execution of more than two hundred inmates a year. And, although Breyten didn't participate directly in any negotiations, the general outlines of a deal were made clear to him: in exchange for a compliant guilty plea and appropriate expressions of contrition, those still in prison on his account would be released, his own indictment would be whittled back, and he could expect leniency, and even magnanimity—a light sentence, and even then the possibility of an early parole. Meanwhile, he was continuing to meet daily with Broodryk, who had taken to insinuating, "Why bother to have legal representation at all; why don't you leave it in my hands? *I shall defend you*."

"HOW IT BECOMES possible for one ultimately to be like the rabbit assisting open-eyed and without kicking at one's own eating," is the rubric under which Breyten would finally characterize this phase of his life in his *True Confessions*.

On November 10, 1975, accompanied by counsel, Breyten appeared in the Pretoria Supreme Court, Judge Piet Cillié, a leading member of the Broederbond, presiding. The prosecutor read out the bill of indictment, after which Judge Cillié remanded the case over for trial eleven days thence. During this period, the regime-controlled media worked themselves into a frenzy of vituperation. Meanwhile, behind the scenes, the crunch negotiations were taking place. A few days before the start of the actual trial, the remainder of those who had been arrested with Breyten (some had been facing sentences of up to twenty years) were released—an early indication, seemingly, that the fix was in.

On the morning of November 21, when the trial began, family members gathered. Yolande had been advised by Breyten's lawyers to go back to Paris, so she was not there; and Breyten's mother felt incapable, both physically and psychologically, of making the trip up from Cape Province. But his father was there, pale and shrunken (he was still recovering from the cardiac episode), clutching his daughter, Rachel, for support. Cloete was there; Jan, of course, was not. And there were countless others. One evening over dinner in Cape Town, Coetzee commented on the number of young women who came each day to observe the trial, longingly—"There was something almost prurient about it"—but his wife, Karin, tried to clarify the point: "The thing you have to realize is that Breyten has always been a figure who can carry a lot of projections. He was almost like a Jesus figure, even physically, for the Afrikaners, this hero who had to be sacrificed so that the rest of us could live." This comment in turn reminded me of something Breyten himself once said to me regarding that early poem in which he'd begged his reader to have mercy on him, since he was harmless. "Perhaps what has always struck me most about the Christ mythology," he commented, "is the harmlessness of the man and the inevitability of his sacrifice. The sheepishness of it all, that he should have let such a damn stupid thing happen to him when it could have been prevented." I mentioned that comment, and Coetzee concurred that the courtroom was positively pullulating with transferences.

The trial itself, once under way, was surprisingly brief—a matter of a few days. The prosecutor began by reducing the indictment substantially. He then worked his way through a parade of cooperative witnesses who laid bare the full folly of Breyten's delusional politics and exploits. His own lawyers barely bothered to cross-examine: they simply pleaded him guilty as charged.

As the hearing moved toward its sentencing phase, on November 25, the defense team finally seemed to rouse itself, calling a young Afrikaner graduate student in literature to the stand and asking her to expound on the significance of Breyten's poetry. She did so, but mainly she *read* some of the poetry: a love song to Yolande, though achingly to South Africa as well ("kissing you leads me to think/ of vineyards gaunt in the sodden winters"); a poem dedicated to his father; and then a third poem ("ma/ I've been thinking/ if I ever come home/ it will be without warning towards daybreak . . . "). By the time she'd finished, there was hardly a dry eye in the house—with the exception of the judge's.

After this, Breyten rose to address the court. Beginning with a summary of his life, he emphasized the theme of love (love of parents, of country, of Yolande), almost suggesting that if only he had been allowed to love Yolande in peace, many years ago, none of this might have happened. He detailed the stages of his political evolution, and then seemed to forswear it all:

I accept the responsibility for what I have done. I know now that the manner and the methods by which I tried to work for the growth of our civilization and our future were wrong, that my behavior was foolish and that things I got mixed up in with good intentions could lead to harm to other people. . . . I am sorry for all the stupid, thoughtless things I did which brought me here and I ask to be forgiven for them.

Breyten went on to express contrition to those whom he might have hurt or insulted "unintentionally or out of thoughtlessness," and, specifically, to Prime Minister Vorster, "for a crass and insulting poem which I addressed to him." He added, "There was and is no justification for it. I am sorry." But he wasn't finished. He proceeded to extend his heartfelt thanks to "Colonel Broodryk [and] the officers who worked under him, for the correct and humane way in which they treated me from the beginning of my detention," adding, for good measure, that "their courteous conduct made these traumatic three months bearable for me." He then concluded, hauntingly, almost creepily, by quoting St. Paul's First Epistle to the Corinthians: "When I was a child, I spake as a child, I understood as a child, I thought as a child: but when I became a man I put away childish things. For now we see through a glass, darkly; but then face to face: now I know in part; but then shall I know even as also I am known."

The spectators watched, drop-jawed, as Colonel Broodryk and the prosecutor both attested to Breyten's perfect contrition, characterizing him as an unfortunate pawn in the hands of sinister forces abroad, and then endorsed the minimum possible sentence.

Judge Cillié now retired to his chambers to consider the sentence, but no sooner had he left the room than the defense dispatched an orderly to fetch him back again: Breyten wished to enter a brief addition to his statement. The spectators craned forward—*this* was going to be interesting. He'd forgotten, it turned out, to express, for the record, his heartfelt thanks to the prison personnel "for their exceptionally correct treatment since I have been with them."

So that was that: surely he'd groveled as much as could have been required by any possible deal. The spectators milled about, awaiting the denouement. They didn't have to wait long. Judge Cillié soon emerged from chambers and announced his sentence:

Nine years' imprisonment, without possibility of parole.

WHAT HAD HAPPENED? Had there been a deal that somehow came unraveled, or had Breyten simply been played for a fool all along? Dumbfounded and shattered, he was led out of the courtroom and taken initially to Broodryk's office. "I was sitting in the corner, facing Broodryk, when two of his colleagues came bursting in—they didn't see me—to congratulate him on the completeness of his triumph," he recalls. "So who knows? On the other hand—and this was a truly horrifying moment—later that same day, he was escorting me back to my cell, he was wearing dark glasses, when suddenly he started crying."

There was a good deal of speculation that Vorster himself had personally dictated the sentence—and, indeed, some indication that between Breyten's final statement and the actual sentencing Cillié had received a phone call from the prime minister in his chambers.

Peter Dreyer, whose account of the trial forms a centerpiece of his masterly South African study *Martyrs and Fanatics*, has an interesting theory. Pointing to a phrase in Cillié's sentencing speech—"In the circumstances now existing, the climate now prevailing"—he notes that during that very week events in the outside world had taken a decidedly dismaying turn, from the regime's point of view. Up till then, the SADF's (and Jan's) Angolan expeditionary forces had been plowing forward, scoring one victory after another. But now they'd bogged down. On November 21, the day Breyten's trial started, the Cubans had completed an emergency airlift of a reinforced special-forces battalion into Luanda, the seat of the newly installed M.P.L.A. (Communist-aligned) government, and already those reinforcements were spreading out into the field. The next day, the *Washington Post* published an authoritative, eyewitness account detailing South Africa's intervention on the side of the MPLA.'s rivals, UNITA and the FNLA. Soon thereafter, Zaire had to suspend its backing of the FNLA. (it couldn't be seen to be on the same side as the South Africans). In the United States, Congress was preventing Secretary of State Henry Kissinger from extending American support to the South African effort—Jimmy Carter had been elected a few weeks earlier on an explicitly anti-apartheid platform. The SADF, including what was soon to be Jan's 32 Battalion, was in retreat on all fronts. Never before had the apartheid regime seemed so isolated. According to Dreyer, Breyten may have merely provided a convenient scapegoat—a readily available, highly visible object lesson through which the regime could intimidate any other potential internal opposition.

Whatever the reason, the outcome of the trial was a disaster for Breyten. Not only had he received a ferociously stiff sentence but also, through his groveling behavior, he had confounded, if not completely alienated, his few remaining allies. Support committees abroad, at the very moment when they should have been jacking up their efforts, were left bewildered by his behavior. (In Holland, his translator now disavowed him, echoing the tone of an ANC campaign of repudiation that was being led by Schuitema's former girlfriend.) Less sophisticated observers—and, in particular, the fans of his poetic persona—experienced a sort of triple whiplash: the initial shock of his arrest, with all its implications; horror at the spectacle of his abject recantation ("No poet of Breyten's caliber would ever dream of apologizing for his work" was a typical comment); and then the jolt of the ensuing sentence, in all its mercilessness.

Breyten himself, meanwhile, was thrown back into the hole. It was November 25, 1975, and he would not see the moon again for five months. Stars, he wouldn't see for years (missing them would become like a "chafing sore" in his mind). He spent most of the next couple of years alone in a narrow, high-ceilinged cell, still, even though he was no longer facing the death penalty, right alongside death row. One evening in Paris, he described that wing of the Pretoria Central prison to me. "The hanging room—the actual chamber where they executed the prisoners—was, of course, the central characteristic of the place. Even though you never saw the room, you could hear it—you could hear the trapdoor opening. It would send a sort of shuddering through the entire building the mornings people were being hanged. And before that you'd hear the singing with all its different qualities. You could definitely hear when somebody sang—and there'd be singing every evening—that that person was going to die in a few days, as opposed to somebody who still had a few weeks or months. And the interesting thing, or the touching thing, when one person sang alone like that in the middle of the night and you knew he was due to be hanged in two days' time, was how you could actually hear the quality of the listening of the other people, because you knew that everybody else in that prison was awake, lying there with their ears cocked close to the bars or the walls, listening. *You could hear the listening.*"

Worst of all, perhaps, was the isolation: having to be alone, in solitary, after everything he had done and been through, with nothing to do but think and rethink the humiliation and the shamefulness of it all. "Isolation has made me sick of myself, and sick of others," he later wrote. His contacts with the outside world were limited to one letter in each direction per month, not to exceed five hundred words and subject to censorship, and one half-hour noncontact visit. This meant that he often had to choose between writing to his parents and writing to Yolande, for example, or hearing from them and hearing from her. His guards used to tease him regarding any new letter's contents, having read it before giving it to him. "On days when I received a letter from Yolande," Breyten recalls, "I would carry it around for hours, *not opening it,* waiting for the warder's touch to dissipate."

Yolande would come to South Africa as often as she could, but her funds were sorely limited. (She was getting no help, for instance, from the ANC) The authorities had a way of rendering even these visits a torment, stalling and bumbling (while the clock was running) so as maddeningly to foreshorten the brief time they had allotted to them; craning forward to eavesdrop on any intimacies the two might attempt to share through the glass partition; subjecting Yolande to a full body search even though the two of them had never come in physical contact, and regaling Breyten with tales of same; peppering him between her visits with lewd speculations ("She's not coming back, Breyten, we hear she's got herself a big *kaffir* lover now, she doesn't need you anymore").

Through the walls he tried to develop relationships of sorts with the neighboring prisoners—but many of them, already in there well longer than he, had gone mad with boredom. Some of his most satisfying relations were with the birds who'd managed to squeeze their way through gaps in the wire mesh overhanging the deep exercise well; long figments of the poet's metaphorical repertory, real birds now became his only intimate friends. One morning he cusped a wounded turtle dove from off the exercise yard's pavement and husbanded it back to his cell, where for days he nurtured it achingly back to health ("The incessant craving in prison to have something or someone to care *for,*" Breyten subsequently told me, "can become almost more overwhelming than the longing to feel cared for oneself.") That bird lasted only a few weeks, however, before the warder's cat ate it.

Breyten returned to his solitude and to the expanse of solitude yawning before him, the truly horrifying dimensions of which only gradually dawned on him. He fell into a deepening depression, succumbing now to a kind of full-fledged slow-motion nervous breakdown.

MEANWHILE, Broodryk was still coming around, serpentine, plying him with fresh possibilities. His situation, after all, wasn't entirely hopeless, Broodryk assured him. It was such a waste, his rotting away like this. Come, friend, come, why not try . . . And so it was that on June 16, 1976—Day One, as it happened, though Breyten would have had no way of knowing about it, of the great Soweto uprising, which was launched by black students in rebellion against the requirement that they matriculate in Afrikaans, the hated language of their oppression—Breyten sat down, at Broodryk's insistence, and wrote a letter to General Mike Geldenhuys, the head of the security police, offering him a deal. "In short, I believe that you can make much better use of me than is at present the case," he wrote. Why not release him, he proposed, after which he would "try—in collaboration with your service—to become a member of the SACP." and inform the police about the Party's machinations. He also offered to inform on Schuitema and Makathini and others: just let him go. "I hope that you will accept my proposal," he concluded, "with the sincerity in which I mean it."

That final sentence is crucial in any attempt to evaluate the significance of the letter. How sincerely *did* he mean it? Was he yet again being too clever by half, trying to wheedle a way out through a deal he had no intention of keeping? Was he already plotting a kind of double or triple agenthood in his own mind? Or was he, understandably, desperate for release and willing to do anything? General Geldenhuys, at any rate, never took him up on the offer, and for good reason. Not even a week later, as Dreyer has pointed out, a young warder named Pieter Groenewald, suddenly racked with misgivings, was spilling his guts to the prison commander—or, anyway, so the prosecution would contend at Breyten's second trial. Breyten, it seemed, had managed to develop a relationship besides the one with Broodryk during those first months of his sentence, and this one made the one with Broodryk seem positively transparent.

Beginning in April of 1976, Groenewald, a twenty-year-old rookie guard, took to whiling away his night shifts by regaling Breyten with unlikely tales of his own prowess and machismo. Breyten, avid for any contact, played along, spinning fantasies of his own. Groenewald said he had followed Breyten's trial and admired his stand, his writings, his courage. Breyten requested paper and pencils, so that he could write and draw. (As bad as the sheer isolation had been this strangulation of his creative impulse. It wasn't just that Breyten was being kept from communicating with the outside world; he was now being kept from creating at all, from expressing himself in ways that had become as necessary to him as breathing.) Groenewald provided him with pencils and blank paper, and smuggled out completed poems and drawings, dutifully sending them on to Paris. (Among these were the pencil drawings of blankets and shoes, of copulations and decapitations, and of "The Orange, Four Times.") Groenewald agreed to smuggle letters out as well, to friends and old allies, both outside and inside the country, many of the latter being the same people Breyten had got into such trouble the first time around.

As the nights passed, in a sort of Scheherazadean folie à deux, the two men began to weave ever more convoluted fantasies of—or plans for (it was hard to tell which)—heroic escapes and subsequent acts of derring-do. (These included, it was alleged, the blowing up of the Monument to the Taal, above Paarl.) But Groenewald presently cracked under the pressure and informed his superiors of their shenanigans—or maybe he had been a plant all along. "Who knows what the hell was going on," Ampie Coetzee subsequently commented. "On the one hand, you have the police's version, and one can never believe a word they say, by definition. And, on the other, you have Breyten's, and he's a poet and, as such, congenitally incapable of merely literal truth." ("The whole thing was obviously a setup," Cloete figures, "and being hopelessly gullible, Breyten fell for it, as usual.") At any rate, from that point forward Groenewald was wired for his nightly conversations with Breyten, and every piece of paper leaving the cell through their supposedly secret channel—including letters, as Dreyer has characterized them, "of stunning indiscretion"—was being routed through the photocopier at secret-police headquarters. The police allowed this charade to continue for several more months, but they were monitoring every letter going in as well, and when those letters grew more and more anxious, urging Breyten to take care—surely something was wrong—the police decided that the game was up. Toward the end of October, they entered his cell to inform him that he was being charged with seventeen counts of violating the Terrorism Act, and that once again he could well be facing the gallows.

This time, however, Yolande took charge of appointing the lawyers, and the new ones proved to be notably competent. More to the point, upon first meeting with Breyten they could immediately infer the extent of his psychological deterioration; the police took eight months to conclude their preparations for the case, during which time Breyten could do nothing but fret, but at least these lawyers now took to visiting him regularly, and slowly they reeled him back in.

The case finally came to trial in June of 1977, amid a new spasm of publicity. Judge Cillié had a prior commitment (improbably, he was heading a state commission on the causes and lessons of the Soweto uprising), and in his place the case was heard by W. G. Boshoff, an altogether more dispassionate arbiter. Breyten's solicitors, meanwhile, had engaged a spectacularly effective advocate, J. G. Kriegler, to handle the actual arguing of their case. When the tapes (recorded from high above Breyten's reverberating well of a cell) proved inaudible, the overwhelming burden of the state's case fell on the improbable shoulders of young Groenewald. Kriegler quietly but mercilessly shredded his testimony—by the end it was hard to tell what had been provocation and what merest delusion.

Breyten himself then took the stand and in a marathon session reconstructed his version of the relationship and the smuggled correspondence, but more important, in the process he was able to reveal details regarding the appalling conditions of his incarceration.

The prosecution, seeing its case unraveling, cynically introduced Breyten's letter to General Geldenhuys with its offer to collaborate. Kriegler calmly rose and asked Breyten about the letter, and Breyten replied that it had just been another admittedly clumsy attempt to maneuver the *boere*. But outside the courtroom damage *had* been done: his activist credentials had been even further tarnished.

The judge ended up dismissing all charges except one, relating to illegal smuggling of correspondence, for which he fined Breyten fifty rand, payable on completion of his sentence. More important, he ordered an immediate rectification of the conditions of his imprisonment for the remainder of that sentence: for starters, he was to be taken away from death row. Kriegler, hugging his client in triumph, admonished, "Now, behave yourself like a good Afrikaner and a good Frenchman." And a few weeks later, Breyten was transferred out of Pretoria altogether (on leaving, he cursed the city's site to hell, vowing never to return) and was transported down to Pollsmoor Prison on the outskirts of his beloved Cape Town.

AT POLLSMOOR, the conditions of Breyten's incarceration improved considerably: he was allowed outside on a regular basis, was no longer confined in isolation, and was given things to do (specifically, he was assigned to the prison storehouse, where he was granted broad clerical responsibilities); and it now became easier for his parents to visit him monthly. That said, Pollsmoor was still one of South Africa's largest prison centers, no less rigorous in its observance of the system's stultifying rules (all visits, for example, remained noncontact, through a glass partition), and at the same time a zone of relentless violence and violation.

Now, however, at the insistence of the Afrikaner professoriat, Breyten was allowed to resume writing regularly—though under highly peculiar conditions. He was permitted to write as much as he liked, but he was not allowed to retain anything he wrote, even for purposes of reference or continuity. At the end of each day, the day's production was confiscated "for safekeeping," with the assurance that it would all be returned to him at the end of his sentence. He never knew whether to believe such assurances (in the end, thanks in part to pressure from his lawyers, they were scrupulously observed), but he could have no doubt that in the meantime his every word was being pored over by regime psychologists and security operatives. The guards even confiscated the blotters in his prison-storehouse office each evening to decipher the doodlings on them

Breyten's was almost a Dadaist endeavor—"a singing death," he once called it. "Writing took on its pure shape, since it had no echo, no feedback, no evaluation, and perhaps ultimately no existence." And yet, even under such circumstances, he managed to produce a body of work of protean vitality, notably including a feverishly enigmatic novel, made up of a series of overlapping short narratives, which he entitled *Mouroir,* a typically Breytenbachian invention, ingeniously yoking the French words for "mirror" (*miroir*) and "to die" (*mourir*). His prison poems eventually filled five volumes—and, reading them, one indeed feels a sense of gazing into a dark mirror, with the themes of a lifetime rising up again, oddly inverted.

> *Laybyes and gauntletmen,*

he starts one poem,

> *allow me to take this leave*
> *of Bengai Bird,*
> *the emaciated dream in the green shirt:*
> *he props up and fondles his wormfat head*
> *and breeds a final poem to bestow upon you,*
> *for example:*
>
> to come out of the hospital you must
> be in a coma . . .

This poem continues for a few more stanzas before reverting to italics at the end:

> *See he is versed in harmfulness—*
> *would you not rather show him mercy?*
> *the feast of words has been consumed*
> *no one is guilty of innocence*

The ache of homesickness is again pervasive, but now it is Paris (rather than the Boland) that is being longed for, and it is reunion with Yolande (rather than his parents) that is being conjured with such startling specificity, as in the case of one poem where he mouthwateringly savors a reunion meal of *couscous mouton* for two at a restaurant on the Rue Monsieur-le-Prince.

There are poems of prison life, some of them rendered with lacerating violence. And then there are (still and always) poems of the Boland, of his youth and his parents and their old age and his fear that they will die before he's released. There is a particularly beautiful ode to his mother, which ends,

> and now you are old, saturated with love and young for ever
> like a fruit tree in the soil:
> I bear your bones in your careening blood
> and the sing-song sounds of your throat:
> *oh mother, bless me before you go!*

The authorities never allowed him to convey that poem to her.

And then suddenly, early in April 1978, she was dead (succumbing to a heart attack while attending the funeral of a friend). Rachel believes that her son's arrest was part of it, "but even more it was the way the enormity of the lie began to dawn on her. She had been raised in a traditional Afrikaner manner: you always took the authorities at their word. But after Breyten's arrest the discrepancies just became too wide—she was always saying we have to go on, we have to go on, but in the end she just couldn't. The state was lying, and her entire belief system crumbled, and within a few years she was dead."

The authorities informed Breyten of her death and then posted a double round-the-clock watch on his cell (a suicide watch? lecherous prurience, the bureaucratic equivalent of rubber-necking?—or just another attempt to drive him mad?) and kept the lights on all night so that he was given nowhere to privilege his grief. He applied for permission to attend the funeral, which was denied and then granted and then denied again. (The event, as it happens, degenerated into a media circus. I am looking at a photograph of the funeral—Rachel is buttressing her devastated father, Breyten is absent, Cloete and Jan are glaring at the paparazzi.)

Jan visited Breyten in his cell soon after, along with Cloete, and then returned seamlessly to his work; a month later, in May 1978, he led a parachute assault of unprecedented scope and ferocity (the largest anywhere, it was claimed, since the Second World War) on the hamlet of Kassinga, a way-station for Namibian refugees or else, depending on who you believed, a SWAPO terrorist training center, deep inside Angola—over six hundred of the base's inhabitants were killed during the raid, the majority of them women and children.

Breyten's father continued to visit him in the months following his mother's death, ramrod straight and increasingly defiant, until one day, two years later and several years before his son's scheduled release, he was felled by a stroke, which left him partly paralyzed and entirely mute.

And the months passed. In September of 1978, Vorster resigned as prime minister, and after that the conditions surrounding Breyten's incarceration seemed to lose some of their personal edge. His situation grew increasingly normal, and he committed no more gross blunders. In April of 1982, when Nelson Mandela and Walter Sisulu, the imprisoned leaders of the ANC, were transferred to Pollsmoor from Robben Island, it fell to Breyten, in his capacity as storeroom clerk, to outfit their quarters, and he did so with particular zeal, though he didn't meet them at this time.

Prison never stopped being a horror for Breyten. And yet on the far side of that horror Breyten found a kind of peace—in fact, the very peace, in a certain sense, that he had been searching for at the Zen center in Paris. "I didn't go into a prison as a form of spiritual exercise," he once told me. "And, believe me, I wouldn't recommend it as such to anyone. But, what with the scattering of the sense of ego, the abdications forced upon one, the grassroots efforts at survival, I really came to understand for the first time what so much of Zen poetry is about: the acuity of observation, the humbleness and immediacy of beauty." He spoke of "growing rich with the richness of the very poor" and recalled, in particular, what it was like, living in that monochrome universe, when all of a sudden "there'd be this explosion of a toffee wrapper, for instance, or a leaf blew over the wall, or even just a thread, a thread of material drifted up over the wall. You cannot possibly imagine the intensity of the experience. *It was as if you'd never seen color before in your life.* So it was always like that in prison—this simultaneous dulling and sharpening, dulling and sharpening. And somehow I survived."

SURVIVAL WAS one thing, rescue another—and his rescue Breyten owed to Yolande. Her efforts on his behalf throughout his incarceration were tireless. In Paris, she ran a small boutique near the Beaubourg, specializing in antique clothing. To supplement her income, she knitted, Penelope-like, the entire time. Twice a year, she closed up her little operation and flew to South Africa, staying with Breyten's parents or with Ampie Coetzee or with other friends, visiting Breyten in prison, and endlessly lobbying journalists, cultural figures, and government officials. "She even got in to talk to some of the top cabinet people," Breyten marvels, "the police and justice ministers, big tough guys towering over her, despising her for being colored and, since she was Vietnamese, obviously a Communist, and *my* wife to boot—where she found the bloody guts to do it, I'll never know." This is, among other things, a love story.

I have spoken with people who feel certain that prison made Breyten and Yolande's marriage, that before prison Breyten had been lurching personally as well as politically, that it took prison for him to realize what he had in her; and that, conversely, the passionate totality of her commitment on behalf of a relationship that was, at the outset, rickety at best had been a revelation to them both.

During the last years of her crusade on Breyten's behalf, Yolande obtained a powerful ally in Frederik Van Zyl Slabbert, an old Stellenbosch rugby star and contemporary of Breyten's, who had shared the platform with him in 1973 at the Cape Town Sestigers conference, had shortly thereafter entered politics, and had quickly risen to become the head of the otherwise "English"-dominated Progressive Party's parliamentary caucus, which was the regime's principal legitimate anti-apartheid opposition. As such, he regularly locked horns, sometimes ferociously, with the new prime minister, P. W. Botha. Slabbert and the prime minister had barely exchanged a civil word in weeks, even though they were required to sit next to each other every day in parliament, when suddenly one evening in the midst of a particularly florid debate, Botha leaned over across the aisle and whispered to him, "Afrikaans is a beautiful language, is it not?" Slabbert replied that it certainly was, and then a few days later took advantage of this momentary outbreak of peace between them to raise the question of Breyten's status.

In part thanks to that, in part thanks to a fresh offensive on the part of the sympathetic local press (inspired by Yolande), in part thanks to the ascension to power (back in Paris) of François Mitterrand's new government with all its cultural pretensions and hence a renewed interest in the fate of this martyred poet and quasi-citizen of France, and in part owing to the whiff of a threat on the part of Breyten's legal team that they might be getting ready to revisit the whole question of the regime's apparent double-dealing at the time of his initial sentencing, things finally began to move. This was early December 1982. Yolande was in the country, with a few days left on her current visa. When release, once again, was beginning to look unlikely after all, Breyten took to consoling himself that he'd at least be getting his Christmas cake in a few weeks' time. "Every year we were allowed to order five hundred grams of cake for Christmas," he explained to me, "but we had to put our order in early, sometime in late October. And that year I had put in for a forêt-noir—fantastic, marvelous cake. And so then on the second of December, I got called in to the prison superintendent's office and was told very brusquely that I was now free, I was being released immediately. And my first thought—the very first thing that flashed through my mind—was, 'Damn it all to hell, there goes my cake!'"

He was handed his various manuscripts—everything in immaculate order—and asked to sign for them. He himself was handed over to an Afrikaans-literature professor, a regime man, who had been visiting him on occasion over the years to discuss his poetry, and who, he was now informed, would be serving as his minder over the next several days. The professor lent him the fifty rand to pay off his outstanding fine. Breyten was asked to avoid publicity. The regime would be announcing his release in a few days but had not yet figured out precisely how to do so, and wanted to keep things quiet until then. And, with that, Breyten was shown to the gate. The minder drove him to the house of some friends, with whom Yolande was staying. Upon answering the minder's knock, Yolande emerged from the house to find Breyten standing by the car. Ever sensible, her first words were "What are *you* doing *here?*" As Breyten says, "That, of course, was a long story."

The minder proceeded to explain to both of them the regime's desire that Yolande return to Paris on schedule a few days hence and that Breyten remain behind for "a decent interval" in order to create the impression "in the public mind" that he was "entirely free." Yolande would have none of it. She'd be leaving in three days' time, and she'd be taking Breyten with her—they'd just better see to it that all the necessary ticketing and papers were in order. Through steely determination, she imposed her will.

After a night together, he and Yolande agreed to meet at the Johannesburg airport in two days. But first, before leaving, Breyten had an errand to do. While Yolande stayed behind to clear up the loose ends of her seven years of half-life there in Cape Town, Breyten and his minder drove out of town, heading just south of Wellington and then eastward, past the two farms of his childhood, the whole "horrendously beautiful" country rushing by—he was, as he subsequently wrote, "seeing everything for the first time, everything for the last time . . . everything was dying, everything was being reborn"—and on to his sister's house, in Grahamstown. She had been notified, and had brought their father over from a nearby nursing home, where he was now living. He was sitting there in her living room, mute (he hadn't said a word since the stroke) and weeping unashamedly. As Breyten went over to embrace him, he stammered Breyten's name, a few more strangulated syllables, and then quite distinctly he spoke the word *"Klaar!"* (It is *finished!* It is *done!*)

And then it was back to Johannesburg to rejoin Yolande, and back to Jan Smuts Airport. This time, no one was there to detain him for an unintended handshake or an unintended prison sentence: he and Yolande just boarded the airplane and were gone.

III

Back in Paris, Breyten tried to retrieve his life, but doing so turned out to be not nearly so simple as ordering *couscous mouton* for two on the Rue Monsieur-le-Prince. "It can be terribly disrupting being forced out of prison like that, having freedom forced upon you," Breyten explained to me several years later, during our conversations in his Paris studio. "Because it's the opposite of what I was saying the other day about how life inside prison consists of the intensification of experience wrapped inside its mortification. Because now, coming out from that zombified world of prison, I felt I was moving into a different sort of zombified world. It was a complete turnabout. I kept feeling that these people really don't know what life's about. *They don't see the colors, they don't hear the sounds*. In prison, being woken up at four in the morning and marched through the yard on your way to work, yes, it was dehumanizing, but on occasion you'd look up into the sky and *you heard that star*—you *heard* it!—and to an extent you continued in that state of heightened awareness for months after your release. It could get to be too much, of course. There was so much more stimulation on the outside that it got to be physically exhausting, and sometimes I almost longed to be back in my cell."

There was of course one cell to which Breyten needed to return—his painting studio—though for several weeks he kept circling it skittishly. "I was afraid, because I hadn't painted for seven and a half years," he said. "And with painting, as with music, you worry that if you don't practice it, a lot of it goes—a lot of the technical ability. I was really scared in front of that first canvas."

I asked him if he still had that painting. He rummaged around in the back and pulled it out. It was dated "February 1, 1983," and the image, competently rendered in dull grays and browns and blues, consisted of his face in a mirror, bruised and pummeled and haggard, with the eyes closed. I asked him why he had painted himself with his eyes closed, and he replied, "It was

Breyten Breytenbach, "February 1, 1983"

all too tender still. I couldn't look at myself yet." (I've often thought about that answer in the years since, and it has seemed ever more magical: he couldn't look at himself, so he painted a picture of himself with his eyes closed. Who/what in such a situation is looking at whom/what? And who are we, where are we, gazing over the shoulder of that regard?)

The act of painting, however, seemed to draw him out, and to heal him. "There was this richness in just basking in the absolute glory of handling brushes and tubes of paint, simply for their own sake," he told me. "And then, of course, there was the hunger for color itself: color quite apart from what it means or any of its associations, just color *as such*—the mad, wonderful yowl of it."

Colors weren't the only mad yowls begging for expression in Breyten's first months out of prison. In May, Yolande and Breyten headed for Palermo, Sicily, where a friend had lent them his apartment for the summer. Breyten took along a tape recorder, and during the ensuing weeks, alone, usually late at night, he proceeded to replicate his interrogations: a darkened room, a bare bulb, the tape spinning. Yolande transcribed the tapes each morning—the exercise was, in part, his way of relating the whole story to her—and the resultant text became the armature for his *True Confessions* ("the implication being that all the other confessions were false," he has commented, adding, "or perhaps, rather, that no confessions are ever really true"). The book proved an uncanny rhetorical exercise, an inquiry not just into his own truths but into the truth-seeking impulse itself, with every comment addressed to a "Mr. Interrogator" who seemed, by turns, God, the Judging Reader, the Void, Jan Vermaak, "Mr. Eye," and finally "Mr. I," Breyten himself.

"One starts such an exercise hoping to purge the horrors," Breyten told me. "But you never do. At best, you come to some terms—you give the memories a shape."

Breyten's first political impulse, in the months after his return, was to shed his South African identity and fixations altogether—never to descend into that particular miasma again. Not that there was any clamor by activists eager for his endorsement. He had been burned, but he had done some burning of his own, and it seemed unlikely that there would ever again be a future for him in anti-apartheid work. He applied for full French citizenship, which, owing to patrons in the Mitterrand government, he achieved in an unusually short time. He tried to become a Frenchman, but the graft never quite took. "I think it's the same with many cultural figures exiled here," he told me, citing as parallel cases Danilo Kiš and Milan Kundera. "There's this initial spasm of what seems like acceptance, but one can mistake being feted for being accepted, and eventually you hit these natural boundaries, the sense that if you weren't born into it they are never really going to let you be a part of it."

As the months passed, Breyten reconnected with his essentially African nature, though at first he addressed such hankerings by plunging into the former French West Africa—Senegal, the Ivory Coast, and the like—rather than dabbling with any manifestly futile fantasies about his own homeland.

Presently, however, South Africa began coming to him, particularly in the form of Slabbert and a parliamentary colleague of his named Alex Boraine, who regularly flew to Paris and tried to persuade Breyten to reengage in the anti-apartheid struggle. Instead, he ended up helping to convince them to leave parliament. Their doing so, a few months later, in a highly public manner and amid vivid denunciations of the ineffectuality of the entire parliamentary charade, proved a decided shock to the apartheid regime's comfortable governing consensus.

Meanwhile Breyten was busy editing his own prison writings. In a kind of obverse schizophrenia to that of his cultural homeland, he somehow imagined that he could continue to be a major organic force in Afrikaans literature without having actually to deal with the only place in the world where that language was spoken. But of course it was not to be. Ampie and his colleagues brought out four volumes of poetry in quick succession, and sure enough, in early 1986 it was announced that Breyten had been selected as the first recipient of South Africa's latest literary honor, the Rapport Prize. He and Yolande were invited back for the awards ceremony, the catch being that it was going to take place in the glitziest civic hall in Pretoria. After a good deal of soul-searching (particularly over having to set foot again in that cursed capital), he agreed to go (although he stipulated that through an elaborate sequence of limousines and gangways and raised platforms he would set foot on the actual ground as little as possible). The address he delivered to an audience of the country's cultural and political élite was perhaps his most scathing yet—it drove foreign minister Pik Botha, seated in the back of the auditorium, into such a foot-wedging frenzy that he ended up destroying the chair in front of him—but according to their prior commitment, *Rapport* magazine subsequently published the text in full. Slabbert escorted the returning hero to Stellenbosch to address a packed auditorium. "Here I am in the capital of Afrikanerdom," he told the students, "where they make the Afrikaners dumb. At the most important moment in our history, our establishment has delivered forth an entirely depoliticized generation." He went on to denounce the South African government as itself "a terrorist organization." Slabbert, at the back of the hall, has told me how at that point he thought, "Oh God, here we go again, another five years!" But Breyten received a standing ovation and was not apprehended.

Later that year Slabbert and Breyten converged on the former slave-processing center on Gorée Island, in the harbor of Dakar, Senegal, where an international musical celebration was marking the tenth anniversary of the start of the Soweto uprising (and, incidentally, Breyten's own most ignominious moment: his ambiguous offer to collaborate). It was there that the two men came up with the idea for their most daring initiative yet.

Much of their next year was taken up with its planning and execution (Slabbert and Boraine working secretly inside South Africa, Breyten performing the necessary liaisons with Danielle Mitterrand, the wife of the French president, Senegal's president Abdou Diouf, and various officials of the ANC-in-exile). Astonishingly, their plan went off without a hitch, and in mid-July of 1987 Slabbert led a delegation of sixty prominent Afrikaners—cultural, political, business, and church leaders—out of the country and, via London, back to Gorée for an unprecedented (and highly illegal) meeting with seventeen top leaders of the ANC. The event made the front pages of papers all over the world, and especially in South Africa, where Prime Minister Botha positively sputtered with rage. And though the convocation was by no means all sweetness and light—the conferees wrangled for hours, for example, about the ANC's continuing commitment to armed resistance—a wall had been breached and the demonized enemy given a face. Slabbert came to think of the Gorée meeting as "the butterfly's wingbeat that precipitated the hurricane." Several years later, Nelson Mandela told François Mitterrand at a state dinner in Paris that Gorée had been one of the keys that unlocked the door, making his own release and everything else possible. Breyten, back in the thick of things, had been one of the event's key instigators. He had been an odd presence at Gorée, not really belonging to either delegation—he was neither any longer a native Afrikaner nor a member of the ANC-in-exile—and, in fact, the entire event represented an edgy, tentative reconciliation between himself and the ANC leaders, some of whom may well have been partly responsible for his seven and a half years of incarceration.

(Actually there were two butterflies flapping in 1987, and Breyten's brother Jan was crucially involved with the second, for almost at the same time as the Gorée meeting, SADF forces were massing for the decisive Angolan incursion that was to become known as "the Battle for Africa," one of the fiercest little wars of the recent period—though it went largely unnoticed by the wider world at the time—pitting Cuban forces and their MPLA and SWAPO allies against the SADF and its UNITA surrogates. In the end the battle played itself out into a kind of grisly stalemate, but that fact in itself proved decisive, both sides finally having to acknowledge that neither could ever prevail militarily and that only negotiations—both within and along the periphery of the apartheid heartland—could ever secure a lasting peace.)

In the short run, the Botha regime expressed its displeasure over Breyten's latest antics by slapping him with a series of visa denials—an action that made it impossible for him to revisit his father, who had suffered a new series of heart attacks, until virtually the last moment. (He was eventually allowed to race to his father's deathbed on a four-day visa.) But Breyten remained committed around the country's edges, and in early 1991 he and Yolande were finally allowed back into the rapidly reforming country for a three-month stay. (It was this visit that became the occasion for his book *Return to Paradise*.) He remained a prickly customer, however, fiercely independent and at times almost defiantly eccentric in his celebration of the individual in the face of any tendency toward hegemonic control, whether National Party– or ANC-inspired. ("Only anarchy can save us from chaos now" was a typical pronouncement from that period.) He even ended up alienating Slabbert at one point by the tenor of his harangues, and the two erupted into a public row, which finally subsided in a wrenching private reconciliation. They agreed that it was the country itself gnawing at their innards, and they reaffirmed their love for each other and their status as each other's essential "good brother."

BROTHERS WERE a recurring theme on the visit I paid to South Africa alongside Breyten in July of 1993. ("Welcome to the land of sour milk and rancid honey," he quipped as our night flight touched down near dawn at Jan Smuts.) He was there mainly to address a convocation at Witwaterstrand University in Johannesburg, but afterward we flew down to Cape Town and embarked on a few days' drive through the Boland haunts of his youth. The countryside down there *is* ravishingly beautiful (imagine Zion National Park wedged between the Napa Valley and Big Sur), and we meandered through Wellington and Paarl, saw the old farm and the old boardinghouse and the pear tree and the Taal monument (still standing), and spoke of his parents and his brothers.

Breyten generally tries to avoid talking about his brothers with journalists; he is almost protective of them. But, amazingly, after everything that has passed between all of them he still keeps up with them.

We visited Cloete in his summer cottage in Montagu, east of Wellington, on the flank of a fragrant hill overlooking a chaparral valley. Their exchanges were gruff and wary and yet surprisingly warm. (Cloete struck me as wry, cynical, despairing, dark-humored, and ostentatiously contemptuous, though by no means contemptible.) Cloete was talking about selling his cottage, because the country was going all to hell. "So why don't you sell it to me, then, instead of to one of the black comrades?" Breyten teased. "You mean to a white comrade instead of a black one," Cloete retorted, mock-witheringly. Although they didn't talk politics—they seldom do anymore—Cloete told us of his latest incarnation: he was now serving as a media adviser to Zulu Chief Mangosuthu Buthelezi's Inkatha Freedom Party, one of the most obstructionist forces opposed to the country's newly evolving order.

On the road east, past Port Elizabeth, toward his sister's place, in Grahamstown, Breyten called ahead a few times to Jan's retirement homestead, in the nearby hamlet of Salem, trying to obtain his consent to our visit. But Jan had no use for American journalists (frankly, he hadn't had since Suez), and while he said he would welcome a visit from Breyten, Breyten was not to bring me. "He's really on a rampage," Breyten related after one of these calls. "All worked up, keeps repeating how 'Big Blood's coming, Big Blood's coming.'" Actually, Jan hadn't simply retired from the SADF; he had been forced out in 1987 after trying to blow the whistle on its UNITA ally Jonas Savimbi (a man whose career and very life he had personally saved on several occasions) for rapacious and patently illegal trafficking in the tusks and hides of endangered Angolan wildlife species. Jan had discovered how tendrils from the ensuing corruption ran high into the South African military's own top command, and when he tried to go public with his information he was summarily stripped of his commission and banished from his beloved 32 Battalion's base.

Breyten and I spent the night at his sister Rachel's home. We leafed through their mother's photograph albums—meticulously maintained but chronologically delirious. Rachel's fifteen-year-old daughter, Anna-Karien, recalled for us her child's-eye view of Uncle Breyten's incarceration ("I just thought you wanted to be alone") and then recited some of the poems of his she'd been learning at school that had especially moved her (the whole scene seemed to move Breyten as well).

The next morning, we headed back to the Port Elizabeth airport, but we gave ourselves an extra hour and detoured by way of Salem, which turned out to be a tiny hamlet—really just a general store, off to the side of which, up a dusty hill, Jan's farmhouse was perched. Breyten went up to the gate while I stayed behind in the car. A few minutes later, Jan's adult daughter came out to fetch me. "When Father heard you were out here, he insisted I come and get you," she told me. "I mean, he's gruff, but he's not a barbarian—he's actually quite kindhearted and very hospitable." And he was. His British wife had prepared tea out on the back porch (they had been hoping that Breyten would come by, but had almost given up), and Jan was regaling his brother with tales of his new life as a farmer, raising chickens and growing olives. They avoided any talk of politics, and, finally, all Jan seemed to want to talk about was the wildlife in his beloved Caprivi preserve and the royal botch that had been made of that onetime Eden. He had just completed a book on the subject, and he arranged for me to get a copy of the manuscript. The entire hour, as he spoke passionately on the subject, I couldn't help recalling Breyten's wistful speculation about the course that Jan's life might have followed if he had only been born a decade later.

We took our leave and raced back to the Port Elizabeth airport, where Breyten boarded a connecting flight back to Yolande, in their Spanish vacation farmhouse. I was to join them there a bit later, but in the meantime I split off for a few last days in Cape Town. That evening, in my hotel, I leafed through Jan's manuscript and found the experience at once absorbing and profoundly unsettling, for two entirely separate narratives seemed to course side by side through its pages, almost oblivious of each other. One was a tale of unending war and mayhem, of soldierly bonding and heroism amid almost incidental carnage. (The flesh-and-blood substantiality of the enemy or "collateral" deaths, at any rate, never quite seemed to register.) The other was a pastoral rhapsody and a passionate witness to the passing of an Edenic preserve (both brothers are drawn to the imagery of paradises lost and squandered); a celebration of elephants and lions and leopards and buffalo and rhino and of the grandeur of nature untrammeled; and an anguished wail at the systematic evisceration of all that splendor. *That* destruction had clearly got to him. Only near the end of the manuscript, and almost in passing, does he seem to draw the connection. "I am all for a 'just war,' but I also have great difficulty in weighing up the justness of war against the wholesale rape of the last outpost of the African savannah. Savimbi may be a better ruler for Angola than dos Santos will ever be," he writes, referring to the beneficiary of more than twelve years of his government's largesse and his own gruesome exertions. "On the other hand, he may not." He goes on to observe how "through a whole string of wars in at least six different African countries" he himself has seldom noted any improvement in governance brought about by violent means, concluding, "To sacrifice the last stronghold of the African savannah for the precarious 'freedoms' promised by Savimbi, which will go unnoticed by at least eighty per cent of the Angolan population anyway, is to my way of thinking, utterly despicable and an offense against God's creation."

Coda

A few days later, I joined Breyten and Yolande in a stout stone farmhouse in the hills outside a small town a few hours' train ride north of Barcelona. It was strange the way, after so much far-flung history, the three brothers had managed to secure virtually identical views from their kitchen windows—an overgrown orchard, the swell of shrubby hills in the mid-distance, the wide sky above, an arid valley falling gently away down below.

Yolande was excited: for the first time since girlhood, she had become fascinated by her own roots, and in a few months' time she and a friend were going to be making a trek back to Vietnam. Breyten seemed pleased by the role reversal. Meanwhile, he was busy in a small painting studio he had had built over the garage: during this last South African trip, he had made the final arrangements for an exhibition of his paintings—the first ever in his homeland—to open that December.

Evening was coming on, and Breyten and I were out back, watching the setting sun blond the surrounding hills. I heard a pair of mellow hoots off in the distance. "Owls?" I asked.

"No," Breyten said, smiling. "Wood pigeons, probably. But we do have owls here. And crows. And quail and nightingales. Well, we have everything." From there he free-associated to Pretoria and the birds that had sustained him in prison. "That's one thing about spending a long stretch in prison," he commented. "You never really get out afterward: part of you is continually being drawn back in."

We were silent a few moments: the sun descended, the light deepened. I asked him whether he ever looked back cringingly on his behavior during those days. "Oh, sure," he said. "There are aspects of my behavior that still leave me appalled. But I also remember that that's what they're continually programming you for—you're being conditioned for self-destruction, they're lacing you with self-disgust, you're being *made guilty*. The whole process is a continual rape of one's own better instincts. So that, sure, it leaves its scar tissue thick across one's sense of self-worth.

"And yet, in a way, I have more confidence in myself than that. Damn it all, so I wasn't able to be perfect. Self-knowledge is not self-abasement or self-rejection. I was, I am, a flawed human being. But that's more interesting than being an iron cast. And there's something to be said for fucking up. In fact, fucking up, if you aspire to be an artist, may be the great creative principle: getting broken, broken wide open, and then delving among the shards. Moving on. Painting, writing—these are always, first and foremost, struggles for authenticity." → Sartre

The sun had set and the world had suddenly gone quite dark. We went back inside. Some of his old gallery-show catalogs were strewn across the kitchen table: research for his forthcoming South African exhibition. And one of them happened to be open to the "Family Portrait"—his triple self-portrait. I smiled, pointing to it. "Ah yes," Breyten concurred. "We had a kid here the other day, and he was looking at that picture, and he asked me why the bird-hand of the old man kept bothering the little boy." He laughed. "I liked that." I asked him how he himself felt about that picture nowadays. "Oh," he said, "you know how it is. That's me, dead at the age of nine. Me, dead at the age of thirty. Me, dead at the age of forty. . . . " (The rumble seat, the goldfish pond, the field plowed under.) "I have sympathy for all of them, as I do for any dead. But they are not me."

↳ Satre's critique of imprisonment

The piece took seven years to write; he first did a radio documentary as a way of avoiding to write the piece;

An Additional Postscript to the Jan Kavan Saga (1999)

One would have thought that by now anyway Jan Kavan's endlessly convoluted saga could hold no fresh prospect for surprise. One would have thought wrong. Last summer (1998), the hapless Mr. Kavan achieved vindication (of a sort) beyond anyone's wildest imaginings (except perhaps his own). K. at last achieved the Castle; Dreyfus was proclaimed pope: Jan Kavan was named foreign minister of the Czech Republic.

When last heard from, in 1996, Kavan had fought his way back into politics as a leading Senatorial candidate of the opposition Social Democratic Party—indeed, the party's foreign policy spokesman—achieving his seat at a moment when Prime Minister Vaclav Klaus's own governance was starting to become increasingly bedraggled: scandalously corrupt and, what's worse, economically inept. In a subsequent set of elections, at the end of June 1998, a coalition led by the Social Democrats captured the leading plurality (though not a majority) of the votes, and there followed a tortuously delicate and extended process of governmental formation.

Things were not rendered any easier for the leader of the Social Democrats, the prospective new prime minister Milos Zeman, by his insistence that Kavan serve as his foreign minister. The prospect provoked a whole new slew of anti-Kavanian media smears, including an allegation in the pages of one of the Senator's most implacable foes, the leading Czech daily *Mlada fronta dnes,* to the effect that he had been declared persona non grata in England owing to his status there as "a convicted liar." (Brandishing a cordial letter, on official letterhead, from his old political ally, the new Labour foreign minister, Robin Cook—"I have taken the precaution of having the official record checked [and] can confirm that there is no suggestion that you have ever been guilty of committing perjury in the UK, or indeed, of any similar offense. . . . As far as I am concerned, you are a valued friend of Britain"—Kavan was able to secure a court-ordered retraction of the first half of the slur, though, bizarrely, not of the second.)

Still, even some of Kavan's former allies had their concerns. President Vaclav Havel, for example, notwithstanding the fact that in years past he himself had been one of those most benefiting from Kavan's tireless efforts, let it be known that he had his doubts about so incendiary a choice—a public misgiving which, if anything, only seemed to further stiffen the independent-minded Zeman's resolve.

Nor was Zeman dissuaded by another quintessentially Kavanian minidebacle earlier in the year: a one A.M. incident on the near-empty streets of downtown Prague, in which Kavan managed to scrape not one but *three* parked cars attempting to maneuver his own parked car out of a narrow squeeze, and then declined to take a breathalyzer test when the police informed him that, as Senator, he wasn't required to. (Typically, this incident got reported in the rabidly anti-Kavanian press as the ostentatiously drunken Senator's having totaled his own and five other cars and then being foiled in his panicky attempt to escape by a furiously righteous mob.) Zeman accepted Kavan's (and the police's) far milder version of the incident, subsequently adding, perhaps facetiously, that it may have only had the effect of costing the Senator an even higher posting as deputy prime minister.

Shortly after his installation in July 1998, I reached Kavan in his improbable new digs in the foreign ministry—the resplendent early Baroque Cernin Palace, perched atop a promontory overlooking Havel's own Hradcany Castle—and he still seemed vaguely dumbfounded by this most recent turn of events. It was by no means obvious how long he'd be able to survive at such heights—lurid exposés of his supposed misdeeds, entirely untethered from requirements of factual corroboration, were becoming a virtually nightly staple across several of the more deeply partisan television shows. But he seemed to be battening down for the long haul, already having accepted invitations to visit the foreign ministers of Germany and Poland (the latter, his longtime Solidarity confederate Bronislaw Geremek), and eagerly anticipating, albeit with a certain degree of irony, how it was he of all people, the veteran END peace activist, who stood to be helping to preside over the Czech Republic's entry into NATO, slated for April 1999.

Meanwhile, the thing that most seemed to awe him was the history of the place: here he now sat, in the very office of Jan Masaryk, the beloved Czech foreign minister who, back in 1948, at the time of the Communist seizure of power, had either leapt or been hurled to his death in the courtyard garden right there down below. There seemed to be a certain conflation as an audibly moved Kavan described the scene—Masaryk's fate momentarily standing in for his own father's. Whereas, of course, though his father was subsequently to suffer a similarly terrible fate at the hands of those very same Stalinists, back in 1948 he'd been serving as their abject apologist in the new regime's London embassy.

I tried that observation out on Kavan and he assured me that matters were even more complicated than that, for his father, who'd long adored Masaryk (having forged an especially close personal bond back during their wartime days together in the anti-Nazi resistance in London), had as a matter of fact been the last person to see the foreign minister alive—or rather, as Jan put it, "the last before the very last." According to Jan, mutual friends in London who'd been dismayed by Masaryk's refusal to resign his position in the face of the gathering Communist coup, and who distrusted the mails and the official diplomatic pouches, took advantage of the fact that Pavel had been called back to Prague for official briefings to use him as conduit for their urgent personal notes to the foreign minister. Pavel met privately with Masaryk late one evening that March, delivered the notes—and the next morning Masaryk was announced dead. In fact, a rumor subsequently even swept émigré circles to the effect that it was Pavel himself who'd personally hurled the foreign minister from the window. That rumor was of course preposterous: Devastated by the news, Pavel returned to London, thoroughly shaken—but he did not resign his own posting. He remained resolutely intent, it seemed, upon sleepwalking toward his own calamity.

Nothing was ever simple in the life of Jan Kavan—nor, it seems, is anything ever likely to be.

Index